STUDIES IN MANAGEMENT

EDITED BY

ANDREW ROBERTSON

National Institute of Economic and Social Research
Senior Research Fellow, University of Sussex
Formerly British Institute of Management

No 8

OWNERSHIP, CONTROL AND IDEOLOGY

Studies in Management

NO. I. BUSINESS ORGANIZATION

by John O'Shaughnessy
Senior Lecturer, the College of Aeronautics, Cranfield

NO. 2. CORPORATE PLANNING

A Practical Guide

by John Argenti
Co-author of *Guide to Management Techniques*

NO. 3. THE MANAGER'S GUIDE TO
INDUSTRIAL RELATIONS

by L. F. Neal
Industrial Relations Director, British Railways Board
and Andrew Robertson
Senior Research Fellow, University of Sussex

NO. 4. THE NUMERATE MANAGER

F. Keay
*Assistant Director of Studies
Ashridge Management College*

NO. 5. BRITISH MANAGEMENT THOUGHT

John Child
Senior Research Officer, London Business School

NO. 6. STAFF REPORTING AND STAFF DEVELOPMENT

E. Anstey

NO. 7. MANAGERIAL AND PROFESSIONAL STAFF GRADING

John Doulton and David Hay

In preparation for the same series

GENERAL MANAGEMENT IN THEORY AND IN PRACTICE

by F. de P. Hanika
Professor, University of Khartoum

THE INDUSTRIAL SOCIOLOGIST'S CASEBOOK

by Joan Woodward
Imperial College

THEO. NICHOLS

OWNERSHIP
CONTROL
AND IDEOLOGY

AN ENQUIRY INTO CERTAIN ASPECTS
OF MODERN BUSINESS IDEOLOGY

London
GEORGE ALLEN AND UNWIN LTD
RUSKIN HOUSE MUSEUM STREET

FIRST PUBLISHED IN 1969
SECOND IMPRESSION 1970

© *George Allen & Unwin Ltd 1969*
ISBN 0 04 338037 9

Printed in Great Britain
in 11 on 12 pt Baskerville
by T. and A. Constable Ltd., Hopetoun Street, Edinburgh

ACKNOWLEDGEMENTS

My thanks are due to Tom Lupton, John H. Goldthorpe, Harold Dellar, and Peter Hardwick. They, like other friends and colleagues mentioned here, have directly or indirectly influenced my work, though they bear no responsibility for what I have written. My thanks are also due to John Child, not only for giving me permission to cite from his (then) unpublished doctoral thesis, but also for the help he has given me in finally preparing the manuscript for publication. Most of all, however, it is appropriate that I acknowledge here my very great debt to Peter Worsley. For me, as for so many others, it was his enthusiasm and evident intellectual excitement which drew me to Sociology in the first place. He has been an unfailing source of encouragement, not least at times when this was most needed. For this I thank him most warmly.

Lastly, I must thank the businessmen of Northern City: they remain, as they wished, anonymous.

CONTENTS

ACKNOWLEDGEMENTS   *page* 7

INTRODUCTION   11

Part I – THEORISTS OF MANAGERIALISM

I   The Managerialism of Berle   19
II   The Managerialism of Burnham   31
III   Dahrendorf and Managerial Theory   40
IV   The Quintessence of Managerialism   52

Part II – TOWARD A RECONSIDERATION OF MANAGERIAL THEORY

V   Some Sources of Confusion   61
VI   Capitalism without Capitalists?   71
VII   Technocracy without Technocrats?   80
VIII Professionalism without Professionals?   84
IX   Managerial Economics   94
X   Social Experience and Values—I   112
XI   Social Experience and Values—II   121
XII   Are 'the Managers' a New Class?   134
XIII Some Concluding Comments   143

Part III – CONTEMPORARY BUSINESS IDEOLOGY

      Introduction   159
XIV   Business Ideology in Northern City   166
XV   Questions of Meaning and Ethics   173

9

10 CONTENTS

XVI   Traditionalism, Professionalism, and the
Ideology of Businessmen   *page* 188
XVII Of Conflict and Organicism, Materialism,
and Social Responsibility   208

APPENDICES   247

BIBLIOGRAPHY   256

INDEX   265

As their critics have sometimes observed there are very few matters upon which sociologists agree. Nevertheless, most would probably agree that it is undesirable for a polarity to develop between the empirical and the theoretical and that, though in one sense it is a nonsense to claim that sociologists are 'value free', it is equally undesirable for their studies of a given economic order to polarize between those which criticize and those which celebrate its excellence, or, as is more often the case, develop in accordance with its dictates. Most would also agree that they should not debar themselves from investigating matters of social and political controversy, or from studying the powerful as well as those over whom power is exercised. When all this has been said, however, and it has been said many times, the fact remains that for sociologists, as for other men, there is often a discrepancy between what is considered desirable and what is commonly practised. And in many respects this observation provides the general starting point for this work.

As far as British industrial management is concerned, for example, one can find a limited number of studies about the social composition, age and education of managers and a mounting literature exists from which one can discover how the manager spends his day. But most studies of the former type fall into the tradition of 'social book-keeping' and as is only to be expected, most of the latter have done little more than to answer the limited questions with which they began. On the other hand, however, a number of macro-theories also exist which, explicitly or implicitly, have been concerned with the possible behavioural and attitudinal consequences of a separation of ownership and control, or 'managerial revolution', in industry.

These macro-theories, which constitute a second and much more general level of enquiry, have received very little attention from British sociologists. More than this, many of the most influential contributions here have not come from sociologists at all, but from economists, lawyers, philosophers, journalists and politicians, and the work of some of those sociologists who have ventured into this field—for example, that of Veblen and more recently, and in a rather different way, Wright Mills— has not always been free from polemical intent. Historically, of course, assumptions about the nature and functions of industrial ownership have found their expression in discussions about the basis of the political order, social stratification, class and class relations, and the specific characteristics of capitalist, as opposed to other types of industrialized society. Indeed, given the long intellectual ancestry of such controversies, and the noticeable extent to which the theories of those concerned with them have, through Comte and Marx onwards, been coloured by their own value preferences, this whole area of discussion might provide a number of fruitful starting points for those concerned with the development of sociology itself. However, it is not our purpose here to present a historical essay of the type the above remarks might suggest.

Similarly, though we provide a brief consideration of the work of Berle, Burnham and Dahrendorf, we do not see it as our main purpose to investigate their work as ideology. Thus, though we will point to the existence of certain ideological undertones in the work of some of these writers, our main reason for considering them is to demonstrate that though they and other recent writers do hold certain ideas in common, which we sum up by terming them 'theorists of managerialism'[1], there are also certain differences between them, and between them collectively, and other writers whom we term 'Marxists'. In fact, it is within the apparent polarity between these two schools of thought that we intend to approach our subject matter, namely, the ideology[2] of the modern British director.

[1] We are using the term 'managerialism' in a narrow sense to refer to a loosely definable complex of ideas about the emergence of a new stratum of business leaders. The term could, of course, be more broadly defined to encompass certain perspectives in the field of political sociology. cf. S. Keller, *Beyond the Ruling Class: Strategic Elites in Modern Society*, N.Y., 1963.

[2] Later on, we will offer a more elaborate definition of 'ideology' but for the present purpose it is sufficient to note that we have generally used the term to refer to the social values and frames of reference of businessmen. We are mainly concerned with directors of joint stock companies involved in manufacturing. Unless the context indicates otherwise, it is to them that we refer when we write of 'managers' or 'businessmen'. Our level of generality allows us to refer to directors collectively but where possible we will look at different types of director, those in larger and smaller companies, and compare directors to senior and other managers.

In proceeding in this way we have been guided by three main considerations. The first of these finds its expression in an attempt to counter the polarity within the sociology of management between empiricism and theory; the second, in an attempt to bring to light the limitations of the economist's fixation with managerial 'motives' and, at least as it stands at present, the sociologist's fixation with class; and the third, in an attempt to point to the existence of a potential, but in our view largely neglected, overlap which is possible between the Marxist and managerialist positions. For us, the third of these matters is by no means the least important because we take the view that there are several respects in which some of the representatives of these two schools of thought 'talk past each other', and we believe that, in the absence of a recognition of this, the controversy in which they are involved threatens to become an arid one.

It should already be apparent, then, that it is not the purpose of this book to provide one more theory of the managerial revolution but to indicate the limitations of our present knowledge, to clarify and, where appropriate, seek to re-define the questions at issue, and to do this within the context of a discussion of directorial ideology. Given the scale of this task it follows, of course, that much of the data cited has been gleaned from published sources. In addition to this, however, we have also made use of some hitherto unpublished data of our own which derive from a study of directors and senior managers in 'Northern City'. This study was conducted in an attempt to throw some light upon the general value orientation and styles of thinking of businessmen but, simply because it refers to the members of only one (local) business elite, we have attempted to confine discussion of it to Part III. Furthermore, given our broad objectives, we have largely confined the report of a short-range 'factorial' analysis of these data to a separate section within Part III itself. The reader is asked to note that though this policy may result in some break in continuity, and the creation of a certain number of loose ends, it has been pursued quite deliberately in order to draw attention to the fact that the Northern City data do derive from just one case study and that the findings presented must therefore be considered as suggestive rather than definitive ones. Quite obviously, we hope that further research will confirm our findings but we have sought to arrange the text so as to draw attention to the fact that the Northern City study is, and can only be, a beginning.

Briefly, the plan of the book is as follows. In Part I we provide a brief and largely non-evaluative[1] sketch of the key postulates of those we term 'theorists of managerialism'. An attempt is made to distinguish between their views and those of their critics. The writers considered do not, of course, exhaust all the possibilities. In the case of those works which (like Galbraith's *The New Industrial State*, London, 1967) largely make public ideas more cautiously advanced by other writers we have, where appropriate, referred directly to these other writers elsewhere in the text.

Following this, and guided by the assumption of some of the above writers, Part II provides a reconsideration of the empirical and theoretical adequacy of certain notions about the occurrence of a separation of ownership and control and its behavioural and attitudinal correlates for businessmen. Consideration is given to the extent to which it is legitimate to regard modern directors as either capitalists, technocrats or professionals and also to the possible significance of some recent developments in micro-economic theory.

In addition to this, an attempt is made to separate out the discussion of class membership and directorial 'motivation' and it is argued throughout that much more attention than has hitherto been the case should be given to the director's normative orientation. Thus, a discussion is provided of the probable forms and possible consequences of the director's pre- and intra-corporate socialization and partly as a result of this, though for other reasons too, it is suggested that the present tendency to dichotomize businessmen into 'propertied' and 'non-propertied' may lead to an important element of over-simplification.

Part III is much more intimately concerned with the businessman's ideology as such. Furthermore, we are mainly concerned there, not so much with management's authority rationale *vis-à-vis* industrial workers but with the businessman's own perception of his role and of the structure and purpose of his company. Given this objective, we have found it necessary to

---

[1] An exception here is Burnham's theory of a managerial revolution. This has already attracted so much (in our view justifiable) criticism that we thought it desirable to remove it from consideration at an early point.

do something more than seek to explain business ideology in terms of a response to structurally generated strains and conflicts because even when, as is generally the case, allowance is made for the part played by certain independently determined factors, this approach tends to place the researcher at one remove from his subject. To adopt it is to run the danger either of reducing the businessman to some kind of robot, who reacts to external stimuli, or of imputing one's own meaning, which may possibly differ from that of one's subject, into the businessman's definition of the situation.

Thus, to point to the existence of one last polarity, this time one that exists within the sociology of knowledge, we have sought to steer a middle course between conducting an opinion survey on the one hand and attempting to relate ideology and social structure in macro terms, on the other. Both lines of development have tended to by-pass what we will have cause to term 'the vexed question of meaning' and consequently it is part of our intention in Part III to begin to grapple with this problem. In particular, we hope to clarify what businessmen mean when they talk in terms of their multiple 'social responsibilities'. For the above reasons, then, the main source of data in Part III is not a national sample of business opinion—which, in practice, would give rise to some difficult methodological, as well as theoretical, problems—but, as we have already indicated, the study of Northern City businessmen, whose responses we are in a better position to interpret. Whether we have understood them aright, only they can say. But if we have been at all successful we hope to have added to the reader's understanding of the British director who, at least in British sociological circles, has remained a much neglected creature.

To begin with, however, we intend to briefly consider the work of Berle. As he himself was later to point out, he and Means 'in no way broke new ground' when their *The Modern Corporation and Private Property* was first published in 1932.[1] Nevertheless, to put it this way is to considerably underestimate their achievement because, as we shall see, much of the on-going discussion about ownership, control and business ideology has its immediate origins in their early work.

[1] *Power Without Property*, London, 1960, pp. 19–20.

PART I

THEORISTS OF MANAGERIALISM

CHAPTER I

THE MANAGERIALISM OF BERLE

BERLE's work deserves consideration here on two counts: first, because together with Means he wrote a pioneer work on the separation of ownership and control, and secondly, because his later work illustrates a tendency to associate the notion of a managerial revolution with the development of 'social responsibility' in business.

The Modern Corporation and Private Property was a pioneer work in the sense that it was the first major attempt to provide detailed empirical data about stock ownership in order to substantiate the claim that shareholders were becoming less influential in the conduct of corporation affairs, and that the 'control' function of ownership was being superseded by that of management. Berle and Means argued that it was consistent with their thesis to expect that as companies grew (and thus issued more share capital), and as at the same time national prosperity increased (and thus more people invested in shares), so the proportion of voting stock held by the largest share-holders would decrease. Thus the changes they saw in the economic system were of a continuing nature. In their estimation:

'Economic power, in terms of control over physical assets, is apparently responding to a centripetal force, tending more and more to concentrate in the hands of a few corporate managements. At the same time, beneficial ownership is centrifugal, tending to divide and sub-divide, to split into even smaller units and to pass freely from hand to hand. In other words, ownership continually becomes more dispersed; the power formerly joined to it becomes increasingly concentrated; and the corporate system is thereby more securely established.'[1]

Briefly, Berle and Means assumed that if the largest share-holder, or group of shareholders, were not in possession of what

[1] A. A. Berle and G. C. Means, *The Modern Corporation and Private Property*, N.Y., 1932, p. 9.

was considered to be a sufficient proportion of votes then a company might reasonably be termed 'management'—as opposed to 'owner'—controlled, and after certain allowances had been made for the use of legal devices, and, where known, special circumstances pertaining to control, the following classification of control situations was used. Corporations which appeared to be owned to the extent of 80% or more of the voting stock by a compact group of individuals were classed as 'private'; those in which the major interest appeared to be larger than 20% but less than 50% were classed as 'majority owned'; those in which 5 to 20% of shares were held by a small group were generally termed 'joint minority-management controlled', and the rest—where there were holdings of less than 5%—'management-controlled'.[1]

By assigning the two hundred largest non-financial American corporations to varying classifications of 'owner-control' or 'management-control' in this way, they were able to state that 44% of them were 'management-controlled'.[2]

Their research led them to believe that 65% of the companies and 80% of their combined wealth were controlled either by management or by a legal device involving a small proportion of ownership and that this indicated 'the important extent to which ownership and control have become separated'.[3]

Some of the results obtained by Berle and Means may be questioned. For example, their classification rested mainly upon the proportion of voting shares held by the largest one, two, or three shareholders and clearly (even if we allow for the fact that the proportion of shares held by a company's shareholders tapers steeply from the largest downwards) their conclusions would have been less startling if they had considered the largest *twenty* shareholders.[4] Then again, their classification of corporations as 'management-controlled' on the grounds that their largest shareholder was another corporation, itself 'management-controlled', is also open to question. And in so far that they cite both 'management-control' and minority shareholder control as evidence of the extent to which ownership is separated from control we can already see that the

[1] A. A. Berle and G. C. Means, *The Modern Corporation and Private Property*, N.Y., 1932, p. 93.
[2] *ibid.*, p. 94.   [3] *ibid.*, pp. 94, 114.
[4] On this point see, P. Sargant Florence, *The Logic of British and American Industry*, London, 1953, p. 192.

use of even this ubiquitous phrase is not without its difficulties.

Nevertheless, *The Modern Corporation and Private Property*
focused attention upon the twentieth century joint stock
corporation and gave some scientific backing to the claims
made for a divorce of ownership and control in industry, and
equally importantly, from our viewpoint, it introduced the
criterion of the proportion of shares held by the largest shareholder, or group of minority shareholders combined, which
has since been the most important index used in empirical
investigations of the relationship between ownership and control
and its significance for company policy. Since the publication
of their work the criteria used in the empirical study of ownership and control in industry have been markedly refined; in
Britain, notably by P. Sargant Florence.[1] The 'statistical
approach' to the relationship of ownership and control is not,
however, without its limitations, so that if we attribute to Berle
and Means the distinction of pioneering a particular field of
study we must also attribute to them the initiation of a form of
analysis which has certain shortcomings.

We should make it plain that what is at issue here is not the
use of statistics as such but the theoretical framework within
which those who have concerned themselves with voting distributions have worked. In particular, and this will be a recurring
theme in the text, we question how far it is applicable to
analyse social power relations in terms of what is essentially a
mechanical analogy. If one is concerned with the question of
interests or, as now seems fashionable, with the 'autonomy' or
otherwise of corporation managements, it is not sufficient
to delimit the field of enquiry to the presence or absence
of shareholder 'control', as measured by figures about
voting concentrations. Yet with the notable exception of
Gordon[2] this is a practice which many contemporary writers
on the separation of ownership and control have tended to
adopt.

The publication of Berle and Means' researchers had led to
the heightening of interest among other American scholars, the

[1] See, *The Logic of British and American Industry*, and *Ownership, Control and Success
of Large Companies*, London, 1961.
[2] R. A. Gordon, *Business Leadership in the Large Corporation*, Berkeley, 1945,
pp. 147, 149–152, 188.

formulation of a particular methodological technique, and ultimately to government investigations of the economy.[1] In addition to all this, however, the thesis put forward in *The Modern Corporation and Private Property* has had other important ramifications so that, today, many theorists of business not only maintain that large corporations are often, in practice, governed by non-propertied managers but further assume that because these managers are not also important share owners, they are guided in their behaviour by a sense of responsibility to society. Thus, we are told that the modern corporation is a 'soulful'[2] or 'benevolent' corporation, and that its leaders are socially responsible.

Berle, himself a lawyer by profession, was clearly already alert to the problems of corporate responsibility, accountability and legitimacy in *The Modern Corporation*, and later his concern with these issues was to have some bearing upon his contention that the modern American business system was one of 'People's Capitalism', 'Non-Statist Capitalism' or 'Collectivism'.[3]

In his work with Means, Berle had clearly stated that the—

'concentration of economic power separate from ownership has, in fact, created economic empires, and has delivered these empires into the hands of a new form of absolutism relegating "owners" to the position of those who supply the means whereby the new princes may exercise their power.'[4]

—and this, for him, in turn raised the legal question, for whom did these managers hold their powers in trust? His own interpretation of the law at that time led him to suppose that they did so for shareholders.[5]

This particular interpretation[6] led Berle into a contro-

---

[1] See, for example, National Resources Committee, *The Structure of the American Economy;* Temporary National Economic Commission, Monograph No. 29, *The Distribution of Ownership in the 200 Largest Non-Financial Corporations*, United States Government Printing Office, Washington, D.C., 1940.

[2] cf. C. Kaysen, 'The Social Significance of the Modern Corporation', *American Economic Review*, May, 1957.

[3] A. A. Berle, *Power Without Property*, 1960, p. 19.

[4] *The Modern Corporation*, p. 124.   [5] *ibid.*, p. 248.

[6] In England, this is still the essence of the legal position. In 1962, as a consequence of a shareholder's objection, the directors of the *Daily News* were ruled *ultra vires* for making an *ex gratia* payment to employees made redundant by the sale of the *News Chronicle* and *Star* newspapers on the grounds that 'this was not

versy[1] with Dodd, another American lawyer, who argued that corporation managers held powers in trust for the community, and later indeed we find Berle himself moving toward an acceptance of this position.[2] But even in *The Modern Corporation* there are signs that he was not fully convinced that the law itself, as then constituted, would always be a necessary deterrent to corporation managements turning the vast economic power at their disposal to the service of their own interests.

Thus, we find him already musing that if as a consequence of the separation of ownership and control managements were actually to become more socially responsible then it would be desirable to change the law. However, one gains the impression that he not only hoped that this would come about but that he thought the development of a more socially responsible business elite was in some way related to a decline in shareholder 'control', this process being a pre-condition to business socializing itself. Thus we find Berle and Means writing:

'When a convincing system of community relations is worked out and is generally accepted, in that moment the passive property right of today must yield before the larger interests of society. Should the corporate leaders, for example, set forth a program comprising fair wages, security to employees, reasonable service to their public, and stabilisation of business, all of which would divert a portion of profits from the owners of passive property, and should the community generally accept such a scheme as a logical and human solution of industrial difficulties, the interests of passive property owners would have to give way. Courts would almost of necessity be forced to recognise the result, justifying it by whatever

---

in the interests of the company'. In the judgment of Plowman, J.: 'The view that directors in having regard to the question what is in the best interests of their company are entitled to take into account the interests of the employees, irrespective of any consequential benefit to the company, is one that may be widely held. . . . But no authority to support that proposition of law was cited to me. I know of none, and in my judgment such is not the law'. *Parke v. The Daily News Ltd., and others* (1962). 2 All E.R. 929 at 948. (In *Greenhalgh v. Arderne Cinemas Ltd.* (1950), 2 All E.R. 1120, Sir Raymond Evershed, M.R., held that the benefit of the company meant the benefit of the shareholders as a general body.) The legal view of business social responsibility was succinctly put by L. C. B. Gower, in a letter to *The Times*, January 30, 1959: 'Directors who subordinate the long-term interests of shareholders to those of consumers, the nation, and the employees are likely to fall foul of the law'.

[1] For a short account of this controversy, see Eugene W. Rostow, 'The Responsibility of Corporate Managements', in E. S. Mason, (ed.) *The Corporation in Modern Society*, Harvard, 1960.

[2] A. A. Berle, *The Twentieth Century Capitalist Revolution*, London, 1955, p. 137.

of the many legal theories they might choose. It is conceivable—indeed it seems almost essential if the corporate system is to survive—that the "control" of the great corporations should develop into a purely neutral technocracy, balancing a variety of claims by various groups in the community and assigning to each a portion of the income stream on the basis of public policy rather than private cupidity.'[1]

In a later work, *The Twentieth Century Capitalist Revolution*, Berle seems to have concluded that the emergence of a socially responsible business elite really was under way. Indeed, as he tells us elsewhere,[2] this book was written on the assumption that the intervening thirty years had seen a change in business behaviour and that, as he had hoped in *The Modern Corporation*, such changes had been for the better.

In both this new work—of which, as Walton and Eells[3] have noted, it is not without significance that the French translation equated the spirit of American capitalism with the *conscience du roi*—and also of course in *Power without Property*, Berle has, however, begun to look at the question of corporate legitimacy in a rather different way. We find that the traditional safeguard against mis-management in the joint stock company (that its leaders be accountable at law to shareholders) is now supplemented by two new concepts, the 'corporate conscience', which restrains managements from acting in their own self interest, or in a socially irresponsible manner, and the 'public consensus', that is public opinion, to which ultimately managements are accountable.[4]

It is true of course that the main theme of *Power Without Property*[5] is concerned with the growth of a new form of institutional investment, of which Berle considers the most significant type to be the pension fund, and we find him expressing disquiet about the concentration of voting power in the hands of a small group of pension fund managers who, if they do intervene in corporate policy, could, he suggests, 'freeze power

[1] *The Modern Corporation*, p. 356. (Galbraith has recently suggested that 'this formidable conclusion . . . expressed in guarded terms . . . Berle's early commitment to socialism'. This is not our interpretation. See, *The New Industrial State*, p. 119.)
[2] See Berle's fo reword to E. S. Mason (ed.) *The Corporation in Modern Society*, p. xiii.
[3] C. Walton and R. Eells, (eds.), *The Business System: Readings in Ideas and Concepts*, N.Y. and London, 1967, Vol. 3, p. 1911.
[4] *Power Without Property*, pp. 90–91, 110.
[5] See also, A. A. Berle, *Economic Power and the Free Society*, N.Y., 1958.

in themselves', and who, if they don't, could 'merely insulate corporate managements from any possible action by or influence of the ultimate beneficial "owners" of the stock', in this case future pensioners.[1] Whichever the case, Berle thought, such an eventuality could upset his own former prediction and hope of American business being responsibly governed by corporation managers for the good of society.

In practice, rule by pension fund managers seems unlikely, and few academics[2] or 'wholesalers of ideas' (journalists, some academics, and professional business ideologists, or P.R. men)[3] have been deeply influenced by this particular theory of Berle's. In Britain, in 1963, public, private and local authority pension funds were estimated to hold only about 6% of quoted ordinaries. Overall, though, institutional investors (insurance companies, investment trusts, unit trusts and pension funds) held about one-quarter of all ordinary, and a similar proportion of all share classes combined.[4] This constitutes a very real potential for influencing policy which the reader should bear in mind in subsequent discussion.

What must mainly concern us here, however, is that other aspects of Berle's work have made an important contribution to the popular sociology of modern capitalism. Quite clearly, with the introduction of the notions of 'corporate conscience' and 'public consensus' Berle had gone beyond asserting that large corporations are controlled by (non-propertied) managers. Indeed he seems to imply that these managers are men of understanding and wisdom who the less competent public must strive to understand, for he writes[5] that—

'Until the community on the one hand or the ritualistic stockholder on the other develop more capacity and inclination for understanding difficult problems and reaching wise personnel decisions, economic power is best located in a sort of government of best minds, ultimately responsible to a community consensus which sets up general objectives, standards of performance and results.'

---

[1] *Power Without Property*, p. 56.
[2] cf. R. M. Titmuss, *The Irresponsible Society*, Fabian Tract 323, London, 1960, p. 74.
[3] For Mills' original (academic) application of this term, see, C. Wright Mills, *White Collar*, N.Y., 1953, p. 130.
[4] See J. G. Blease, 'Institutional Investors and the Stock Exchange', *District Bank Review*, Sept., 1964, p. 43; for a comment on the American situation, see J. Lintner, 'The Financing of Corporations', in E. S. Mason (ed.) *The Corporation in Modern Society*, pp. 127–201.   [5] *Power Without Property*, p. 109.

The above should not of course be taken to imply that Berle purposely introduced the concepts 'corporate conscience' and 'public consensus' with the aim of insulating corporation managements from charges of irresponsibility and self interest, once the traditional safeguard of management accountability to ownership had withered. In fact, as we have already noted, he seems to have genuinely believed that there had been real changes in the corporate control situation and that the 'purely neutral technocracy', which he had envisaged in *The Modern Corporation*, really was emerging at the time he published *The Twentieth Century Capitalist Revolution* and *Power Without Property*. Like one influential group of American writers on management, he reasoned that after the war there had been a transformation of the recruitment, functions, and responsibilities of corporation leaders—and thus a revolution in the behaviour of capitalist institutions.

The Editors of *Fortune*, for instance, have argued that though James Burnham's *The Managerial Revolution* had portrayed the trend to a controlling management class accurately enough, it had quite wrongly 'conveyed the idea that somehow the corporate manager is destined to become the Western equivalent of a King Farouk or perhaps an unusually forward commissar'. In reality—and here we think Berle would agree—

'The corporate manager neither is, nor is becoming, anything of the kind. He is part of a group that enjoys power only so long as it does not abuse it—in other words, precisely so long as it does not exercise power the way men used to before the capitalist transformation.'[1]

At this point, of course, we are not concerned with the ideology of businessmen, as such, but rather with writers who have theorized about business, some of whom, and here we would include Berle, may have helped to form, or at least explicitly to conceptualize, a business ideology. However, it should be noted that the attention Berle focused upon the occurrence of a separation of ownership and control had a two-sided significance for the representation of the role of the corporation leader and of the corporation within modern society.

On the one hand, *The Modern Corporation* used systematically

---

[1] The Editors of *Fortune* in collaboration with Russell W. Davenport, *U.S.A.: The Permanent Revolution*, 1951, p. 180.

gathered data to dispose of the notion that giant business was controlled by giant capitalists: on the other, however, and as a direct consequence of this, it attributed very great power indeed to the new managers, or as Berle and Means then called them, 'the new Princes'. It is, perhaps, an open question whether the publicizing of the first of these conclusions was or was not welcomed by businessmen. But, as far as the second conclusion is concerned, there can be no doubt about its undesirability. It simply transferred the attributes of corporate power from owner to manager, and with this, of course, it also transferred to the alleged new holders of power the need to lay claim to be recognized as disinterested and responsible men.

It is for this reason that Berle's later works, *The Twentieth Century Capitalist Revolution* and *Power Without Property*, are of importance to us here. In these, he built upon his earlier notion of a separation of ownership and control to suggest not only that the managers are now in control but that there is reason to hope they will control responsibly.

By postulating the existence of a 'corporate conscience', Berle, in effect, provided the corporation and its leaders with some protection against suspicion of, or attacks upon, their use of power. Thus, we can see that though Berle was primarily concerned with the analysis of business structure and behaviour, a side effect of his work has been the formulation of what may be used as a rationalization or ideology by which the directors of corporate policy may justify their position and behaviour. It is all the more important to note this here since the ideology of corporate power which Berle's analysis led him to provide is similar in some respects to the views put forward by some present-day corporation leaders.

This does not mean, of course, that we believe businessmen read Berle—and then pronounced themselves 'socially responsible'. The sociology of ideas is a good deal more complex than this and many American and British businessmen had talked in terms of social responsibility long before any of Berle's works were published. Indeed, it is likely that the comments of contemporary businessmen and his close association with the business world provided the initial impetus behind his ideas. His work is not therefore important to us here because it bears a direct relationship to the growth of an ideology among businessmen—quite possibly such a relationship operated the other way round—but because even such a brief review of it as we have provided inevitably introduces us to one particular aspect of business ideology with which we will be concerned, namely, the notion of 'social responsibility', and because, in addition to this, it also provides an explanation of why business-men should adhere to this ideology at all. As we have seen, Berle suggests that they do so because the separation of owner-ship and control makes possible the emergence of some sort of 'neutral' and thus presumably disinterested elite.

Of course, simply because this has been a brief review, care must be taken not to oversimplify Berle's position (or rather positions, for he has shifted this from time to time over the years). In practice, for example, it is often difficult to decide how far he believes modern corporate leaders to be guided by an actually functioning 'corporate conscience' and how far by a prudent regard to the 'public consensus'. Nevertheless, we find it difficult to read his work without concluding that to some degree at least he does consider the former to be important and that, in his view, its emergence is causally related to the separation of ownership and control. Indeed, if we may be permitted what at first sight must appear a rather fanciful comparison, it would seem to be on this point that his analysis of the modern corporation begins to deviate from a much earlier set of suppositions and prescriptions about industrial society which was latent in the work of Comte. Lest the comparison seems all too fanciful, however, it might be appropriate to recollect that, as Aron[1] has observed, Comte is in many ways the (unacknowledged) symbolic patron of the poly-technician-managers, and also, of course, of the theorists of meritocracy.

Both Comte and Berle take the concentration of economic power as a datum, the former implying private ownership in general and the latter share-ownership in particular, to be necessary and inevitable. Both of them further imply, to cite Aron's exegesis of Comte, that private ownership is 'tolerable only when conceived no longer as the right to use and abuse, but as the exercise of a collective function by the few whom fate or merit has singled out'.

---

[1] *Main Currents in Sociological Thought*, London, 1965, Vol. I (trans. R. Howard and H. Weaver), pp. 70–72.

But if both writers are in agreement that industrialists must regard their role as a 'social duty' it must be remembered that, for Comte, the precise form taken by ownership in industrial societies was virtually a matter of indifference so that, as Aron again points out, he was completely deaf to the argument that the concentration of capital should itself imply the public character of ownership. There are perhaps traces of this type of thinking in Berle's thought too—hence his use of terms like 'Collectivism'. But in his case an apparent rejection of the public/private dichotomy amounts in no small part not to a denial that such a dichotomy exists but rather to an affirmation that it does—and that the twentieth century revolution has placed modern corporate capitalism, the capitalism of the people, not just capitalists, into a position between these two extreme possible cases. For Berle, it appears, the precise form of ownership and in particular its degree of concentration, and thus 'control' potential, is itself a factor facilitating the emergence of a new corporate business elite which acts on the basis of public policy rather than private cupidity and which will, it is to be hoped, have a sense of social duty.

We can see, then, that Berle and Means' work not only provided a descriptive analysis of modern corporate capitalism which was of the first importance in its own right. In addition to this, it contained the beginnings of a prescriptive analysis which, more fully developed in Berle's own later writings, itself rests on the assumption that the withering of the powers of property ownership is connected with the advent of new men of business, the managers, who, it is hoped, will strive to balance a whole complex of competing interests and not merely further the interests of the beneficial ownership, the shareholders.

Such views have, of course, constituted an important growth point for a burgeoning literature which, sometimes by way of a rather crude inverted-Marxism, and sometimes by more subtle arguments, has sought to establish that the managers of today are not the (seemingly by definition) irresponsible capitalists of yesteryear—and that, as a consequence of this, the large modern corporation is in process of socializing itself. True or false, we take the ideological potential of such views to be self-evident and since the similarity between Berle's own views on this matter and those of some modern businessmen will become apparent later on we intend to conclude our brief comments upon his work at this point. We will turn now to a consideration of Burnham's book *The Managerial Revolution*.

We think that Burnham, like Berle, can be meaningfully termed a 'theorist of managerialism'—but as we shall see, many of his ideas are out of keeping with those we have considered so far.

CHAPTER II

THE MANAGERIALISM OF BURNHAM

The Managerial Revolution

As we have seen, the central argument of *The Modern Corporation* was that shareholder control of large private corporations would gradually diminish. As a consequence of this the managers would cease to act as mere agents for the owners and would develop policies of their own. In that work Berle expressed the hope that, in future, freed from shareholder control, the managers would become responsible arbiters of the public good and his later works suggest that he now believes that this has happened.

Both Berle and Burnham were concerned with the consequences of bureaucratization in large scale industrial organization. Both were concerned with the role of managers. And both predicted their rise to power. Nevertheless, Berle and Burnham are not saying the same thing, nor indeed are they even writing about the same managers.[1]

Berle wrote about *private* industry and predicted the emergence of a *neutral management elite*. Burnham, on the other hand, was mainly concerned with *state enterprise*, and predicted the rise of a *new ruling class*.[2]

Berle took the new managerial ideology seriously: Burnham, on the other hand, quite clearly used the term in a derogatory sense and implied that the idea of 'technocracy', though 'at a more primitive level', served the same function as Stalinism and Nazism.[3] Then again, whereas Berle generally confined his thesis to the emergence of a new management-controlled economy, Burnham went much further and envisaged the emergence of a managerial society, and ultimately, a

---

[1] For a similar distinction between the views of Berle and Burnham, see E. S. Mason, 'The Apologetics of Managerialism'. *The Journal of Business*, Vol. xxxi, No. 1, Jan., 1958.

[2] James Burnham, *The Managerial Revolution*, London, 1962, pp. 73–74, 87.

[3] *ibid.*, p. 75.

managerially dominated world. As far as he was concerned *The Modern Corporation* provided no more than a new viewpoint from which to see the mechanism of the managerial revolution.[1] In his view, both democratic capitalism and socialism were to be replaced by a new managerial society. Stalinism in Russia, Nazism in Germany, and even the New Deal in America, were all moving in the same direction.[2] There might, he conceded, be a Russian way, a German, and an American way,[3] but a transition was definitely under way '*from* the type of society we have called capitalist or bourgeois *to* a type of society which we shall call managerial'. In fifty years after the First World War the new order would be consolidated.[4]

Burnham's theory of a new managerial class is based on three major propositions. First, he assumed that the corporate state would be an enduring feature of all industrialized societies. Secondly, he argued that state ownership of the means of production would lead to the emergence of a powerful stratum of managers. And thirdly, he assumed that because such managers performed indispensable functions, and because they had access to the means of production, they would inevitably exercise power in their own interests. In his view,

'control over access is decisive, and, when consolidated, will carry control over preferential treatment in distribution with it: that is, will shift ownership unambiguously to the new controlling, a new dominant, class.'[5]

He assumed that it was in accordance with an 'historical law' that those who 'control' (initially for others) will control eventually for themselves. Thus, since the basic instruments of production were to be directed by 'the managers' it followed that they would be the ruling class. But the relationship between bureaucracy and power is not as simple as Burnham would have us think.

A Short Critique of Burnham's Theory

Chapter 7 of *The Managerial Revolution* asks the question 'Who Are The Managers?' In this chapter Burnham's answer is

---

[1] James Burnham, *The Managerial Revolution*, London, 1962, p. 93.
[2] *ibid.*, p. 231.
[3] See his comments on 'The Russian Way' (chap. 14), 'The German Way' (chap. 13), 'The Future of the United States' (chap. 16).
[4] *The Managerial Revolution*, p. 73.   [5] *ibid.*, p. 93.

quite clear: 'the managers are simply those who are, in fact, managing the instruments of production nowadays'.[1] Elsewhere, however, he widens this definition to include those who are 'actually managing, on its technical side, the actual process of production, no matter what the legal and financial form—individual, corporate, governmental—of the process'.[2] It would be sufficiently ambiguous if Burnham stopped here: but he did not. He goes on to include the 'European managerial politician' and 'managers, in and out of government, along with their bureaucratic and military colleagues'. And in addition to this, he refers to 'the bureaucrats (for which we may read "managers")', and then contradicts himself by asserting that it is not 'the bureaucracy but the managing group which is becoming the ruling class'.[3]

Other students of Burnham's work have criticized his lack of clarity. Thus Cole has criticized him for supporting his argument 'by shifting at caprice from one definition of his terms to another'.[4] And Gerth and Mills[5] and Dahrendorf[6] have argued that Burnham simply calls 'the managers' those who are powerful. There is no lack of evidence to support the views of these critics and it is quite clear that Burnham's thesis must be rejected on these grounds alone. But his theory has several other major defects.

First, there is the argument that the managers will become the next ruling class because they are indispensable. Since the reader cannot be sure exactly who 'the managers' are, it is difficult for him to evaluate their importance. Whichever group Burnham really refers to, however, this particular argument is a poor one. As Weber put it, if indispensability were the basis for class rule then slaves would be masters.

A second major limitation of Burnham's thesis is that many of his assumptions (e.g. his prediction, in 1940, that Germany would continue to win the war, and his later prediction, in 1944, that the Russians would dominate the world) have been proved

---

[1] *ibid.*, p. 78.   [2] *ibid.*, p. 81.

[3] See H. H. Gerth and C. Wright Mills, 'A Marx for the Managers,' in *Reader in Bureaucracy*, (ed.) R. K. Merton *et al.*, 1952, p. 173.

[4] G. D. H. Cole, *Studies in Class Structure*, London, 1955, p. 55.

[5] 'A Marx for the Managers', p. 173.

[6] R. Dahrendorf, *Class and Class Conflict in Industrial Society*, London, 1957, p. 87.

C

wrong. As Orwell[1] demonstrated, Burnham consistently projected the eddies of world history into tidal waves. This procedure often led him to the wrong conclusions which he later used to corroborate his theory. Of course, the fact that some of his predictions were wrong is not sufficient reason to invalidate the whole of his theory. Unfortunately for Burnham, however, this is not the only ground upon which his theory may be criticized.

As Bendix has argued, the very concept of a managerial ruling class begs the question whether 'the managers' of, say, industry, government and trade unions constitute one cohesive ruling class simply because they are 'managers'.[2] The answer to this question is quite clearly that they do not.

In short, then, there are four major reasons for rejecting Burnham's theory. First, he does not define who 'the managers' are; secondly, he assumed that class rule was based upon indispensability; thirdly, some of the predictions he used to corroborate his theory have been proved wrong; and fourthly, there is no reason to expect the emergence of a unified ruling class which is based upon the interests of 'managers' *qua* 'managers'.

Since Burnham's theory has already been heavily criticized by other writers we do not intend to deal with it at length here. There is, however, one further point which we will make. This is that despite his protestations that he was not writing a programme of social reform, or making 'any *moral* judgment whatever',[3] Burnham's theory cannot be fully understood unless we also understand something of his political position at the time it was written. Burnham had been a Trotskyist and some writers have interpreted his work as the means employed by a publicly committed intellectual to break with his past.[4] Whether this was so or not, *The Managerial Revolution* can be

[1] See his essay, 'Second Thoughts on James Burnham', reprinted in *The Collected Essays*, London, 1961.
[2] R. Bendix, 'Bureaucracy and the Problem of Power', in *Reader in Bureaucracy*, pp. 119–120.
[3] *The Managerial Revolution*, p. 19.
[4] See, for example, P. M. Sweezy, *The Present as History*, N.Y., 1953, chapter 3. (In this context it is of some interest that, with the exception of his more pessimistic conclusion, Burnham's analysis closely parallels that of Rizzi. See Bruno Rizzi, *La Bureaucratisation du Monde*, Paris, 1939; cf. N. P. Mouzelis, *Organisation and Bureaucracy*, London, 1967, p. 32.)

read as an anti-communist polemic,[1] and there can be no doubt that it provided an admirable vehicle for the views of a man who was equally disillusioned with both soviet communism and capitalist democracy. But if Burnham rebelled against Marxism, Marxism had left its mark on Burnham.

As Young has pointed out, 'Marxism is here in the language'[2] —but its influence was more pervading than this. Indeed, in a very special sense Burnham had put forward a 'Marxist' analysis. Marx had argued that the proletariat would overthrow capitalism just as the bourgeoisie had overthrown feudalism. By substituting 'the managers' for 'the proletariat', Burnham was able to retain the (to him) familiar Hegelian dialectic: this enabled him to fight the Marxists on their own ground. But this lingering attachment to a 'Marxist' mode of analysis caused major problems. It is, for example, the essential and special characteristic of a *managerial* ruling class that it is non-propertied—and the whole point of Burnham's analysis is that he predicts the emergence of such a class. Yet Burnham suffered from a trained incapacity to dissociate the concept of 'control' from that of 'ownership'. Thus, he felt bound to support his claim that 'the managers' are to be the next ruling class by asserting that they have 'ownership'. This resulted in his nonsensical statement that,

'if there is no control, then there is no ownership. The central aspects of the control which is ownership are, as we have seen, control over access to the object in question and preferential treatment in the distribution of its products. If ownership and control are in reality separated, then ownership has changed hands to the "control" and the separated ownership is a meaningless fiction.'[3]

As Dahrendorf[4] has argued, Burnham's inability to distinguish property from authority (as evidenced by his reiteration of the formula that 'ownership means control' so that 'those who control *are* the owners') implies that 'the head of the state would have property in "his" state'. Indeed, at an earlier point in the text Burnham makes it quite clear that, 'the state—that is the

---

[1] As Michael Young suggests in his preface to the 1962 (Penguin) edition of *The Managerial Revolution*, p. vii.

[2] *ibid.*, p. viii.

[3] *ibid.*, p. 91. (Burnham tells us that it was a 'basic deficiency in the analysis of Berle and Means' not to realize this.)

[4] *Class and Class Conflict*, p. 141.

institutions which comprise the state—will, if we wish to put it that way, be the "property" of the managers'.[1]

So far, we have attempted to make two fundamental points. The first was that Burnham's managerialism is radically different from Berle's, the second, that Burnham's theory is, in any case, of limited value. Since his theory is so obviously weak, the reader might ask why we have bothered with Burnham at all. The answer is that he was the popularizer of managerialism.

Burnham as the Publicist of Managerialism

What Berle and Means had done for the academic world, Burnham did for the masses, or more accurately their leaders. It is largely as a result of his influence that the phrase 'managerial revolution' is now used by journalists, economists and politicians with a greater degree of ambiguity and assurance than perhaps any other.

Nowhere has the influence of Burnham's work been greater than in the British Labour Party. At the time of the first post-war Labour government 'references to Burnham (were) scattered through Labour literature, and (found) their way into Labour speeches on the floors of Parliament'.[2] By 1957, the main tenets of managerialism had been incorporated into party policy in the pamphlet *Industry and Society*, which declared that many of the large corporations were management-controlled or 'ownerless'.[3]

By 1964, the party had committed itself to an election campaign which was largely based upon an appeal to the developing stratum of technical workers and managers.[4] The consequent legislation enacted by the 1964 and 1966 governments—and indeed the absence of certain legislation—bears

---

[1] *The Managerial Revolution*, pp. 91, 93, 74.

[2] R. A. Brady, *Crisis in Britain: Plans and Achievements of the Labour Government*, London, 1950, p. 563.

[3] cf. C. A. R. Crosland, *The Future of Socialism*, London, 1956, chapters 1, 3, 17.

[4] This was not of course a logical development, for it was the 'managers' and technicians which were appealed to, rather than the directors and senior 'technocrats', who were, presumably, the main subjects of Burnham's work. It is noticeable, however, that the managerial thesis is very much mixed up with notions about embourgeoisement and that both of these theories are often associated in political and journalist circles with further notions about an emerging meritocracy.

witness to the extent that managerialism had been accepted by the Labour Party.

As we suggested earlier, however, the growth of managerialist thought has not been confined to the Labour Party. Since the war it has been widespread in the 'quality Press'. Anthony Sampson, formerly an *Observer* journalist, has done much to help this trend with a recent best-seller[1] and his old paper has continued to describe industrialists as 'typical products of the managerial revolution' and to allot increased news space to their activities. In the first seven months of 1949 'Pendennis' referred to only six businessmen in his *Observer* column: for the same period in 1959, 131 were mentioned.[2] In 1969, the publicity given to businessmen is so great as to require no documentation —after all, today, even *The Times* has a business supplement.

Quite clearly, the growth of managerialism in post-war Britain is not a direct product of Burnham's work: yet it is equally clear that the publication of *The Managerial Revolution* was an important factor in this development. However, to understand the full significance of Burnham's work we must retrace our steps a little. We have already seen that his work was frequently cited in Labour Party literature and in the speeches of party members at the time of the post-war Labour government. But the surprising thing is that the particular kind of managerialist thinking which took root was much more in keeping with Berle's thinking than with Burnham's. As Brady[3] put it:

'one would gather from these references that businessmen in Britain are being led, as though by the unseen hand of some technological logos, to encompass broad social ends which are not only no part of, but are actually contrary to, the narrow objectives of their early entrepreneurial intentions.'

In other words, even though Labour thinkers may have cited Burnham, the actual ideas which they expressed had more in common with Berle's notion of a 'neutral technocracy', which pursued broad social aims, than with Burnham's own conception of a self-interested managerial 'ruling class'. Paradoxically, then, Burnham's success as a publicist resulted in the acceptance, not of his own, but of Berle's managerial theory.

[1] A. Sampson, *The Anatomy of Britain*, London, 1962.
[2] See R. Samuel, 'The Boss as Hero', *Universities and Left Review*, 1959, p. 26.
[3] *Crisis in Britain*, p. 563.

Part of the reason why Burnham succeeded in popularizing Berle's ideas, rather than his own, is to be found in the way in which he presented his argument. As we have seen, even his definition of who 'the managers' are is imprecise. In view of this, one can only conclude that vagueness was Burnham's greatest asset. *The Managerial Revolution* is so loosely conceived that it could be used to explain a number of social changes and, indeed, could be applied to a multitude of 'managers'.

So far, by outlining Berle and Burnham's main postulates we have suggested some of the divisions and nuances which distinguish their two managerial models. We have also noted the different ways in which both of them have contributed to the present state of managerial theory. However, it would be quite wrong to assume that the difference between these two writers represents the most important division in contemporary economic and sociological writings about the implications of the joint stock company: it does not. The crucial division in writings about the joint stock company and the nature of modern capitalism is between those, on the one hand, who postulate that either a 'divorce of ownership and control' *or* a 'managerial revolution'[1] has occurred and those, on the other hand, who refuse to accept that such a divorce exists, or—if they admit its existence—minimize its importance. In short, the fundamental division of opinion is between *managerialists* and *non-managerialists*.

Thus, now, having pointed to certain important differences within managerial theory we intend to put this whole body of thought within a broader perspective.

To do so we will refer to a classification of writers on this subject which was first put forward by Dahrendorf. After we have considered Dahrendorf's classification (which will demonstrate quite clearly that managerialism is only *one* type of theory about contemporary capitalism) we will then proceed to briefly outline his own views. We will do this because, as we shall see, Dahrendorf himself can be termed a managerial theorist and because his work provides a particularly explicit expression of certain assumptions which are only implicit in

---

[1] To be strictly accurate, Berle writes of a 'separation of ownership and control' whereas Burnham writes almost exclusively of a 'managerial revolution.' However, in writing, we have found it more convenient to use the terms interchangeably.

other managerialist writings. Berle was a corporation lawyer, Means an economist, and Burnham a philosopher, but Dahrendorf is a sociologist and any sociological analysis of the separation of ownership and control must begin with a consideration of his work.

CHAPTER III

DAHRENDORF AND MANAGERIAL THEORY

Dahrendorf's Classification of Theorists on the Separation of Ownership and Control

DAHRENDORF, in his work *Class and Class Conflict in Industrial Society*, distinguishes between two major categories of thought about the separation of ownership and control. He terms these the 'conservative', and the 'rather more radical', views. Briefly, the radical school supports the notion of a separation of ownership and control (or managerial revolution), and the conservative school opposes it. In view of their usual political connotations the selection of these terms is unfortunate. It is not the nomenclature of these schools of thought which primarily concerns us here, however, but their usefulness and internal consistency as conceptual classifications.

The Conservative School. The interpretation offered by the conservative school is not, in Dahrendorf's view, very prevalent in the West nowadays. He claims that on the whole there is 'an astonishing degree of consensus among sociologists on the implications of joint stock companies for the structure of industrial enterprises, and for the wider structure of society.[1] And most of them, in his view, incline to the 'more radical' interpretation. Traces of the conservative view are, however, to be found in the work of C. Wright Mills.[2]

Despite Dahrendorf's belief that this view is 'clearly contrary to Marx's own analysis'[3] it has been put forward almost exclusively by members of the political left[4] and, above all, by

---

[1] *Class and Class Conflict*, p. 42.

[2] *ibid.*, p. 43. (Examples of Mills' work on this subject are: *Power Elite*, London, 1959; *White Collar*, London, 1951; and 'A Marx for the Managers', in R. K. Merton (ed.) *Reader in Bureaucracy*.)

[3] *Class and Class Conflict*, p. 43.

[4] But see N. Davenport, 'Mr Crosland Gets it Wrong', *Spectator*, January 11, 1963, and the same author's *The Split Society*, London, 1964.

those on its Marxist and Neo-Marxist fringe.[1] Often, as in the case of Wright Mills' own work, the views held by the 'conservative' school have been put forward in such a way that they have gained popularity at the expense of clarity. However, the key postulates of this school have been neatly summarized by C. A. R. Crosland.[2] These are that ownership, and particularly institutional ownership, is still sufficiently concentrated to ensure control: that owner-control is reinforced by an elaborate system of interlocking directorates; and that even to the extent that managers do exercise control, they do so in the interests of the owning class. In the view of these writers, then, there has not been a divorce of ownership and control so much as a 'managerial reorganization of the propertied classes into the more or less unified stratum of the corporate rich'. This follows because 'the chief executives and the very rich are *not* two distinct and clearly segregated groups'.[3]

The Radical School. As we have already noted Dahrendorf contrasts the 'conservative' school with a 'rather more radical view'. He tells us that Marx was the founder of this school and that his interpretation has been followed by Burnham, Geiger,[4] Renner[5] and Sering.[6] However, since Dahrendorf's *own views* are in consonance with what he takes to be the 'Marxist' tradition, they provide an admirable illustration of the key postulates of the 'radical' school.

[1] Examples of left-wing writing on this subject can be found in the following British and American works:

S. Aaronovitch, *The Ruling Class*, London, 1961;
R. Blackburn, 'The New Capitalism', in P. Anderson (ed.) *Towards Socialism*, London, 1965;
M. Barratt Brown, 'The Controllers', *Universities and Left Review*, No. 5, 1959; 'The Insiders', *Universities and Left Review*, No. 3, 1958;
P. A. Baran and P. M. Sweezy, 'Monopoly Capital', *Monthly Review*, Vol. xiv, Nos. 3 and 4, July–August, 1962. (For a fuller account see the same authors' *Monopoly Capital: An Essay on the American Economic and Social Order*, N.Y., 1966);
G. Kolko, *Wealth and Power in America*, London, 1962, chapter 4;
P. M. Sweezy, *The Present as History*, N.Y., 1953, chapter 3;
D. Villarejo, 'Stock Ownership and Control of Corporations', *New University Thought*, Chicago, Autumn 1961 and Winter 1962.

[2] C. A. R. Crosland, *The Conservative Enemy*, London, 1962, p. 69.
[3] C. Wright Mills, *The Power Elite*, pp. 131, 147.
[4] Theodor Geiger, *Die Klassengesellschaft im Schmelztiegel*, Cologne and Hagen, 1949.
[5] Karl Renner, *Wandlungen der modernen Gesellschaft: zwei Abhandlungen über die Probleme der Nachkriegszeit*, Vienna, 1953.
[6] Paul Sering, *Jenseits des Kapitalismus*, Nurnberg, 1947.

To begin with, Dahrendorf points out that more than two-thirds of all companies in advanced industrial societies are joint stock companies; that their property exceeds four-fifths of all property in economic enterprises and that 'the enterprise owned and run by an individual, or even a family, has long ceased to be the dominant pattern of economic organisation'. Furthermore, he argues, the shares of joint stock companies are dispersed fairly widely, so that,

'three per cent of the population of the Federal Republic of Germany, and approximately eight per cent of the United States, own one or more shares of joint stock companies. Probably the proportion in other countries is somewhere between these extremes.'[1]

Having noted this dispersion of stock in several highly industrialized countries, Dahrendorf goes on to argue that the very spread of shareholdings makes the rights of property ineffectual, so that ownership is superseded by management. In his view, 'the separation of ownership and control involved both a change in the structure of social positions and a change in the recruitment of personnel to these positions',[2] so that 'the roles of owner and manager, originally combined in the position of the capitalist, have been separated and distributed over two positions, those of stockholder and executive'.[3] The 'positions, roles and outlooks' of the managers and of the stockholders 'are far from identical'.[4] Thus, for Dahrendorf, as for the 'radical' school as a whole, the joint stock company brought about a complete break with earlier capitalist traditions: '*by separating ownership and control, it gave rise to a new group of managers who are utterly different from their predecessors*'.[5] In short, then, Dahrendorf describes the emergence of a new kind of industrial order in which ownership and control are separated and for which the term 'capitalism' is no longer appropriate. A new class of managers had emerged to replace the old owner-managers. These managers are bureaucrats who owe their position to their managerial ability instead of property ownership. Their different social background, training, and

---

[1] *Class and Class Conflict*, p. 42. We will examine the situation in Britain in later chapters but even at this point one must raise the question whether the figures cited are evidence of dispersion or concentration.
[2] *ibid.*, p. 43.   [3] *ibid.*, p. 44.   [4] *ibid.*, p. 47.
[5] *ibid.*, p. 42. (My italics.)

experience, make them both think and act differently from their predecessors, the owner-managers or capitalists.

So far we have used Dahrendorf's classification of 'radical' and 'conservative' views in order to distinguish between the two major schools of thought about a separation of ownership and control. We have used his own work as an example of the 'radical' view. However, whilst we accept the essentials of his classification we think that his use of the two terms 'radical' and 'conservative' tends to obscure rather than clarify the nature of these two schools of thought. Thus, in all future references to this distinction we intend to use the terms *'managerialist'* and *'Marxist'*. We do not mean to imply by this that all those who reject the managerial revolution thesis are Marxists (for example, C. Wright Mills was not), but many of them are, and in our view the type of analysis which such theorists generally employ is closer to Marxism than anything else. As we have already seen, however, it is not possible to regard managerialism as one homogeneous theory. Berle on the one hand, and Burnham on the other, represent a division of opinion within managerialism itself, for they have imputed different motives to 'the managers'. Thus, Burnham assumed that the managers would be self-interested, whereas Berle argued that their actions were governed by a 'corporate conscience', that they were 'neutral' and that they sought to fulfil a variety of social responsibilities. Since we are partly concerned with the study of business ideology, and since businessmen are more likely to portray themselves as 'socially responsible' than as 'self-interested', this distinction is, for us, an important one. Henceforth, we will therefore term the Berlian type of managerialism 'non-sectional', and the Burnhamian variant, 'self-interested' or 'sectional'.

There is one more comment we must make about Dahrendorf's classification of theorists. This concerns the role he attributes to Marx as the founder of the 'radical' school. Quite clearly, if he were right about this it would be impossible to deny that Dahrendorf himself was in the 'radical' tradition, and the use of his terms would be partially justified. However, we think he was wrong.

Such a view is inconsistent with the totality of Marx's work. It is quite true that Marx wrote of the 'transformation of the actually functioning capitalist into a mere manager, an administrator of other people's capital, and of the owners of capital into mere owners, mere money capitalists'.[1] However, it is, in our opinion, more than *'merely a step'* from this kind of analysis to Renner's thesis that the 'capitalists without function' *yield* to the 'functionaries without capital', and that this new ruling group of industry bears little resemblance to the old 'full capitalists'.[2] Though Marx wrote that the joint stock company would lead to 'removing the owners from the sphere of production'[3] he also made it quite clear that it had—

'brought matters to such a point, that the labour of superintendence, entirely separated from the ownership of capital, walks the streets. It is, therefore, *no longer necessary for the capitalist to perform the labour of superintendence himself.'*[4]

There are other reasons which make Dahrendorf's interpretation of Marx debatable (e.g. his interpretation of why Marx argued that the joint stock company would lead to the 'abolition of the capitalist mode of production within the capitalist mode of production itself').[5] However, we are not concerned here to argue 'what Marx really meant'. Our sole purpose is to demonstrate that Dahrendorf's assertion that Marx was the founder of the 'radical' school is open to question. This provides us with an additional reason to reject the nomenclature—though not the content—of his classification.

So far, we have considered Dahrendorf's classification of theorists on the separation of ownership and control. We have disagreed with this argument that Marx was the founder of the 'radical' school. We have also substituted the terms 'managerial' and 'Marxist' for the two major groups of theorists, and within the first group have distinguished between models which attribute to managers 'non-sectional' or 'self-interested' motives. As a consequence of this we can see that non-sectional managerialism is but one sub-type of managerial theory as a whole.

We have also noted that Dahrendorf himself may be termed a managerialist. Thus, in order to illustrate some of the wider assumptions of managerialist writers we will now examine Dahrendorf's own views on class structure and society, and on the relationship between corporate managerialism and business

[1] *Capital*, Chicago, 1909. Vol. III, chapter XXVII, pp. 516–517.
[2] Cited in *Class and Class Conflict*, p. 43. (My italics.)   [3] *ibid.*
[4] *Capital*, Vol. III, chapter XXIII, p. 455. (My italics.)
[5] We take this point up in passing later on in Chapter V

ideology. As we will see, his work has the great virtue that it makes explicit much of what has been left implicit in the works of other theorists of this school. In addition to this, he presents his views within the context of a rigorous sociological theory.

Dahrendorf: Class Structure and Society

It is possible that since the nationalization of certain industries in Britain the 'average man' has concluded that 'there'll always be bosses'. In this respect, our fictional average man and the sociologist Dahrendorf have much in common. The crux of Dahrendorf's argument is that class may best be defined in terms of *authority relationships*. Starting from this fundamental assumption, he goes on to argue that capitalism is only one kind of industrial society and that the term 'capitalist' is only applicable where the legal owner of the factory is at the same time the practical manager of production and the supreme commander of his workers.[1] It is after making such implicit or explicit assumptions that many other writers (e.g. Berle) have gone on to claim that modern industrialized societies (especially America but also Britain) are no longer capitalist, so that other terms like 'People's Capitalism' or 'Non-State Socialism' are now more appropriate.

Many writers have gone on from here to argue that the conflict of interests which was endemic to 'old-type capitalism' is no longer present in today's 'management-controlled' corporation. They assert that in the modern corporation the controlling managers do not have the same relationship to property, the same interests or even the same personal motivation as the old 'full capitalist' who both owned and controlled his own company. Thus, they argue that since the managers are not property owners the conflict of interests between owners and workers is no longer present. Such writers tend to make the initial and crucial assumption that highly industrialized societies, and especially the USA, are 'classless'.[2]

However, it must be emphasized that Dahrendorf does not share this particular viewpoint: the major function of *Class and*

---

[1] *Class and Class Conflict*, p. 40.

[2] Some indication of how far this development has gone in America can be gathered from the title of the article by B. Selekman, 'Is Management *Creating* a Class Society?', *Harvard Business Review*, January–February, 1958, p. 37. (My italics.)

Class Conflict was to establish that authority is the major determinant of class and also of *class conflict*. Most managerialists (and almost by definition those who put forward a non-sectional type of theory) have assumed that *property* is the cause of conflict and that it therefore follows that the interests of (non-propertied) managers are not in conflict with those of employees. But Dahrendorf argues the very opposite to this, namely, that property ownership, or lack of it, is not the sole constituent, or even a necessary part of class. Thus, for him, the absence of owner-managers in industry is virtually irrelevant to the fundamental and original conflict situation. But though his views on this subject must be sharply distinguished from those of most other managerialists, in other respects he has much in common with them.

One aspect of his sociology of class structure which Dahrendorf shares with other managerialists is his concept of several—not one—ruling classes. The whole of his work rests upon the assumption that authority determines class. As a consequence of this, he argues that it is useful to assume that within every 'imperatively co-ordinated association' authority relationships determine the existence of a dominant and a subservient class. Thus, industry, church, and state all have their ruling and subservient groups. Furthermore, Dahrendorf argues, it follows from this that ruling groups should initially be regarded as no more than ruling groups within separate and defined associations. In theory, therefore, 'there can be as many competing, conflicting, or co-existing groups in society as there are associations'. Thus, the expression 'ruling class' in the singular may be quite misleading. And 'whether and in what way certain associations—such as industry and society—are connected in given societies is a matter for empirical analysis'.[1]

Unfortunately, though he quite properly states that whether there is any connection between the leaders of industry and other associations is a matter for empirical verification, Dahrendorf himself does not put forward any evidence. He moves from an assertion of the *theoretical possibility* of a plurality of ruling classes to the implication that modern advanced industrial nations are *in fact* 'pluralist' societies. In the absence of any empirical data about the relationship of industry and society, we may at least presume that, for him, any

[1] *Class and Class Conflict*, p. 198.

connection between government and industry is not one of property. This is self-evident since he believes in a separation of ownership and control in industry. We assume, then, that he takes the ties of ownership and property interest to be either non-existent or ineffectual.

The essence of Dahrendorf's work upon class structure and society (as it concerns us here)[1] may be summarized as follows.

Theoretically, ruling groups may only exist within separate institutions. There is, for example, 'no axiomic relationship between the managers or capitalists of industry, and the ministers or higher civil servants of the state'.[2] Even the existence of any such relationship 'does not legitimatize the formulation of a general law' that the rulers of industry are the rulers of the state. If this law were to be advanced as a hypothesis, 'then it was refuted by the first government of a labour party in an industrial society'.[3]

The notion of a 'pluralist' society, in which the differences between dominant groups are emphasized, rather than the interests common to them, is one widely held by other managerial theorists and generally it is expressed in terms of Galbraith's concept of 'countervailing power'.[4] Thus we are presented with a view of society in which the corporation is but *one* powerful institution among others. What power corporation leaders have is countered by the power of organized labour, customers, government, the local community, shareholders and other groups—and many writers believe that corporation managers respond to this 'countervailing power' by fulfilling responsibilities to employees, customers, the local community, and so on. As one group of writers put it:

'the class struggle in America . . . is not a struggle between the proletariat and bourgeoisie. It is a struggle between functional groups possessing concentrated power—a struggle to control the products of industry. These groups . . . are Big Labor, Big Agriculture, Big Little Business, and Big Business. Of them all, Big Business, if only because it is subject to the most pressure, exercises

---

[1] His belief that class action is noticeably lacking in contemporary society led Dahrendorf to modify some of his earlier analysis in a recent Noel Buxton lecture at Essex. (*Conflict After Class: New Perspectives on the Theory of Social and Political Conflict*, London, 1967.) However, his original interpretation of the ownership-control problem appears to remain intact.

[2] *Class and Class Conflict*, p. 141. [3] *ibid.*, p. 143.

[4] J. K. Galbraith, *American Capitalism: The Concept of Countervailing Power*. London, rev. ed., 1957.

its power with a strong and growing sense of responsibility. It has led the way to the formation of a kind of capitalism that neither Karl Marx nor Adam Smith ever dreamed of.'[1]

In short, when managerialists write of *business in society* they, like Dahrendorf, think in terms of pluralism, and of counter-vailing power—that is essentially of a *conflict* situation. When, however, they write of *business as a society*, and examine the relationship between management and men, they, unlike Dahrendorf, tend to think in terms of natural co-operation— that is essentially of a *non-conflict* situation. Dahrendorf is at least consistent since he entertains the possibility that conflict may develop both *within* the industrial enterprise and also *between* the ruling class of business and other ruling classes. Other writers, however, whilst they are eager to assert that businessmen may have their power delimited by other groups *outside* the enterprise, are equally keen to imply that there is no conflict of interests *within* the enterprise itself.

Quite obviously such theories are in keeping with the views of many businessmen and, indeed, they have a high degree of ideological potential. Large corporation directors often assert that their interests are identical with those of their employees, which means that 'we must do away with this idea that there are "two sides in industry".' They are also prone to depict themselves as some sort of powerless—or indeed 'suppressed'— minority. If only they were freed from 'government/union *interference*' we would all be much more prosperous; customers would have cheaper goods; employees would have higher wages and the balance of payments crisis would be over. Such views are given a large measure of support by most (non-sectional) managerial theories.

As we have noted, Dahrendorf would not claim to support this view. Nevertheless, he does suggest that the separation of ownership and control has led to certain changes in the nature of business ideology.

Managerialism and Business Ideology

Dahrendorf maintains that as a consequence of the separation of ownership and control, and the emergence of a new dominant

[1] The Editors of Fortune in collaboration with R. W. Davenport, *U.S.A.: The Permanent Revolution*, citing Wilcox, p. 68.

class of managers, there has occurred a 'significant change in the basis of legitimacy of entrepreneurial authority'.[1]

Whereas, he states, the manager's right 'to command and expect obedience accrues in part from the property rights delegated to him by the shareholders', the manager, 'unlike the 'full capitalist', can ill afford to exercise his authority in direct and deliberate contravention to the wishes of subordinates'. Because of

'his more immediate contact with the participants of production, he has to seek a second, and often more important, basis of legitimacy for his authority, namely some kind of consensus among those who are bound to obey his commands.'[2]

In this sense, he argues, 'the "human relations" movement is nothing but a symptom of the changing basis of legitimacy of entrepreneurial authority *once ownership and control are separated*'.[3] He claims to find support for this view in Bendix' *Work and Authority in Industry* which suggests that an ideological change has occurred so that modern management now claims an identity of interests among all participants in production, instead of basing unlimited authority on the interests of a ruling class, and he argues that Bendix' work 'lends considerable support to my thesis that *the separation of ownership and control involved a change in the basis of authority*'.[4] At this point we are not concerned with the validity or otherwise of Dahrendorf's views: there is, however, one point which we must make. This is that we think it unlikely that Bendix' work does in fact lend support to Dahrendorf's thesis.

It is quite true that in *Work and Authority in Industry* Bendix uses the terms 'entrepreneurial ideology' and 'managerial ideology'. But—as he is careful to explain elsewhere[5]—he only uses these terms in order to contrast two stages of industrialization. He uses the term 'managerial' for the 'mature' (as opposed to the 'early') stages of industrialization because, in this later period, the necessity for planned and impersonal methods of

---

[1] *Class and Class Conflict*, p. 44.
[2] *ibid.*, pp. 44, 45. This in our view begs the question of which 'managers' are being referred to, consequently we return to the questions of corporate director-employee contact in a later discussion of class (see Chapter XII).
[3] *ibid.*, p. 45. (My italics.)
[4] *ibid.* (My italics.)
[5] 'A Study of Managerial Ideologies', *Economic Development and Cultural Change* Vol. v, No. 2, January, 1957, pp. 120–121.

D

managing the work force leads to an emphasis upon labour management. What Bendix is saying is that modern business has *management problems* and that these cannot be so readily solved, nor in the same way, as they were in the earlier stages of industrialization. Thus, he writes that

'any new challenge to the position of employers and managers will tend to be met by appeals which justify the managerial as well as the other practices of business leaders.'

Bendix' argument that the contemporary business has to solve management problems of bureaucratic organization is of the utmost importance: but in our view (and in our reading of Bendix, in his view too) this is nothing to do with a *separation of ownership and control*. In Britain, for example, this problem is not peculiar to 'management-controlled' companies like ICI and Unilever—it is equally common to both large private companies, like Ferranti and Pilkington's, and also to those joint stock companies which even managerialists believe to be owner-controlled', like Ranks and Woolworth. Despite this, however, it is characteristic of managerialist writers that they believe that changes in the 'control' situation of joint stock companies have led to significant changes in business ideology and practice.

Some, such as Crosland, have pointed out that the separation of ownersip and control, taken by itself, makes less difference to society than is sometimes supposed because the goals of growth, profits and personal wealth are common to managers in Birmingham, Detroit and even Kharkov. But even he argues that because

'the new managers do not have the same relationship to private property as the old owners (though also for other reasons), there are significant differences in the nature of the profit-goal and degree of responsibility with which economic power is exercised. These differences constitute one feature of present-day, as opposed to capitalist, society.'[1]

Others, epitomized by the editors of *Fortune*, have not been so cautious. They believe that 'the history of US capitalism . . . (has shown) . . . that the moral conviction of men can change the course of capitalist development'. They argue that 'at the bottom of the change is simple morality' and that 'the manager

---

[1] *The Conservative Enemy*, p. 92.

is becoming a professional in the sense that like all professional men he has a responsibility to society as a whole'.[1] It can be seen, then, that Dahrendorf, Crosland, and the editors of *Fortune* place differing degrees of emphasis upon the significance of the separation of ownership and control for company policy and ideology. Like all those we term 'managerialists', however, they do consider that it is important.

So far we have considered the works of Berle, Burnham, and Dahrendorf. These writers are among the most important proponents of this school of thought and, as we have seen, there are certain differences between them. Despite such differences, however, there can be no doubt that there are several fundamental ideas which are held by all of them. These fundamental ideas which are the key postulates of managerialism will now be briefly outlined in the following chapter.

[1] *U.S.A.: The Permanent Revolution*, pp. 68, 69, 79.

CHAPTER IV

THE QUINTESSENCE OF
MANAGERIALISM

So far we have referred to the works of Berle, Burnham and
Dahrendorf in order to illustrate the nature and content of
managerial theory and to distinguish between its various subdivisions. As we have seen, managerialism is a body of theory
about business structure and behaviour. In several respects its
non-sectional variant is similar to the socially responsible
ideology advanced by some businessmen and, indeed, as a theory
it puts forward an explanation of why such a business ideology
has developed.

At the root of the theory is the assumption that a separation of
ownership and control has occurred. This proposition is generally
supported by statements that the large industrial joint stock
company has led to a dispersion of shareholding and a consequent diminution in the proportion of votes held by the largest
shareholders. In addition to this it is claimed that the increased
financial and technological complexity of modern business
has weakened the shareholder's ability to intervene. Indeed,
some writers[1] have gone even further than this and argued that
shareholders have no *desire* to govern, since 'the majority are
ignorant of business—40% of shareholders are women—and
the remainder too busy with their full-time jobs elsewhere'.
The main point which concerns us here, however, is that
managerial theorists have not been content to merely assert
that a separation of ownership and control has occurred. They
have also argued that because the 'new managers' have a
different relationship to private property, they also have
different interests and objectives to the 'old capitalists', and
therefore pursue significantly different policies.

It appears that as long as industry was believed to be

[1] See, for example, C. A. R. Crosland, *The Future of Socialism*, London, 1956,
p. 353.

52

controlled by owner-managers, or 'capitalists', then the relation-ship between individual motivation and company policy was treated as a straightforward one. Thus, it was generally held that the owner-manager made company decisions in accordance with his own self-interest and even after the publication of *The Modern Corporation* many economists continued to ignore the view that managers (not capitalists) generally took the important policy decisions. As Florence reports, they continued to use the term 'entrepreneur' and to assume that businessmen were 'risking' their own wealth.[1] Gradually, however, the idea of a separation of ownership and control took hold and, today, there are probably rather fewer economists who would accept Katona's[2] view that the non-propertied manager's identification with his company is so great that there may be no good reason to reject the idea that he maximizes profit. Instead, it is now often assumed that the emergence of a new managerial stratum has raised problems about reconciling some of the classic postulates of economic science with a realistic modern theory of the firm. Thus, a contemporary American economist[3] has summarized the view of many of his colleagues as being that,

'control has passed from ownership's hands into the hands of management; management personnel is more highly specialized and selected for professional competence; its motivations are substantially different from those of the owner-capitalist; its areas of discretionary action and the character of the limitations that bound that area differ markedly from those relevant to the enterprise of an earlier capitalism . . . (hence) . . . the term "managerial".'

An acceptance of this viewpoint has led some economists to follow Keynes,[4] who was one of the first to argue that the dissociation of ownership and control would result in a form of satisficing behaviour. According to this interpretation, the manager is more concerned to pursue an easy life than to maximize profit—though from time to time he will make accommodations to potentially awkward groups if they awaken

[1] P. Sargant Florence, *The Logic of British and American Industry*, London, 1953, p. 300.

[2] G. Katona, *Psychological Analysis of Economic Behavior*, N.Y., 1951, p. 197.

[3] E. S. Mason, 'The Apologetics of Managerialism', *The Journal of Business*, Vol. xxxi, No. 1, January, 1958, p. 1. For a similar summary see: C. Kaysen, 'The Social Significance of the Modern Corporation', A Report of the Papers and Proceedings of the American Economic Association, *American Economic Review*, May, 1957, p. 312.

[4] J. M. Keynes, *Essays in Persuasion*, London, 1931, pp. 314–315.

him rudely enough. Other economists have reacted rather differently. By retaining the classical postulates of self-interest and rationality, and by assuming that the separation of ownership and control has given the new managers some scope to exercise their own discretion, they have concluded that the non-propertied director is just a different kind of economic man. Kratz,[1] for example, has sought to predict company performance on the basis of whether managers are paid by straight salary, commission or some other method. Still others have moved away from regarding the manager exclusively as an economic man and argued that his 'motivation' makes it unlikely that he will be as interested in profit maximization and dividends as he will be in expanding sales or pursuing company growth.[2]

In view of the fact that there has been very little systematic empirical investigation into the motivation of businessmen, economists who adopt the above views have shown an astonishing degree of consensus about what these actual motives are and many of them agree that when translated into operational objectives these 'motives' result in the pursuit of growth. Indeed, as can be seen by reference to the work of Marris[3] and Williamson,[4] this particular objective plays a major part in recent contributions to the theory of the firm in both England and America. And since both these writers have broken out of their disciplinary straitjackets, and attempted to account for psychological and sociological variables, we will return to the possible implications of their work for the analysis of business ideology at a later point. For the moment, however, it is sufficient for our purposes here to note that they, like some other economists, whose views we mention above, fall into our category of 'sectional managerialists'. This being so, it is exceedingly unlikely that many corporate directors will choose to publicly identify themselves with the key actors in such theories of the firm in the same way that their predecessors may have identified themselves with the entrepreneurial figure in classical economics.

[1] L. A. Kratz, 'The Motivation of the Business Manager', *Behavioural Science*, Vol. v, 1960, pp. 313–316.

[2] cf. W. J. Baumol, *Business Behavior, Value and Growth*, N.Y., 1959.

[3] Robin Marris, *The Economic Theory of 'Managerial' Capitalism*, London, 1964.

[4] Oliver E. Williamson, *The Economics of Discretionary Behavior: Managerial Objectives in a Theory of the Firm*, N.J., 1964.

As we have seen, however, the new concern with the motives of non-propertied businessmen has also led to the development of a different, 'non-sectional', type of managerial theory. It is a characteristic of this type of managerialism that the 'motives' of non-propertied directors may lead to the pursuit of operational objectives which are in conflict with the interests of shareholders. But this variant of the theory has not only overthrown the notion of the self-interested capitalist, it has dispensed with the notion of the self-interested manager too. This procedure, in common with certain observations of the sectional managerialists, has led to greater emphasis upon the non-economic analysis of economic behaviour but, in doing so, it has also resulted in a large element of (favourable) *moral* evaluation. Thus, the old notions about ruthless, self-interested individualism have been turned upside-down and some writers have depicted the modern non-propertied director as a responsible, disinterested or even, following Berle, 'neutral' arbiter. There seems little doubt that non-sectional managerialists believe that the managers have changed business and that they have done so for the better. They argue that,

'corporate managements, being self-appointed and responsible to no visible group, are free to choose their aims and in the typical case . . . subordinate the old-fashioned hunt for profits to a variety of other, quantitatively less precise but qualitatively more worthy, objectives.'[1]

Managerialism, then, has a Berlian tradition and a Burnhamian one. But it is the quintessence of managerialism that the adherents of both its sectional and non-sectional variants not only share the belief that a separation of ownership and control has occurred but, put simply, they believe that it matters, and that it has resulted in changes in business behaviour and, by extension, in business ideology.

It should, of course, already be clear that non-sectional managerialism has a high ideological potential for businessmen and given this any attempt to study modern business ideology must concern itself with the extent to which businessmen do in fact believe in their own social responsibility. However, since so much of the literature about the modern corporation and the

---

[1] This summary is offered in P. A. Baran and P. M. Sweezy, 'Monopoly Capital', *Monthly Review*, Vol. XIV, Nos. 3 and 4, July and August, 1962, pp. 138–139.

'new managers', social responsibilities is of a prescriptive, rather than descriptive, nature,[1] and since, in addition to this, we consider the practice whereby some non-sectional manager-ialists have inferred structure and behaviour 'backwards', from the publicly declared self and structural representations of businessmen, to be methodologically unsound, we intend to centre our own analysis of social responsibility as a business ideology upon the findings of our own study of Northern City businessmen.

It should be understood at this point, however, that we have no quarrel with the proposition that an actor's 'definition of the situation' affects his behaviour. But we believe that there is room for a much fuller investigation of how businessmen do define their role, their obligations and responsibilities (i.e. of what they mean by 'social responsibility') than has yet appeared in the literature. The Northern City study clearly has its limitations but it does have the advantage of being based upon systematically gathered data and it is hoped that it may throw some light upon this important question, a discussion of which is provided in the last chapters of this work.

In the immediately following chapters, however, and especially when, in Chapter IX, we consider managerial eco-nomics, we will be much more closely concerned with sectional managerial theories. Since it is unquestionably a fact that the modern giant corporations are not managed by giant capitalists it will not be part of our intention in these chapters to 'prove' or 'disprove' the notion that ownership is increasingly separated from control. Nor do we regard it as part of our purpose to challenge the micro-economists on their own ground and produce yet another theory of the firm. However, the following chapters are very much concerned with the notion of a sepa-ration of ownership and control and given, as we will argue, that this process is best regarded as a matter of degree, the argument will be advanced that its implications for the value systems of businessmen are by no means as clear as sometimes thought. In what follows, then, by giving more attention than has been usual in managerialist writing to what Marris[2] has

---

[1] For a cross-section of the vast amount of literature of this kind see, *The Business System: Readings in Ideas and Concepts* (3 Vols.) (eds.), C. Walton and R. Eells, N.Y. and London, 1967.

[2] *The Economic Theory of 'Managerial' Capitalism*, p. 53.

called 'the "external" sociology of the manager's position', and also of course to the 'internal' sociology of the firm, we hope to clear the way for a consideration of contemporary business ideology which does not regard its relationship to a separation of ownership and control as axiomatic.

To make one thing quite clear, however, we must emphasize that it is not our intention to put forward a general theory of managerial capitalism. On the contrary, since we believe that our present state of knowledge has been retarded more than necessary by a literature which is polarized by attempts to provide such general theories, on the one hand, and by the accumulation of facts without theory, on the other, we will be much more concerned to convince the reader that some of the already existing theories could benefit from qualification, that some commonly accepted 'facts' are open to different interpretations and, not least, that some of the crucial information necessary for a general theory is simply not yet available. Thus our main efforts will be directed toward the redefinition and clarification of questions at issue and where possible toward putting forward short run hypotheses of our own, some of which we will later attempt to test against the Northern City data.

So far, however, we have confined ourselves to spelling out some of the main themes of managerial theory. But since we have already dropped several dark hints that all is not well in the managerialist analysis of Berle, Burnham, Dahrendorf, Florence and others (nor indeed in the analyses of Mills and other 'Marxist' writers) it is clearly incumbent upon us to preface our reconsideration of managerial theory with some explanation of the sources of the confusion we claim to exist.

PART II

TOWARD A RECONSIDERATION OF MANAGERIAL THEORY

CHAPTER V

SOME SOURCES OF CONFUSION

In the preceding pages we outlined two contrary schools of thought about the relationship between ownership and control in advanced industrial societies. We stated that managerial theory, and particularly its non-sectional or Berlian variant, is conformable to a socially responsible business ideology. This ideology is both imputed to and espoused by some businessmen. We further emphasized that some theorists who believe that a separation of ownership and control has occurred *also* believe that this separation provides an important explanation for the development of the 'new' ideology of social responsibility among businessmen. It is this belief which makes a consideration of the notion of a separation of ownership and control essential to this work. It is the purpose of Parts II and III to provide just such a consideration.

There are, however, four important observations which must preface any assessment of the arguments for or against the theory of a managerial revolution. These are, that the debate has been conducted in the absence of sufficient empirical data, that it is characterized by a prevalence of semantic confusions, that it is a political debate, and that the two major groups of protagonists have different logics of analysis.

Paramount among the above is the fact that despite the research which has been done on ownership and control we still lack knowledge about the control situation itself. Many of the important facts about the industrial decision-making process remain unknown. This is of the first importance because if we are to substantiate or reject the claim that managers control the large corporations we need evidence from a whole series of detailed descriptive studies.

We need to know who takes what decisions where and when, and with what objectives in mind. We require detailed information about the parts played in the decision-making process by senior management as opposed to the board of directors. We need detailed knowledge of which groups supply which information to those who take decisions; and which advisory groups have their way and which do not. In addition we need to know much more about the role and influence of different types of director. Above all we need to know whether any one category of director (e.g. propertied; non-propertied-managerial; non-propertied-technical) is generally dominant or generally holds power of veto. If such a group could be found then we could ask some all-important questions. Why is it that its members have power? In short, what is the basis of their power?

For the most part, the answers to these questions have not been found and, even if they were, we still severely lack studies of the relationship between the manager's personal motivations and beliefs and the interests of the shareholders. It is indeed ironic that the influential American industrial sociologists who characterized the 'human relations' approach (and who assumed 'harmony', sometimes apparently to the exclusion of conflict) should not have investigated further one factor which they take to legitimate their orientation—the 'disinterested', 'non-propertied', 'professional manager'. One finds that studies of, say, the restriction of output of shop floor workers, or even Russian managers, come more readily to mind than similar studies of American or British managers. However, even assuming that we had such knowledge, we know very little of what the *shareholder* wants from his investment. Obviously, he wants a profit—but what sort of profit, and do large shareholders think differently from small ones? And to which shareholders, if any, do directors accommodate their policies—large ones, the many smaller ones, present ones, future ones?

It follows from the absence of such empirical data as we mention above that, for the most part, *all* participants in the ownership-control controversy have been forced to rely upon *inferences* drawn from industrial and social structure. This, of course, is not a fully satisfactory approach to the problem. But this situation will remain until a greater proportion of industrial sociologists turn their attention from aiding the operation of a given power structure to analysing that power structure itself and until corporations open, not only their shop floors but also their boardrooms, to the sociologist. There are signs that both these events will come about but, in the meantime, the majority of work on ownership and control must rest on no more than unsubstantiated hypotheses. Much of its credibility rests on facts and figures which, whilst perhaps true, may not be relevant. That is to say, they are not only often open to different interpretations—as are most 'facts'—but in the absence of further crucial evidence neither the managerialist nor any other interpretation can be effectively tested. This, however, brings us to a related point.

The case for a separation of ownership and control has often been buttressed by what may be termed 'secondary evidence'. By this we refer to variables which are assumed to be associated with a change in control from shareholders to managers but which, in practice, may be independently determined. Examples of such secondary evidence are the frequency with which levels of company re-investment or 'plough back', enlightened welfare and personnel policies—and indeed a socially responsible business ideology—have been cited as confirmation of a changed control situation. It will in fact be a common theme throughout Part II that many such inferences drawn from social and industrial structure may be misleading or invalid ones.

A second observation which must be made by way of introduction to our subject concerns the prevalence of semantic confusions. It is of fundamental significance that even such key terms as 'manager', 'control', 'power' and 'capitalism' are often left undefined or given contradictory meanings by different writers. Sometimes, as with Burnham, they are given various meanings by the same writer. Since some managerial theorists posit that we are moving from one type of society to another the last of these terms, 'capitalism', is of particular significance. One may, of course, like Dahrendorf or to a lesser extent Crosland, view capitalism as an aggregation of capitalistic enterprises, that is, enterprises owned *and* managed by the same persons.[1] If one does this, however, the term 'capitalism' is no longer appropriate once the legal owners cease to be the practical managers of their property in a substantial area of the economy. In short, it implies that despite the existence of

[1] cf. R. Dahrendorf, *Class and Class Conflict*, London, 1959, p. 40; C. A. R. Crosland, *The Future of Socialism*, 'Is Britain Still a Capitalist Society?', pp. 62–68. However, it must be noted that Crosland makes this only one point in a six point definition.

extra-industrial power which has been conferred by property ownership one would not speak of a 'capitalist' society. In this respect the writer does not believe Dahrendorf's very strict definition of capitalism to be an adequate one. But irrespective of its merit as a definition it must be emphasized that it conflicts with what we will term the Marxist conception of capitalism. 'Capitalism' means different things to the managerialist Dahrendorf and the Neo-Marxist Blackburn.[1]

The Marxist conception of capitalism is a much wider one. It refers to a system of production in which the ownership of private property plays a dominant role. And at a more fundamental level the Marxist assumes that the prime mover of capitalism is *capital* and that those who have capital have power. Yet the personal absence or presence of the *capitalist* is not regarded as proof or disproof of the existence of *capitalism*. *The capitalist* is a mere 'personification' of the movements of *capital* which dominate the *capitalist* system. As Blackburn puts it, 'the essential alienation of capitalist society is that it is presided over not by man, but the market'. It is of course because Dahrendorf was either unaware of, or unable to accept, this interpretation of Marx that he makes the error of categorizing him as a managerialist. For our part, however, we accept this interpretation of Marx and think it was his view that once the *capitalist* became personally removed from his factory then *capital* appeared in its purest form so that the antagonism between *labour* and *capital* would become sharpened. Stripped of mere 'personifications', the conflict of *capital* and *labour* would appear in its purest form . . . the revolution would be pending.

Dahrendorf interprets Marx's 'the abolition of the capitalist mode of production within the capitalist mode of production itself' to indicate his acceptance of a managerial society. In our view it does not; it represents the cumulation of the forces of capitalism—capital and labour—in the purest form of antagonism, that is, departicularized, fundamental and perceivable conflict. The above is merely what we—and more importantly, some Marxist theorists—understand Marx to predict as a consequence of the joint stock company form. As a statement of fact we find it leaves much to be desired. It implies a determinist notion of history in which capital moves

---

[1] cf. R. Blackburn, 'The New Capitalism', in *Towards Socialism* (ed.), P. Anderson, London, 1965, p. 117.

almost of its own volition. It is a sociology without human action. Here, however, we are merely concerned to use 'capitalism' as an example of the type of semantic differences, and thus confusions, which exist between the Marxist and managerialist schools. Later on, we will have cause to discuss the other semantic confusions which we mention, those concerning the terms 'power' and 'control'.

Thus far we have made two major observations. First, that the inadequacy or inaccessibility of much essential data has limited most of the work on ownership and control to the level of unsubstantiated inferences drawn from structure. Second, that the controversy over ownership and control is often characterized by semantic confusions; we have used the term 'capitalism' as one obvious illustration of this. We will now proceed from outlining differences in the definition of the term 'capitalism' to make two further points which are closely associated with such differences.

The first of these points, and the third major observation which we wish to make by way of introduction, is that these different definitions of capitalism are quite closely associated with political differences. Furthermore, the ownership-control debate is not only an 'academic' controversy but also a political one. However, this does not mean that, in Britain, it is the political right which is pro-managerialist and the left which is anti-managerialist. It is true, of course, that one *can* find right-wing economists who complain that large corporation managements plough back profit to the possible detriment of share-holders and there is no lack of criticism of such managements on the grounds that, not being large shareholders themselves, they are not sufficiently preoccupied with making profit for others. But city and financial journalists, who presumably study the market, show no inclination to shy away from 'management controlled' companies and at least one of them has written that—

'in my investment work I have always tried to avoid the shares of companies which have a public school banker in the Chair because I know that the money influence will be predominant and that the scientist-technician on whom our industrial future depends will be conspicuous by his absence from the Board.'[1]

[1] He adds, with evident chagrin, that he has 'found this simple investment rule almost impossible to follow' since such companies are so few that 'they would not fill a page of an investment folio'. See N. Davenport, *The Split Society*, London, 1964, p. 177: cf. Blackburn, 'The New Capitalism', p. 131.

E

As far as the parliamentary right, the Conservative party, is concerned, however, the truth of the matter would seem to be that it has scarcely concerned itself with the ownership and control controversy at all. Quite obviously the party is against nationalization. Again, quite obviously, the notion of a pluralistic society, in which all have a property-stake, is part of its ideology. Yet, with the exception of some faint-hearted encouragement for 'wider-shareholding' and generalizations about a 'property-owning democracy' the party has remained remarkably reluctant to argue who actually controls British industry today. Or, at least, the Conservative party has remained remarkably quiet on this issue when compared to the Labour party.

To locate the actual participants in the ownership-control controversy in Britain we must look not to conflicts between the two major parties—but to conflicts within the Labour movement itself. It is here that the most prolonged and explicit division of opinion has occurred and there are good reasons that this should be so.

After the Second World War the absence of high levels of unemployment, the greater visibility of prosperity, and the decline of traditional imperialism all contributed to discussion on the left about whether capitalism had overcome, or at least accommodated, its contradictions. All this, and in addition dissatisfaction with the limited changes achieved by nationalization, made imperative a reassessment of left-wing political and economic theory. Of necessity, the left had to answer the question 'Is this still capitalism?' The ownership-control situation has been a common reference point to which all hues of socialist have turned in order to find the answer.

The leadership of the Labour party, for their part, would generally seem to have believed that ownership and control are increasingly separated and to have accepted the case which, as we have already noted, was argued by the party intellectuals Strachey and Crosland, and eventually incorporated into party policy by the pamphlet *Industry and Society*. For these writers, and for the Labour party leadership, the belief that Britain had a management-controlled economy was confirmation that industry itself could be 'managed' by government. And since the belief that managers are more manageable than capitalists has become endemic to the thinking of the Labour party's leadership we may infer that their acceptance of the separation of ownership and control thesis has served to complement and corroborate their wider politico-economic theories and policies. For them, the removal of the capitalist from capitalism has been a factor in legitimating policy.

One problem of all moderate, gradualist and reformist parties is to answer charges made by the more extreme left that their policies operate *within* a given structure. Once they had espoused the notion of a 'managerial revolution' the Labour party was able to retort to such critics that public ownership was no longer a prerequisite to a socialist society and that the economy was manageable. In short, the structure itself had changed.

If, however, we imply that there were good reasons for the party leadership to be interested in the 'managerial revolution' this is equally true of their most vocal left-wing opponents on this issue, the New Left.[1] Inspired as they have been by the sociology of C. Wright Mills, and permeated in varying degrees by Marxian economics, the New Left has been anxious to establish that Britain is *still* a capitalist society. If New Left intellectuals accepted that ownership and control were in fact separated this could weaken their theoretical justification for radical as opposed to reformist political policies. After all, their radical political philosophy rests in no small part on their analysis of the alleged significance of private capital and capitalist relations of production. They are not satisfied to accept the existence of several discrete ruling classes and the occurrence of a managerial revolution would mean, for them, that it was difficult for them to substantiate the existence of one dominant class, or (in their own terms) 'power elite'. The evolution of a non-owning industrial elite would not merely upset one aspect of their total picture of a power elite—it could make problematic the essential source of its power.

C. Wright Mills' work, *The Power Elite*,[2] has often been criticized for his inability to explicitly define the source of power in anything more than 'institutional position'. But his Neo-Marxist disciples in the British New Left quite clearly

---

[1] i.e. those writers who published in or have been associated with either the *New Left Review* or its two precursors *The New Reasoner* and *Universities and Left Review*.

[2] C. Wright Mills, *The Power Elite*, N.Y., 1956.

believe that the source of the power elite's power is rooted in property ownership. It is for this reason that the New Left, and of course other more 'orthodox' Marxists,[1] regard managerialism as an attack on their sociology of power. For them, managerial theory does more than raise questions about the structure of society and the nature of the ruling class. It raises the fundamental question which, in some respects, their use of the term 'power-elite' allows them to side-step, namely, whether there is a propertied ruling class at all.

We do not intend to depict New Left and Labour party intellectuals as mere creatures of their own ideology but we do wish to stress that both parties to this *political controversy* find one or other interpretation the more pleasing as *political men.* Both parties are prone to cite 'the facts' about the ownership and control relationship to defend their wider politico-economic perspectives: and, *vice versa,* their political and economic beliefs rest to some degree upon their interpretation of this relationship. Thus, both managerialists and non-managerialists use the 'true facts' about the control situation to substantiate other discretely different theories: on the one hand, the manageability of the economy, on the other, the nature of class structure. It is partly because the ownership-control debate does operate within two different political matrices that the controversy has continued for so long.

This brings us to our fourth introductory observation. The controversy is not merely characterized by a lack of crucial information, nor by the prevalence of semantic confusions, nor even by the different political interests espoused by its participants—but in addition by the fact that the two sides often do not share a common logic of analysis. Managerialists and Marxists have different analytical systems and at times even use different methods of investigation.

Managerialist methodology, as represented in Florence's *Ownership, Control and Success of Large Companies,* rests partly on a mathematically derived theory of probability.[2] The voting potential of the largest shareholders is calculated and then the

[1] Nearly all their popularized publications seem bound to mention this issue; cf. M. Dobb, *Capitalism Yesterday and Today,* London, 1958; J. R. Campbell, *Some Economic Illusions in the Labour Movement,* London, 1959; S. Aaronovitch, *Monopoly,* London, 1955; and the same author's *The Ruling Class,* London, 1961.
[2] cf. L. S. Penrose, 'Elementary Statistics of Majority Voting', *Statistical Journal,* 1946, Part I.

probability of their being able to control is assessed in terms of the mathematical theory. Allowance is made for familial ties between shareholders, cases where large shareholders are also directors, and so on. Where Marxists have used this type of methodology they have tended to accept a lower threshold of significance than the managerialists.[1] What is much more important, however, they have always supplemented it with a *class analysis*. They have defined managers in terms of their *class position* and in relation to their *class interests*. The managerialist asks, 'who controls?': the Marxist asks 'in whose interests?'[2]

Managerialists write of 'management-controlled corporations' and of 'self-perpetuating oligarchies of managers'. Marxists write of managers as the 'agents of the propertied few' or as 'part of the propertied class'. The two parties operate within different parameters of analysis. Even the time perspective is different. The Marxist regards the growth of a managerial stratum as an historically developed division of labour within the capitalist system itself. The managerialist (we exclude here the ex-Marxist, Burnham) studies the relationship between ownership and control at one point in time.

The managerialist and Marxist forms of analysis are both useful and legitimate ones. Both, as we shall see, can shed light on particular aspects of the modern corporation. But both have their limitations if we wish to clarify the relationship between ownership and control in industry. To do this we not only need more information, we need a greater degree of precision and a more refined sociological form of analysis. Whereas it would be pretentious to claim that we will provide the reader with this in what follows, it should be noted that we regard the observation that 'Marxists' and 'managerialists' have conducted different sorts of analyses to be an important one. It allows us to proceed with an analysis of our own, in

[1] Thus, Villarejo takes ownership of 5% of shares as his criterion and Barratt Brown uses Penrose's work to argue that 6% of the votes is sufficient for control. By contrast, Florence raised his criterion from 20% in *The Logic*, 1953, to 30% in *Ownership, Control and Success*, 1961. (See Villarejo, *New University Thought*, Autumn, 1961, pp. 54–55; Barratt Brown, 'Crosland's Enemy—A Reply', *New Left Review*, March–April, 1963, pp. 24–25.)

[2] For a general discussion of the implications of 'intra' and 'extra-unit' orientations in modern sociological theory, of which this difference is but one example, see, G. Poggi, 'A Main Theme of Contemporary Sociological Analysis: its Limitations and Achievements', *British Journal of Sociology*, Vol. XVI, No. 4, Dec., 1965, pp. 283–294, especially pp. 288–289.

which, in many important respects, these two schools of thought
can be treated as complementary rather than contradictory.
However, before any synthesis can be attempted the facts
themselves must be set straight and for this reason Chapters VI,
VII and VIII are concerned with attempting to answer some
important questions about capitalists, technocrats and professionals.

CHAPTER VI

CAPITALISM WITHOUT CAPITALISTS?

BOTH types of managerialists agree that the diminishing share ownership of large corporation directors is evidence of a separation of ownership and control. There are two reasons for this. On the one hand, it is argued that if the large corporation director is non-propertied he will not act *qua* shareholder but *qua* manager: that is, his interests will be different from those of the owner-manager and consequently 'his' corporation will pursue different policies. On the other hand, it is argued that a decline in directorial shareholding means that large shareholders are less likely to sit on the boards and thus 'control' policy. We will consider sociological implications of the second argument later on but, for the moment, we wish to examine the evidence for the thesis that the large corporation director *is* non-propertied. To do so we will refer in detail to Florence's work—*Ownership, Control and Success*.

This work is probably the most recent and detailed large-scale attempt to present the relevant historical and comparative data. We refer to it because we believe it doubtful whether our replication of the Herculean labour performed by Florence and his research team over several years would merit the exertions it demanded. But a further reason for referring to Florence's work is that in *Ownership, Control and Success* he has moved from a former rejection of the managerial thesis toward a partial acceptance of it. In his earlier work he had written that 'the managerial revolution has not proceeded as far as is sometimes thought (or stated without thought)' and that 'proclamation of the managerial revolution should perhaps, for the present, be postponed'.[1] In *Ownership, Control and Success*, on the other hand, he refers to a 'managerial evolution if not revolution'.

Florence has formulated his conclusions with great caution but nevertheless this later work has become a common source to

[1] *The Logic of British and American Industry*, London, 1953, pp. 193, 202–203.

which managerialist writers have turned in order to substantiate their case[1] and not all of them have been as cautious in
citing Florence's conclusions as he was in formulating them.
What concerns us here, however, is that his work established
the following major facts, all of which are frequently cited by
managerial theorists as evidence for a separation of ownership
and control.

First, he found an inverse relationship between size of
company (in assets) and the percentage of ordinary shares
owned by the board. The percentages of ordinary directorial
shareholding by size of company were as follows: smaller
companies 2·9%, medium companies 2·1%, very large
companies 1·5%.[2]

Secondly, for the same size ranges, the proportion of directors
among the twenty largest shareholders was 30%: 21%: and
16%.[3]

Thirdly, Florence found that the (median) average percentage of directors' ordinary holdings in the very large companies
had fallen from 2·8% in the year 1936 to only 1·5% in 1951.[4]

Facts such as these are widely acclaimed by those writers who
believe that the diffusion of share ownership on the one hand,
and the decline in directors' shareholding on the other, underlie
the inevitability of a managerial revolution. Control, they argue,
now rests in the hands of new men with new motives. When
Florence's work is presented in this manner it begins to appear
as if some inexorable force is at work. As a consequence of this
directorial holdings inevitably decline, control of the boards by
shareholder members becomes increasingly unlikely and even
those directors who do own shares do not do so *qua* shareholders,
but *qua* managers, whose interests and satisfactions are not
related to share ownership but to salaries, expense accounts,
the pursuit of growth, sales maximization, and so on.

But what do we mean by a corporation head acting *qua*
shareholder or *qua* manager? Although the percentage of shares
held may vary from company to company most directors do
own shares in their own companies. Indeed, a specified mini-

---

[1] See, above all, C. A. R. Crosland, *The Conservative Enemy*, London, 1962,
chapter 5, 'Insiders and Controllers'.
[2] Florence, *Ownership, Control and Success*, p. 191.
[3] *ibid.*
[4] *ibid.*, table IVg, p. 104. (These figures do not relate to companies which
though 'very large' in 1951 were not so in 1936.)

mum holding is usually a legal qualification for office—though an exception here is Unilever which abolished the qualification in 1956. Furthermore, if we are concerned with the *motives* of present-day directors (and not merely the *control potential* of large shareholders) it is possible that the *percentage* of ordinary capital owned by the board is not a very satisfactory measure. What is required is an estimate of the actual *wealth* which directors have at risk in their companies or, more precisely, of that proportion of their income which derives from share ownership—and not the percentage of *all* ordinary shares which they own. The problem of taking the percentage ordinary holding of directors to indicate their financial interest may be clearly demonstrated by the case of Unilever in 1951.

At that date a 0·1% holding had a *nominal* value of *circa* £13,600.[1] Such a holding could hardly be termed a minimal one—even though it represents only one thousandth part of all ordinary shares. Furthermore, were we to allow for the cost of purchasing such a fraction at market prices then its actual value would be much greater. In addition to this obvious limitation of using the percentage there are others. For example, the same percentage holding may conceal wide differences between two companies if they have different amounts of share capital—and indeed it may not reflect the amount of wealth at risk in one company at two dates if the total issued capital has not been constant.

In order that we may gain an approximate measure of the *wealth* which directors have invested in their own companies we have therefore translated Florence's percentage figures back into their equivalent *nominal* values.[2] When this is done (see Table 6.1) we find that the directors of all his 'Very Large' companies collectively owned £22,700,000 in 1936 and £19,400,000 in 1951. These figures relate only to *nominal* values and as such they are of little meaning to the economist.

However, while we recognize that it would be foolish to make

[1] Here we have converted Florence's data back into equivalent nominal values; cf. *Ownership, Control and Success*, Appendix A.1., p. 208.

[2] The data was re-worked from Florence, *Ownership, Control and Success*, Appendix A.1, pp. 196–217. We have excluded nine of the 98 companies which Florence presents as having £3 million or over tangible assets in 1951. Six were excluded because they were not formed at 1936; two because their directors held preference shares; one company (Tobacco Securities Trust) was excluded because of its complicated voting rights.

comparisons over time from figures such as these, they do place
the discussion of directorial share ownership on a concrete
footing. Put simply, they do indicate that large sums of capital
were invested in the largest corporations by at least some of
their directors as late as 1951.

However, the contention that the modern director has little
economic interest *qua* shareholder cannot be tested by reference
to the *total* investment at risk for *all* directors. Nor can it be
tested by citing the holdings of the 'average' director who, in
this case, owned shares to a nominal value of £21,000 in 1951.[1]
Clearly, some boards, and some directors, will own more shares
than others and given a skewed distribution, an arithmetic
average will mislead more than it informs. Thus, in order to get

TABLE 6.1

*The Nominal Value of Directors' Ordinary Shares
in Companies with Assets of £3 million or Over*

	(1)	(2)	(3)	(4)	
Year	No. of Companies	No. of Directors	Total Ordinary Investment for All Boards (£)	'Average' Board's Ordinary Share Ownership (3/1) (£)	'Average' Director's Ordinary Share Ownership (3/2) (£)
1936	89	896	22,728,490	255,376	25,367
1951	89	934	19,351,570	217,433	20,719

a better measure of the wealth which directors have at stake in
their companies we have re-worked Florence's percentage data
for each company in Table 6.2 and translated this back into
nominal values. In this table we have found the 'average'
director's holdings for each company. This means that should
one director out of, say, ten hold an exceedingly large amount,
then this will give an inflated 'average' figure. This does not
effect the issue unduly if we confine ourselves to the study of
particular companies because the average figure then indicates

[1] Marxist writers are fond of citing the Oxford Institute of Statistics survey
which showed that, in 1955, directors of companies held shares to an average value
of £28,000. This figure, like the one given above, is based on an arithmetic
average. Both Aaronovitch, *The Ruling Class*, p. 22, and Blackburn, 'The New
Capitalism', p. 117, cite this figure. See L. R. Klein *et al.*, 'Savings and Finances
of the Upper Income Classes', *Bulletin of the Oxford Institute of Statistics*, Nov., 1956,
table viii, p. 308. (It should also be noted that there is no reason to assume that
the 'directors' in this study are those who manage the major corporations.)

that there is at least *one* wealthy director in that company. The figures in the table relate only to the nominal value of ordinary shares which are registered in a director's name, they do not relate to preference or other forms of stockholding and of course they exclude any holding the members of a board may hold in other companies.

Now despite their obvious limitations these figures leave no doubt that the modern director generally has a financial stake in his company's shares which is very small when compared to

TABLE 6.2

Classification of Companies by the Nominal Value of their Directors' Ordinary Shareholdings

Value of 'Average' Director's Nominal Shareholding (1)	No. of Companies	
	(2)	(3)
	1936	1951
Less than £1,000	14	18
£1,000–£2,999	18	21
£3,000–£4,999	9	13
£5,000–£9,999	14	9
£10,000–£24,999	16	11
£25,000–£49,999	4	6
£50,000–£99,999	7	6
Over £100,000	7	5
	89	89

Source: The nominal share values have been re-worked from Florence, *Ownership, Control and Success*, Appendix A.1.

Notes: Column (1) refers to the total board holding in each company divided by the number of directors at each date. Columns (2) and (3) refer to the same companies as those in Table 6.1.

the £millions of a Leverhulme or Nuffield. They serve as a sharp reminder to 'Marxist' writers that, in practice, the 'average' director who owns £28,000's worth of shares is not to be found in many boardrooms. Furthermore, if we look at the very largest companies in Florence's sample, i.e. those with assets of over £50 million (see Table 6.3), there is evidence in at least three companies (BAT, ICI, and Dunlop) that big corporation directors sometimes own very small proportions of ordinary shares indeed.

There are, however, certain indications that the diminution of directorial shareholdings may not be quite such an inexorable process as some writers would have us believe.[1] For example, though Florence found that the number of directors with no more than the legally required minimum of shares decreased between 1936 and 1951 he found this process to be more characteristic of the 'smaller' and 'medium' sized companies than of the very 'large'. In 1951 the proportion of companies with *no* directors holding no more than the legal minimum was 47% for the smaller, 47% for the medium, and only 27% for

TABLE 6.3

The Nominal Values of the Board and Average Director's Ordinary Holdings in Six Companies with Assets of over £50 million in 1951

Company	Assets	Issued Ord. Share Capital (£m)	% of Ord. held by Board	Nominal Value of Board's Ord. Holding (£)	No. of Directors	Nominal Value of 'Average Director's' Holding (£)
Lever Bros	193·7	13·6	23·2	3,055,200	24	131,466
Imperial Tobacco	123·3	37·6	4·2	2,256,000	34	46,447
Courtauld	63·1	24·0	1·2	288,000	18	16,000
British American Tobacco	143·2	23·8	0·2	47,600	17	2,800
Imperial Chemical Industries	236·9	60·6	0·1	60,600	17	3,565
Dunlop Rubber	51·5	12·9	0·03	3,870	10	387
				5,711,270	120	

the very large.[2] However, though share options may have become more popular after 1951 they have, if anything, probably become less so in recent years. In America, three out of four companies have such schemes[3]; in Britain, a 1969 report on business salaries found them to be 'almost non-existent.[4] Thus provided one assumes that corporation directors are rational animals, the implications of this situation for their economic motivation is quite clear: one would predict they had much

[1] See, for example, C. A. R. Crosland, *The Conservative Enemy*, p. 69.
[2] Florence, *Ownership, Control and Success*, pp. 187, 191.
[3] Marris, *The Economic Theory of 'Managerial' Capitalism*, p. 67.
[4] *Top Salaries in the Private Sector and Nationalised Industries*, p. 7.

more to gain from their ample salaries and emoluments than from the dividends and capital gains accruing from their shares.

In passing, however, one might note that the case of Dunlop indicates that either directors are not rational animals, or that they are not exclusively self-interested, or that other factors play an important part in the treatment of shareholders. In many respects Dunlop is the epitomy of the 'management-controlled' company. In 1951 the board collectively owned only 0·03% of ordinary; the top 20 vote-holders held only 9·6% of the votes (whereas a clear 80% of Florence's £3 million or over companies had 20 shareholders owning more than 10% of the vote); and yet, over the period 1936–51, Dunlop shareholders did better than those in all but 15 of the 83 companies for which Florence had data.[1]

So far, however, we have only considered the possible significance of the nominal value of directorial shareholding (as opposed to the percentage of shares owned by directors) for their economic interests and motivation. But directorial shareholding may also be considered in another light.

Non-sectional managerialists, and, as we have seen, Berle in particular, have placed some emphasis upon the role of 'public consensus' and the 'corporate conscience'. The figures we have cited in the preceding pages therefore give rise to another question, namely, what bearing may directors' share-ownership have upon them developing a 'conscience' toward shareholders? The phrase 'stockholder-orientated conscience' has been coined by Marris[2] to cover just this eventuality. However, Marris was mainly concerned with the economic analysis of the firm as a system in its own right and we will be much more concerned with business ideology, which focuses our attention rather more upon the representation of the firm as a system significant to others located in external systems. For this reason we are rather more closely interested in the possibility of a 'shareholder conscience' existing than it was necessary for Marris to be in his own analysis—and in our view the evidence we have considered

---

[1] *Ownership, Control and Success*, Appendix A.1. Dunlop's performance cannot be explained by its being 'owner-controlled' prior to 1951. In 1951 the largest twenty shareholders owned 9·6% of the votes (1936—5·1%), the largest single shareholder held 2·3% (0·6%), the board held 0·03% (0·09%), and in neither year were any directors among the top twenty vote-holders.

[2] *The Economic Theory of 'Managerial' Capitalism*, p. 54.

so far does more to confirm than to reject the hypothesis that such a conscience may exist.

As we have seen, it is quite true that the collective ordinary share ownership of most large corporation boards of directors is only a very small percentage of such firms' ordinary shares and it must be further accepted that the nominal value of such directors' holdings disqualifies them from being termed 'capitalists' in any meaningful sense. But, in fact, neither of these observations fully bear out the claim that modern large corporation directors are 'non-propertied'. This becomes apparent once we look *outside* the corporation and consider the distribution of wealth in British society.

We find, for example, that in 1963 the Inland Revenue classified only 18·5 million of the population as wealth-holders. Yet, of these, 77% had wealth to the value of less than £3,000[1] —the average wealth of those with less than £3,000 being estimated at about £100[2]. Thus, even in terms of the nominal value of their ordinary shareholdings in their own companies, large corporation directors must often belong to a small propertied stratum of British society. If we were to include the shares they hold in other companies, different forms of investment which they may have in their own company, and other forms of wealth, this fact would emerge all the more clearly. But even on the basis of the figures advanced so far we feel justified in stating that large corporation directors, as a group, do have a stake in industrial share ownership and that they are probably more likely to own industrial shares than the members of other occupations.

After all, it must not be overlooked that only an estimated 1·8 million (or about 5% of the adult population) hold industrial or commercial stocks.[3] In comparison with the population as a whole, then, and even when compared to shareholders generally,[4] there is some justification for regarding directors as 'men

---

[1] *107th Report of the Commissioners of Inland Revenue*, 1963–64, Cmnd. 2572, table 145. (The 1966 figures, the latest available, show no appreciable change: cf. *110th Report*, Cmnd. 3508, 1968, table 185.)

[2] 'Still No Property-Owning Democracy', *The Economist*, January 16, 1966.

[3] *How does Britain Save? A Summary of the Results of a Survey Conducted for the London Stock Exchange by the British Market Research Bureau Limited*, London Stock Exchange, May, 1966, pp. 5, 9.

[4] Despite the time-lag, and problems pertaining to the figures involved, this is strongly suggested by a comparison between the London Stock Exchange's estimates of the ownership distribution of all commercial and industrial shares and

of property'. They constitute an important segment of the small minority group of shareholders.

It does not necessarily follow from this that large corporation directors will experience an overwhelming desire to serve the interests of, say, boarding-house widows with small investments in their companies. Nor does it necessarily follow that they will regard themselves as shareholders rather than managers or administrators. It does seem improbable, however, that they will treat shareholders badly, in the sense of serving their interests in a way that is incompatible with their own expectations as shareholders in their own or other companies. This gives some grounds for presupposing the existence of a directorial conscience for the interests of shareholders. Whereas the existence of such a conscience may not constitute an immediate and specific input to the day-to-day decision making process it may well constitute a limiting boundary within which directors choose to pursue their own 'personal' interests and value preferences. We will return to this possibility later on.

For the moment, however, since the evidence reviewed above quite clearly supports the contention that the 'capitalist' has gone out of 'capitalism', the question arises of whether, as many writers also contend, he has been replaced by the 'technocrat'. We consider this and allied propositions in the following chapters.

---

our own estimates (cf. Table 6.2, col. 3) of the ordinary share ownership of large corporation directors in their own companies. This indicates that 66% of shareholders (and 20% of large corporation directors) held shares to the value of less than £1,000, 23% of shareholders had holdings between £1,000–£4,999 (38% of directors) and 11% of shareholders had holdings of £5,000 or over (42% of directors). See, *How Does Britain Save?* p. 27.

CHAPTER VII

TECHNOCRACY WITHOUT TECHNOCRATS?

IN practice, there is some evidence to suggest that the majority of directors have not been to university. Studies by the Institute of Directors in 1959,[1] 1965[2] and 1966,[3] and a study by Abrams in 1960,[4] all found that eight out of ten directors did not have university degrees. Less reliable studies by Copeman[5] in 1955, Clark[6] in 1966, and our own Northern City survey all suggest a proportion in the region of six out of ten.

A university education is not always a necessary pre-condition to technocratic status but it generally is, and in any case there is scant evidence to suggest that many directors hold *either* a university degree *or* any other kind of formal qualification. Barritt has shown that 74% of directors in companies with assets of £500,000 and over had no qualifications at all.[7] And the three studies by the Institute of Directors found approximately 60% of directors were not 'qualified'—even when an Arts degree was counted as a qualification.[8] To quote *The Director's* 1959 survey,

'the striking feature is the relatively small proportion with a University Degree and the high number who think that experience alone qualifies them for a directorship . . . (it would seem that) . . . business is not learned at school but depends largely on training on the job. The professional, academic man as yet plays a minor part in industry.'

[1] 'The Life and Times of a Director', *The Director*, Oct., 1959, p. 301.
[2] 'The Anatomy of the Board', *The Director*, Jan., 1965, p. 88.
[3] 'The Director Observed', *The Director*, April, 1966, p. 85.
[4] M. Abrams, 'The Elite of Tomorrow', *The Observer*, September 4, 1960.
[5] G. H. Copeman, *Leaders of British Industry*, London, 1955, p. 100.
[6] D. G. Clark, *The Industrial Manager: His Background and Career Pattern*, London, 1966, p. 43, table 3.17.
[7] D. P. Barritt, 'The Stated Qualifications of Directors in Larger Public Companies', *Journal of Industrial Economics*, Vol. v, 1956–7, pp. 220–224.
[8] *The Director*, 1959, p. 301; *The Director*, 1965, table 3; *The Director*, 1966, p. 85; see also, Clark, *The Industrial Manager*, Appendix II, table 40, p. 189.

Now, of course, the membership of the Institute of Directors contains a large number of smaller companies and it might therefore be objected that the above figures hide the fact that there are more technocrats (or qualified directors) in larger companies. *Prima facie*, there is some evidence to support this view. In Table 7.1 we can see that the proportion of non-

TABLE 7.1

The Percentage of Directors Without Qualifications
by Size of Company

Size of Company (Capital)	Directors Without Qualifications %
Less than £50,000	67·57
£50,000–£100,000	66·58
£100,000–£250,000	62·76
£250,000–£500,000	56·03
£500,000–£1 million	46·31
£1 million–£5 million	50·79
£5 million or more	43·14

Source: This table was supplied to the writer by courtesy of E. D. Foster, Editor of *The Director*, and J. L. Jolley and Partners who conducted the 1965 survey.

qualified directors falls as we move from smaller to larger companies. Closer analysis of the Institute's data also confirms that there is an increase in the proportion of directors with Science qualifications as we pass from smaller to larger companies. However, given a hundredfold increase in company size (from £50,000 to £5 million plus) the proportion only increases from 3% to 9%.[1] A more recent survey of *The Times* 'Top 300' companies indicates that less than one out of three private directors have Science qualifications—41% having no qualification equivalent to an ordinary degree, compared to only 12% of those in nationalized industry.[2]

Indeed, the decreased proportion of non-qualified directors in large companies is only partially connected with this small increase in those with Science qualifications. Equally, if not more important, are the increased proportions of those with Accountancy qualifications and Arts degrees. Only 3·5% of small company directors hold accountancy qualifications compared to 14·6% of those in large companies. The fact that

[1] See, *The Director*, 1965, table 3.
[2] National Board for Prices and Incomes, *Top Salaries in the Private Sector and Nationalized Industries*, Cmnd. 3970, table 22.

15% of large corporation directors have Arts degrees compared to only 4% in smaller companies is, if anything, a reminder that there are few technocrats even in the boardrooms of large companies. And since one out of six large company directors are 'qualified' only in the sense that they have an Arts degree, this means that the figure of 43% in Table 7.1 is a considerable *underestimate* of those 'not qualified' for *management*. If further evidence were required to question the thesis that large company directors are 'technocrats' it is to be found in the fact that in 1965 *The Director* found only 1·4% of those in companies with £5 million or more capital to have Ph.D's.

TABLE 7.2

The Percentage of Managers not Qualified in Science or Technology by Position and Size of Company

Management Level	Less than 2,000 Employees	2,000–20,000 Employees	Over 20,000 Employees
	%	%	%
Top Management	65	68	73
Middle Management	68	67	75
Junior Management	64	74	77

Source: Adapted from *Management Recruitment and Development*, H.M.S.O., 1965, Appendix III, Table 11.4. (The response rate for the smallest companies was only 27%; this contrasts with 95% for the largest, and 74% for the medium-sized companies.)

There is, of course, the possibility that there are more technically qualified men in the lower echelons of the management hierarchy. Some evidence for this is to be found in a P.E.P. survey[1] which reported in the early 1950's about eight out of every ten graduates going into industry had taken degrees in science or technology and also in Clark's[2] work which revealed that four out of five graduate managers in the North-West had taken such subjects. However, even Clark's survey indicates that about 55% of managers in private industry do *not* hold technical qualifications[3] and a recent N.E.D.C. report[4] suggests that, irrespective of position or size of company, the majority of managers are not qualified in technical or scientific subjects (see Table 7.2). There does seem to be enough evidence

[1] P.E.P., *Graduate Employment*, London, 1956, p. 114.
[2] *The Industrial Manager*, p. 37.
[3] *ibid.*, table 3.11, p. 38; table 3.23, p. 50.
[4] Though see note to Table 7.2.

to confirm that the proportion of technically qualified managers has increased in the last 10 years[1] but even so it does not automatically follow that the technically qualified will be represented proportionately in future boards of directors. On the basis of their management survey the Acton Society developed a scale for ranking 'Advantageous' and 'Disadvantageous' factors in promotion: 'Technical Qualifications' came bottom in the 'Advantageous' category—at the top was 'Arts degree, Oxford or Cambridge'.[2]

In fine, it is exceedingly difficult to argue that the large corporation director is technically qualified. In addition, it is by no means certain that there will be a radical increase in the proportion of such directors in the near future. Managerialists have argued that we have 'Capitalism without Capitalists': in historical perspective there is some evidence for this. But, for Britain at least, the notion that the 'capitalist' has been replaced by the 'technocrat' is not borne out by fact. If this be technocracy it is 'Technocracy without Technocrats'.

Thus far we have seen that *some* directors do have large holdings in the stock of the large corporations and that it is possibly erroneous to consider even most directors as 'non-propertied'. We have also seen, and this is quite certain, that the majority of directors are not, in any meaningful sense of the word, 'technocrats'. However, the possibility remains that they may be—or may consider themselves to be—'professionals'.

---

[1] cf. Acton Society Trust, *Management Succession: The Recruitment, Selection, Training and Promotion of Managers*, 1956, table 9, p. 12; R. V. Clements, *Managers: A Study of their Careers in Industry*, London, 1958, Appendix II, table 17.

[2] *Management Succession*, p. 28.

CHAPTER VIII

PROFESSIONALISM WITHOUT PROFESSIONALS?

As we saw earlier many of the ideas which make up the Berlian variant of managerial theory rest upon the assumption that the modern manager is a 'professional'. *If this is to mean anything it must imply that the manager's skill rests upon an established body of knowledge and that his conduct is governed by norms which derive from a source independent of his source of income.*[1] We will consider the ethical aspects of management behaviour later on.[2] But here we will confine ourselves to an examination of the proposition that the manager's skill is derived from an established body of knowledge.

Since the war there has been an increasing interest in management education: it is now widely believed that a high level of management education can be instrumental in the achievement of a high level of productivity. This argument is due in no small part to the conclusions arrived at by the 66 teams which went to America under the Marshall Aid Plan. As Hutton reports 'practically every Productivity Team' emphasized the contribution of 'the American system of higher education in general and, in particular, by that part of it which is devoted to administrative studies'.[3] In the words of *The Economist*,

---

[1] For a similar interpretation see, Bernard Barber, 'Is American Business Becoming Professionalized? Analysis of a Social Ideology', in E. A. Tiryakian (ed.), *Sociological Theory, Values, and Socio-cultural Change*, N.Y., 1963, pp. 121–145. For a very definite assertation that the I.I.A. is a professional association and that British management is on the way to being professionalized, see Edward Meigh, 'The Implications of Membership of a Professional Body', *The British Management Review*, Vol. 12, No. 3 (reprinted in H. W. Vollmer and D. L. Mills (eds.), *Professionalization*, N.J., 1966, pp. 153–168).

[2] For a statement of the difficulties in depicting businessmen as egoistic and professionals as altruistic, see Parson's classic essay, 'The Professions and the Social Structure', *Social Forces*, Vol. 17, No. 4, May 1939, pp. 457–467.

[3] G. Hutton, *We Too Can Prosper: The Promise of Productivity*, London, 1953, pp. 43–44.

the Anglo-American Council on Productivity 'has probably had a continuing effect upon the younger generation of British managers that will be felt for many years'.[1] However, this was written in 1952 and even by 1963, 15 years after the Anglo-American Council on Productivity had been set up, there were, strictly speaking, still no British business schools. Lord Franks, reporting on the then existing state of management education, had felt bound to state: 'It is all needed and more'.[2]

More recently, however, there has been a spate of development in management education. In 1965 there were 17 universities which provided some form of management training and the development of two business schools was under way. Nevertheless, provision for management education is still limited and the fact that such courses have been more common in technical colleges and colleges of commerce than they are in universities is probably symptomatic of their low status as academic subjects. Certainly, provision for management education is poor when compared to that in the established professions[3] or even when compared to the American situation, where students of business administration are the largest single undergraduate group.[4]

In Britain, management education is still limited, and given the dearth of such courses in the past it seems highly probable that the majority of contemporary directors have little or no experience in this field. Indeed there is some evidence to suggest that a sizeable proportion of modern-day directors are anti-management education and, above all, anti-management theorists. If the directors we interviewed in Northern City are typical of others, then this would certainly appear to be the case.

Of the 65 directors and senior managers who we interviewed in Northern City 61 had experienced no formal management training prior to taking up their first management position. Nor had many of them attended management or specialist courses since they became managers. When asked—'Have you

---

[1] *The Economist*, September 13, 1952.

[2] *British Business Schools*, British Institute of Management, 1963.

[3] The Urwick Management Centre has estimated that there are approximately 19,000 places (or 105,000 man-weeks capacity) in organizations of all types whch provide management courses of over a week in length. See *Management Recruitment and Development*, Appendix VIa and Appendix VIII, table 1.

[4] W. H. Whyte, *The Organisation Man*, London, 1957, p. 84.

attended any management courses since becoming a manager?'
—41 of the 65 replied that they had not.

Since they had experienced little participation in professional
management bodies and had undergone little or no management education, it might be supposed that these businessmen
would lack a favourable attitude to management bodies in
general. In an attempt to see if this was so, we asked them,
'What is your opinion of management bodies?' No attempt
was made to relate the question to any specific institution
and the fact that all but 11 found it possible to give their
opinion may perhaps indicate that the question did tap a
pre-existing attitude complex. In Table 8.1 we have classified
the responses to this question into broad categories.

TABLE 8.1

Views on Management Bodies in Northern City

General Approval	10
Qualified Approval	10
Pro-latent but Anti-manifest Functions	22
Rejection	12
D.K.; no experience; lack of knowledge	11
	—
	65

As can be seen from the table, a dozen respondents flatly
denied that management bodies had any value at all: for the
most part they did so on the grounds that 'you can't teach
management', or that 'they only tell you what you already
know'. But even though those who rejected management
bodies did so on the grounds that, in the words of one, 'potted
management is no substitute for experience', it would be quite
wrong to assume that the opposite to this was believed by those
whose attitudes we have classified under 'general approval'.

In fact, only one of those specifically stated that management
skills *could* be taught and implied that a body of knowledge
existed which 'help(s) people obtain management skills more
efficiently than trial and error'. The majority only went so far
as saying that 'I suppose it helps them see the wood from the
trees'. And the fact that the director just quoted referred to
'*them*' is perhaps significant: in general, participation in
management bodies, and courses in management training,

were considered, at best, possibly useful for *other* people. In practice, then, 'approval' was indicated in only the most non-specific sense and the phrase 'wood and trees'—which was reiterated throughout the interviews in many different contexts (and which management education supposedly helped to distinguish between)—is hardly tantamount to a high level of commitment. Of those whose attitudes were of 'Qualified Approval', two were in favour of management bodies when they confined themselves to running *specialist* courses. The rest replied that 'it's all right for younger men', and three added—to quote the words of a senior manager who *lectured* in management—'the type that go will never make managers anyway'.

In short, the majority of interviewees whose replies are classified as showing 'General' or 'Qualified' approval had opinions which make it doubtful that they considered themselves professional managers—and even more doubtful that they accepted the existence of a useful body of management theory. This impression is strengthened when we consider the largest category of response.

To do so, we have used the rather awkward term 'Pro-latent but Anti-Manifest Functions'. This exactly summarizes the views of the largest number of respondents—and, in addition, though this was not always made explicit, it reflects the attitude of most of the directors we interviewed. In short, we refer here to the view that even though management bodies have little to offer *in themselves* they do provide an opportunity to make contact with other managers and facilitate the discussion of common problems.

Now, it is, of course, quite common for members of all professions to attend conferences and meetings in order to meet other colleagues: sometimes, no doubt, this occurs *despite*, rather than *because*, X or Y is to lecture. However, the attitude we found in Northern City went further than this. It rested on the assumption that management is the 'practical art'—or, as some would have it, the 'artful science'—of practical men. The 'theoreticians', which many of these directors associated with 'management bodies', were 'too airy-fairy', 'too theoretical', 'all talk and no do'. Attendance at professional management functions was therefore regarded as valuable 'only in so far as it brings you into contact with others in the same line'.

Knowledge, that is to say, 'practical know-how', was regarded as almost a monopoly of the individual and other directors who shared the same problems—and dealt with them successfully.

These directors and senior managers had deeply rooted beliefs that their firm, industry, labour force and so on were 'different'. Indeed, upon making contact with a company it was almost certain that the interviewer would be told that 'of course this company is a little idiosyncratic' or that 'we have special problems here'. Thus management bodies and theorists who were concerned with industry and organization in *general* were anathema to many of these businessmen. They denied the authority of 'those who teach rather than do', and their emphasis upon the latent functions of management bodies was tantamount to a rejection of their manifest functions.[1]

Indeed, we believe that many of these businessmen were determined to deny the usefulness of management education and management theory—almost irrespective of its content. Although they were prepared to accept that 'specialist' courses (which generally referred to techniques akin to time and motion study) were useful, they were hostile to the teaching of social science and organization theory.[2] If they thought the content of 'human relations' courses (which they associated with 'management bodies)' was congruent with their own experience, they criticized them as 'commonsense'; they only taught you 'what you already know'. If they thought these courses taught something other than this, they were criticized for being too theoretical—'too airy-fairy'.

In short, there are several reasons why Northern City businessmen cannot be regarded as professionals. They lack professional management qualifications and were seldom members of professional bodies. They have a low level of participation in such bodies. And, most important, they deny

[1] Four of the 22 classified as accepting only the latent functions of management bodies did so on different grounds to the rest. They expressed the view that attendance at management functions 'helped people to come out', 'to meet others and mix more'. All four had come up from the shop floor.

[2] For an indication of what (in the main progressive) managements think should be taught to such courses see the N.E.D.C. report, *Management Recruitment and Development*, Appendix vib. It should not be forgotten that much of the past, and some present teaching on 'human relations' courses has been of inferior quality. Nor should it be forgotten that even in the Hawthorne plant foremen were busy 'human relating' prior to the experiments. See H. A. Landsberger, *Hawthorne Revisited*, Cornell University, 1958, p. 21.

the legitimacy of such bodies and very rarely accept even the *existence* of a body of management theory. In addition, they read very little management literature[1] and had ambivalent attitudes to management consultancy which, presumably, is the epitome of professionalized management. Nor, it seems, did they think of themselves as professionals. When asked, 'Do you regard yourself as a professional?' 28 replied that they did not and a further 17 said that they couldn't answer—which to some degree indicates that they didn't think of themselves as professionals either.[2]

Thus the major conclusion to be drawn from answers to this question is that 47 of the 65 did *not* regard themselves as professionals. However, the reasons given by the remaining 18 who *did* regard themselves as professionals are worthy of some further study.

In half of these cases (9), although it was replied that they did regard themselves as professionals, little interest or enthusiasm was shown. It is doubtful whether they would identify themselves as such outside the interview situation and in any case most of them took the term 'professional' to apply to socio-economic position. For example, one director replied, 'Yes, I think you could say we're professionals. After all we're no worse off than doctors'; another, after making some derogatory remarks about dentists, went on to argue that it was wrong that they had a higher status than businessmen.

The other half of those who replied that they were professionals qualified their response to indicate that they were not professional *managers*. Accountants said they were professional accountants, engineers that they were professional engineers, and so on. The only *management* group to identify itself in this way were personnel managers and directors. As one of them put it: 'I feel capable of tackling any personnel job—but not marketing, sales, production and the rest of it'.

[1] For example, 52 of them had not heard of Elton Mayo and said that the 'Hawthorne Experiments' meant nothing to them: cf. the much earlier report by L. Urwick and E. F. L. Brech, 'The Pioneers of Scientific Management: The Hawthorne Investigations', *Industry Illustrated*, Nov. 1944, p. 12; M. Argyle and T. Smith, *Training Managers*, Acton Society Trust, 1962, p. 21; C. Bursk and D. T. Clark, 'Reading Habits of Executives', *Harvard Business Review*, 1949, p. 345; W. Guzzardi, *The Young Executives*, N.Y., 1964, p. 170.

[2] In addition one man replied that 'management should be a profession but isn't'; another, that 'there is such a thing as a professional manager but I'm not one, I had to come up the hard way'.

This type of argument is interesting since it is contrary to the hopes of some management educationists, namely, that managers should be good 'all-rounders'.

However, the results of this question and others which we asked about professionalism all point to the conclusion that, at least in Northern City, most directors and senior managers neither were, nor regarded themselves as professionals. And while we cannot treat Northern City as a microcosm of business as a whole it seems improbable that it is the only 'backwater' in an advancing ocean of management education. For example, Clark found that younger managers were more likely to have received some management education than older men but only 52% of managers aged 39 or less had received some such education, and managers in private industry were generally found to be less educated in this respect than those in the public sector. His findings about 'top managers' and 'directors' were broadly in line with our own since only 28% of the 'top managers' and 23% of the directors in his sample had experienced any form of management training. A national survey of directors in 1966 put the percentage having attended a formal management course even lower at 21%.[1]

Furthermore, given the limited and late development of institutions concerned with higher management education, it appears inevitable that for some time to come many large corporation directors will have undergone only a minimum of professional training. Given also the present state of organizational studies in Britain, it will be some time before we may speak of the existence of even loosely co-ordinated body of management theory. Indeed, some social scientists may be too anxious to minimize the criticisms of many businessmen: businessmen are concerned with the practical application of the social scientist's work and inevitably the former's ability to predict is still often inadequate for their purposes.

So far, then, we have considered some of the evidence for the view that the modern large corporation director is a non-propertied technocrat and/or professional. We are led to conclude that the facts do not bear out these assumptions and that, today, and probably for some time to come, the description of British directors as 'non-propertied', 'techno-

[1] *The Industrial Manager*, pp. 123, 124, 126, 127; 'The Director Observed', *The Director*, April, 1966, p. 85.

cratic' or 'professional' will be less than satisfactory. It is possible, of course, that some managerial theorists would find nothing in our conclusions which is at odds with their own position, for they might well regard Britain as no more than one special case of 'retarded development'.

Given that today's large corporation director is more likely to have some technical qualifications and management training than his predecessors, and given that he is less likely to be a majority shareholder in his own firm, there is clearly something to be said for this view. Even so, such an argument is less than satisfactory in so far that both the assumption that a discretely new professional managerial class will emerge and also the often related assumption that ownership will, in practice, become (almost inevitably) separated from control, tend to overlook differences in the class structure and culture of different highly industrialized societies. (To cite the most obvious example: in the USA 17% of the population, as opposed to 5% in Britain, own shares).[1]

As we imply further on, many of the changes which have occurred in British society can be regarded, for the most part, as changes which have occurred *within* a more or less enduring structure of that society and for our purposes we find it much more meaningful to regard them in this way, than as indications that, as Clark[2] suggests, a 'new class' is coming into existence. As we shall see in the following chapter the findings of contemporary theorists of the firm (who are explicitly 'managerialist' since they assume that business behaviour can only be understood if one accepts the proposition that new men ('the managers') have new motives) do not necessarily conflict with this interpretation. But before proceeding further—and especially since we have emphasized (see Chapter V) that many of the questions at issue in discussions about the consequences of a separation of ownership and control are lacking in clarity—we should perhaps make clear just what has and has not been our main concern in Chapters VI, VII and VIII.

Directorial share ownership, which we discussed in Chapter VI, has, for example, been considered in the literature to have

---

[1] cf. *How does Britain Save?; Shareownership U.S.A.*, The New York Stock Exchange, 1965; Dept. of Applied Economic, Cambridge, *The Owners of Quoted Ordinary Shares: A Survey for 1963*, (No. 7 in *A Programme for Growth*) London, 1965, p. 42.

[2] *The Industrial Manager*, p. 153.

significance in at least four analytically separable respects. These are (i) whether it is sufficient to allow directors to be termed 'capitalists', (ii) whether it is sufficient to indicate that the very largest shareholders in a company 'control', (iii) whether the proportion of directorial income streams deriving from shares is great enough to permit the conclusion that 'managers' will maximize profit for the same reason that the capitalists of old are popularly thought to have done and (iv), whether the present level of directorial share ownership necessitates that they be termed a 'new class'. Now, so far, we have mainly confined ourselves to a consideration of the available data for questions (i) and (iii) and we will return to this latter set of questions (i.e. related to (iii)) in Chapter IX. We have, however, also touched upon the question of whether 'the managers' are a new class (iv), and we will also have cause to consider this more fully later on (see Chapter XII). We have not, on the other hand, given much consideration to question (ii) and nor do we intend to.

In Britain, Florence has already provided ample evidence—e.g. that the median percentage of votes held by directors of 'very large' corporations is only $1 \cdot 5\%$—to indicate that the very largest shareholders are not usually directors and vice-versa. Thus even though one can quibble with his method of classifying control situations, and to some extent with the basis of his sample, which excludes traditionally 'owner-controlled' industries like steel and shipbuilding, any attempt to do this is, in our view, beside the point. As far as we are concerned these are established facts and we are much more interested in attempting to consider what consequences they may have for the behaviour and more particularly the attitudes and values of present-day directors than with asking questions about whether a vote holding of $x\%$ or $y\%$ or $z\%$ is sufficient to ensure 'control'. This question can, in any case, only be answered by the empirical observation of behaviour. The study of company share registers and of the *Directory of Directors* are, at best, poor substitutes for this. There is, however, one further matter which is related to the extent to which directors own shares, even if they are not always among the *top twenty* shareholders. This particular aspect of the problem has not been listed above because with the exception of Marris, very few writers on the ownership and control situation have concerned themselves with it at all. But since it is possible that share ownership may have significance for the director's value system —which does *not* imply that it will necessarily constitute an immediate and specific element in his economic motivation (as is implied in (iii) above)—we did provide a brief discussion along these lines in Chapter VI and we will have cause to return to it in most of the following chapters in Part II.

The discussion in Chapter VII was, of course, quite simply concerned with the extent to which directors and managers hold technical or scientific qualifications. However, the 'political arithmetic' of technocracy ought not to be confused with the sociological implications of the fact that a category of science-trained managers now exists. Consequently, we will discuss the extent to which such managers may adhere to distinctively different norms and values (i.e. the extent to which they may have an 'external' professional identification group), the probability that they will retain this upon becoming directors, whether in fact they will become directors if they do and related issues in the following chapters. It should be noted, however, that our discussion of such matters will of necessity be based upon very little empirical data and consequently it will be presented in passing rather than separately in the text.

In the present section the discussion of the extent to which businessmen may be termed 'professional' has, as stated earlier, been largely confined to a consideration of whether their skills can be said to rest upon a formally transmitted body of knowledge and also of course to the question of whether they regard themselves as professionals. But in addition to this, questions also exist about whether those businessmen who have taken part in some form of professional management activity have different frames of reference, and different conceptions of their own role and of the role of business in society, to those who have had no such experience. We provide some suggestive findings on this point, which once again we have been forced by lack of other available data to base on our own Northern City study, in Chapter XVI.

CHAPTER IX

MANAGERIAL ECONOMICS

THE Berle and Means thesis expected substantial changes in the dividend policies of corporations as managements became more secure in their control position and, as Lintner[1] reports, in later versions this thesis emphasized not only an increasing reliance by non-financial corporations on internal funds but also freedom from dependence on outside capital markets. In the last decade, however, Berle and Means' assumption that the separation of ownership and control would lead to changes in business behaviour has begun to be explicitly incorporated into economic theories of the firm. But unlike Berle, and perhaps partly because the notions of rationality and self-interest have been so fundamental to economic science, few of the authors of these theories have given much weight to 'social service' or 'social responsibility' as probable operational objectives for the new non-propertied managers.

Nevertheless, because the writers who have put forward such theories share the assumption that in consonance with the emergence of the new role of 'manager' there appear expectations, motivations, criteria of success, corporate policies, and even ideologies, which differ from those of the old owner-manager, they must clearly be classified as 'managerialists'. Furthermore, since the general procedure which they have adopted is to substitute more sophisticated notions about managers' economic (as well as psychological) costs and rewards for hitherto over-simplified notions about capitalistic self-interest it is equally clear, as we noted earlier on, that their work falls into our category of 'sectional' managerialism.

In this chapter, then, the main purpose of which is to examine the bearing of modern economic theories of the firm upon the identity or otherwise of shareholder and directorial interests—

---

[1] J. Lintner, 'The Financing of Corporations', in E. S. Mason (ed.), *The Corporation in Modern Society*, 1961, pp. 183, 185.

which is clearly an indispensable preliminary to any consideration of contemporary business ideology—we will generally confine ourselves to those economic theories of the 'sectional' type. Furthermore, because there is some consensus among theorists of the firm that modern corporate leaders are likely to value growth as an objective, we will concentrate more specifically upon this view rather than examine the work of those writers who have been more concerned with the question of whether businessmen 'maximize' or 'satisfice'.

The latter concept is by no means unambiguous. For example, one might apply it to a situation in which—given full information and no uncertainty about outcomes—businessmen choose not to maximize but to do something less than this.[1] In this sense, one is referring to some form of satiation. On the other hand, it may also be used to refer to cases where—given lack of information and uncertainty about outcomes—profit maximization is not consciously attainable. In this sense, reference is typically to the 'rules of thumb' which develop in the absence of any one, unique, solution being available.[2]

Clearly, and despite an emphasis on planning,[3] most businesses are *not* characterized by a lack of uncertainty and most businessmen *are* concerned with resolving conflicts between sub-goals, and may therefore be said to be 'satisficing' in the second sense. But we suspect this has ever been the case. Thus, given this, and the ambiguities associated with the term 'satisficing',[4] we intend to concentrate upon recent developments in 'managerial', rather than 'behavioural', theories of the firm.[5] In so far as we will be concerned with behavioural theories, we hope to do something other than to explore the implications of the fact that there *is* learning and adaptation in economic organizations. As will become clearer in the remaining chapters of Part II, we wish to draw attention to the existence and nature of organizational culture—to the

[1] cf. H. A. Simon, 'Theories of Decision Making in Economics and Behavioral Science', in *Surveys of Economic Theory*, Vol. III, N.Y. and London, 1966, p. 10.

[2] cf. R. M. Cyert and J. G. March, *A Behavioral Theory of the Firm*, N.J., 1963.

[3] cf. J. K. Galbraith, *The New Industrial State*, London, 1967.

[4] For a fuller discussion, see R. Marris, *The Economic Theory of 'Managerial' Capitalism*, London, 1964, pp. 266–277.

[5] F. Machlup, 'Theories of the Firm: Marginalist, Behavioral, Managerial', *American Economic Review*, Vol. LVII, No. 1, March, 1967, pp. 1–33.

normative framework within which the above processes of decision-making take place.[1]

Two major works of the type we have in mind were published in 1964 by Marris,[2] in England, and Williamson,[3] in the USA. Both these writers make it quite explicit in the titles of their works that they are to be regarded as contributions toward a *managerial* theory of the firm. Furthermore, though Marris would seem to place less reliance on the rather unsystematic literature about managerial motivation he, like Williamson,[4] has followed R. A. Gordon's earlier work[5] in accepting that the quest for salary, security, status, power, prestige and professional excellence may all constitute immediate determinants of managerial behaviour.

In Marris' case a consideration of these objectives suggested the theory that (non-propertied) managers maximize the rate of growth of their firms (i.e. the growth rate of gross assets) subject to the constraint of maintaining a reasonable minimum valuation ratio. Such behaviour, he argued, facilitates the satisfaction of those wants associated with scale (salary, power and prestige) and, at the same time, by insuring against take-over bids and guarding continuity of employment, also satisfies the need for security.[6] The introduction of the notion of 'expense preference'[7] makes for a neater link between assumptions about managerial motivation and behaviour in Williamson's theory but his argument is of substantially the same type as Marris'.

He posits that the firm is operated so as to maximize size of staff, emoluments and discretionary profit, subject to the constraint that reported profit is at least equal to a minimal acceptable level expected by shareholders.[8] Williamson associates staff expansion with the quest for salary, dominance,

---

[1] cf. the dominant (psychological) emphasis of J. G. March and H. A. Simon, *Organisations*, N.Y., 1958.

[2] *The Economic Theory of 'Managerial' Capitalism.*

[3] O. E. Williamson, *The Economics of Discretionary Behavior: Managerial Objectives in a Theory of the Firm*, N.J., 1964. (For a short review of the theories of both Marris and Williamson, and their intellectual predecessors, see A. A. Alchian, 'The Basis of Some Recent Advances in the Theory of Management of the Firm', *Journal of Industrial Economics*, Vol. 14, Nov., 1965, pp. 30–41.)

[4] cf. *The Economics of Discretionary Behavior*, pp. 29–30, *The Economic Theory*, p. 47.

[5] *Business Leadership in the Large Corporation*, pp. 305–316.

[6] *The Economic Theory*, pp. 47–48, 55.

[7] *The Economics of Discretionary Behavior*, pp. 33–34.   [8] *ibid.*, p. 37.

security and professional achievement, and considers increasing emoluments to be an indirect source of prestige and status. The earning of discretionary profit (i.e. that which exceeds the minimum acceptable level of profit demanded) is held to be associated with managerial self-fulfilment and, since Williamson accepts that increases in emoluments and staff size are tied to physical growth which, however financed, is tied to profitability, the quest for discretionary profit is held to be indirectly associated with satisfaction of all the other above wants as well.[1]

Williamson accepts that some of the evidence he uses to corroborate his theory might indicate that the management first selects that physical combination of factors that maximizes profits and then absorbs some amount of profit as cost. There are, however, no *a priori* grounds for supposing that managers who behave as he, or Marris, or indeed Baumol[2] suggest that they do will inevitably maximize profit in the sense that classical capitalists were supposed to do.

Nevertheless, questions do arise about whether profit maximization, as an objective in itself, is now, or ever was, typical of the owner-manager, or entrepreneur, and whether, and to what extent, changes in business behaviour can be attributed to differences in the motivation of 'managers' and 'capitalists'. Williamson,[3] for his part, points out that whereas profit maximization was a useful assumption in classical economics and is, in certain circumstances, still applicable today, its plausibility probably owed more to the antecedent postulate of perfect competition than to the validity of its inferences about capitalistic motivation. Marris, too, makes the point that capitalists probably had a variety of objectives and that these may have had as large a non-pecuniary content as those of the modern large corporation manager.[4]

There is, of course, much to recommend this view for in many cases the pursuit of profit itself may only serve as a means to diverse ends. It is possible, however, that one can go even further than this. Thus, if, like Marris and Williamson, one assumes that freedom from outside interference is a necessary pre-condition to the exercise of discretion by business leaders,

[1] *ibid.*, pp. 34–37.
[2] W. J. Baumol, *Business Behavior, Value and Growth*, N.Y., 1959.
[3] *The Economics of Discretionary Behavior*, p. 18.
[4] *The Economic Theory*, p. 59.

G

then, given similar conditions of imperfect competition, it could be argued that the owner-manager will have greater opportunity to further his non-pecuniary and non-profit oriented objectives than his 'managerial' counterpart. (By definition, he will not have to 'look over his shoulder' at his company's shareholders.)[1]

It is a strength and also in a sense a weakness of Williamson's theory (since he calls it a 'managerial' one) that these observations do not necessitate the formulation of a new, alternative, 'capitalistic theory of the firm'. Instead, his theory can incorporate more realistic assumptions about the objectives likely to be favoured by propertied directors by positing that these enter into a preference function which is not necessarily dominated by a profit component.[2] Having said this, it must, however, be noted that, in contrast to more popular versions of managerial theory, both Williamson's and Marris' theories avoid giving the impression that non-pecuniary objectives, and indeed any form of non-economic motivation, are characteristic of modern non-propertied directors alone.

Neither of these writers would have much sympathy for the view that, in contrast to managers, 'owners of most business firms are single-mindedly and wholeheartedly dedicated to the total profit-maximizing ideal'.[3] In practice, however, neither of these writers, though this is true to a lesser extent of Marris,[4] have paid much attention to the probable (non-profit) objectives of traditional capitalists and modern owner-managers.

Marris does suggest that the bureaucratic environment of the modern corporation is likely to direct emphasis from the character of the goods and services produced to the skill with which production activities are organized. But he does not raise the possibility that the 'traditional capitalist' was more closely concerned with technical competence than is the case with the modern non-propertied director whose technical function is often separated off into specialist departments like R. and D. Nor does he do more than briefly explore[5] the

---

[1] cf. *Attitudes in British Management: A P.E.P. Report* (first published as *Thrusters and Sleepers*, 1965), London, 1966, p. 44.

[2] *The Economics of Discretionary Behavior*, p. 48.

[3] L. A. Kratz, 'The Motivation of the Business Manager', *Behavioral Science*, Vol. v, 1960, pp. 313–316.

[4] *The Economic Theory*, pp. 59–60.   [5] *ibid.*, p. 10.

implications of the fact that, in the ideal-typical case, the 'traditional capitalist' owned and managed a firm which he or his family had created, and which bore his name.

This might suggest that he, or his modern successor, the propertied director, would derive substantial satisfactions from the expansion of assets, sales, and other indices of organizational size in much the same way as contemporary non-propertied 'managers' are assumed to do. In short, growth, rather than profit maximization, might be an important objective for both of them.

Then again, it is possible, given the common existence of large-scale organization, that the modern propertied director who is actively involved in management may also derive 'professional managerial' satisfactions from the pursuance of his duties.[1] If this were in fact the case the term 'managerial' would be confusing, for it fails to distinguish between (a) economic satisfactions which are 'managerial' in the sense that they are not 'capitalistic' and (b) satisfactions which may be so termed because they derive from organizational involvement. However, it is sufficient for our purposes here to make the point that, were more 'realistic' assumptions to be made about 'capitalistic' motivation, the policy characteristics of management-controlled companies might not appear so distinctively 'managerial' as some more popular writers are apt to assume.

The fact is, however, that we lack systematic studies into business motivation and those studies and observations which are available,[2] perhaps partly because some of them have been concerned to show that modern corporate leaders are not the oversimplified economic men of classical theory, shed little light upon the motivation of *propertied* directors. For this reason the suggestions we make above about the motivation,

---

[1] Several instances of this were found in the Northern City study.

[2] See, for example:

C. I. Barnard, *The Functions of the Executive*, Harvard, 1938.

A. H. Cole, *Business Enterprise in Its Social Setting*, Harvard, 1959.

R. A. Gordon, *Business Leadership in the Large Corporation*. Berkeley and Los Angeles, 1961.

M. Haire, E. E. Ghiselli and L. W. Porter, *Managerial Thinking: An International Study*, N.Y., 1966.

G. Katona, *Psychological Analysis of Economic Behavior*, N.Y., 1951.

H. Leibenstein, *Economic Theory and Organisational Analysis*, N.Y., 1960.

V. A. Thompson, *Modern Organization*, N.Y., 1961.

objectives and non-economic satisfactions of owner-managers can only be considered as more or less plausible possibilities.[1] McClelland,[2] of course, has provided some evidence for the view that businessmen originating in the highest stratum of society, and those with kinship ties to property owners (and such people approximate to the managerialist conception of the propertied director), may have a lower need for achievement. However, the bearing of McClelland's evidence on this point is only of a suggestive nature and, in any case, it remains an open question what policies propertied directors would choose to fulfil this need, no matter how intensely it might be felt.

Questions also remain about some aspects of the work on more specifically 'managerial' motivation. Thus, even a short review of the literature, like that presented by Williamson,[3] raises questions about whether some of the 'motives' (e.g. salary) can properly be termed motives at all, and how certain apparent contradictions (e.g. desire for salary and the performance of a social service) are resolved.

Studies more immediately concerned with the psychodynamics of businessmen reveal even greater contradictions. Henry,[4] for example, found that the successful American executive was 'a man who has left home' and whose 'ties and obligations to his parents were severed': he adds, 'we find the relationship to the mother to be the most clearly broken'. Other researchers[5] have concluded that the successful executive had experienced a happy home life in his earlier years and argued that this was conducive to the development of security and self-confidence. Yet Rogers,[6] in a study of managers in 'Universal', a large British firm in the domestic appliances field, attributed their success to a desire to serve their (hard-working, loving and understanding) mothers,

---

[1] Though see *Time* magazine's interview with Lord Thomson (*Time*, December 8, 1961); P. W. S. Andrews and E. Brummer, *The Life of Lord Nuffield: A Study in Enterprise and Benevolence*, Oxford, 1955, p. 220; O. F. Collins, D. G. Moore and D. B. Unwalla, *The Enterprising Man*, Michigan, 1965.

[2] D. C. McClelland, *The Achieving Society*, London, 1961, pp. 264–265, 269, 279–280, 378.

[3] *The Economics of Discretionary Behavior*, p. 30.

[4] W. E. Henry, 'The Business Executive: A Study of the Psycho-dynamics of a Social Rôle', *American Journal of Sociology*, Vol. LIV, Jan., 1949, pp. 286–291.

[5] R. M. Wald and R. A. Doty, 'The Top Executive—A Firsthand Profile', *Harvard Business Review*, July, 1954, p. 53.

[6] K. Rogers, *Managers, Personality and Performance*, London, 1963.

and to triumph over their (ineffective, often absent, and apparently unloved) fathers.

At first sight, studies such as these would appear to have little consequence for contemporary theories of the firm. They are, after all, primarily concerned with managerial psycho-dynamics, rather than with linking such driving forces to probable operational objectives. However, two of them do contain potentially important findings which have generally been neglected by managerialist writers.

Henry,[1] for example, noted that successful American executives represented 'a crystallization of many of the attitudes and values generally accepted by middle-class American society'. Such an observation should not, of course, surprise us. It does, however, raise the possibility, suggested even more strongly by Rogers' work, that no matter how complex managerial psycho-dynamics may be, they do not necessarily lead to conflict with the shareholder interest. Thus, we find that 'Alexander', a key figure in Rogers' case study of 'Universal'—and a 'manager' in the non-propertied sense—is quite clear that the function of a chief executive is to 'accept the fundamental responsibility, in there, pitching for profits for his shareholders'. He adds, 'if he doesn't want to do that, he must get out'.[2]

Now, so far, by commenting upon the possible motivation and non-pecuniary objectives of owner-managers, and by briefly considering some of the literature about managerial motivation and psycho-dynamics, we have suggested that there are some grounds for supposing that both types of businessmen may share broadly similar frames of reference. At the very least, it seems improbable that all their motivations, objectives and satisfactions are mutually exclusive ones. Quite probably some of the authors of managerial theories of the firm would not disagree with such a conclusion but they have paid little attention to this line of argument. The main reason for this is that, generally speaking, they have been more immediately concerned with a slightly different problem, namely, the probable outcome of situations in which non-propertied directors—who are thought unlikely to pursue policies exclusively designed to maximize profit—are separated from their

---

[1] *American Journal of Sociology*, Jan., 1949, p. 291.
[2] *Managers, Personality and Performance*, p. 106.

shareholders, whose interests, as Williamson puts it, are unambiguously tied to greater profit.[1] This particular problem directly raises question about the identity or otherwise of shareholder-management interests in the large modern corporation.

Prima facie, this problem would seem to be resolvable by asking four questions—What are the interests of non-propertied directors? What power do they have to ensure these interests are served? What are the interests of the shareholders? What power do they have to ensure these interests are served?

To formulate the problem in this way does, however, give rise to even more, equally important, questions. For example (1*a*), are interests to be treated as imputed abstractions which are definitionally served when policies exist which maximize them to the full, or (1*b*), are they to be treated as the empirically evidenced expectations of the parties concerned? Is the identity or otherwise of the interests of these parties to be assessed exclusively in terms of the relationship between the two of them (2*a*), or, are their interests to be judged in relation to their identity or otherwise to those of other members of society? (2*b*). Is power to be regarded exclusively as an activity, in the sense of 'control' (3*a*), or, is power also to be considered as social power which, when legitimated, may find its expression in the frame of reference which one actor has transmitted to another? (3*b*).

The importance of this last set of questions derives from the fact that much of the face validity of managerialist theory is based upon answers to the first alternative in each case (1*a*, 2*a*, 3*a*).

If, for example, we treat the shareholder interest as synonymous with the abstraction of profit maximization (1*a*), then, clearly, it follows that this interest is not served. If we confine ourselves to asking whether there are differences between the interests of shareholders and non-propertied directors (2*a*), then, again, it is quite clear that these are not identical. And if we consider power exclusively in the sense of 'control' (3*a*), then, once again, there is much to suggest that shareholders do not generally control directors.

As we have seen, however, these particular 'answers' result from asking a particular set of questions. These, in turn, can be seen to derive from a particular interpretation of what is

[1] *The Economics of Discretionary Behavior*, p. 24.

meant by a 'separation of ownership and control'. The distinguishing features of this interpretation are, (a) that *separation* is taken to imply autonomy from shareholders and, (b) that *control* is interpreted in terms of active intervention. Yet, as Baldwin[1] puts it, the premise that managers are in fact autonomous is 'nearly as simplistic and inapplicable to modern corporate reality as are earlier models based on the entrepreneur'.

Quite clearly, we must ask ourselves whether 'managers' may, in Marris' phrase, have a 'conscience' towards shareholders and we must also ask whether shareholders are totally ignorant, completely fractionized or entirely passive. The answer to this second question is that they are obviously not: as Williamson[2] has argued, 'they will ordinarily be in a position to mobilize their forces should profits fall below some minimum acceptable level'.

We could, of course, like Villarejo,[3] proceed from this last point to an exploration of the extent to which the distribution of votes in the large corporation confers control potential upon shareholders. To do so, however, would deflect attention from that which most concerns us, namely, the much neglected sociological study of the modern corporation director.

If, on the other hand, we pursue an alternative course we may be able to complement the predominantly intra-unit orientation of theories like those of Marris and Williamson with a consideration of the proximity of shareholder-management interests when viewed in the context of the wider social system. This entails that we pay some attention to the director's normative orientation and to those prescriptive[4] elements of his role which derive from sources other than his professional membership group. We intend to proceed with this line of enquiry in subsequent chapters. Before we do so, however, there are four additional observations which ought to be made.

[1] W. L. Baldwin, 'The Motives of Managers, Environmental Restraints and the Theory of Managerial Enterprise', *The Quarterly Journal of Economics*, Vol. LXXVIII, May, 1964, p. 239.

[2] *The Economics of Discretionary Behavior*, p. 36.

[3] D. Villarejo, 'Stock Ownership and the Control of Corporations', Part II, *New University Thought*, Autumn, 1961, pp. 54–55.

[4] For a distinction between the *descriptive* aspect of rôle (how actors behave in a particular position) and the *prescriptive* aspect (how others expect them to behave) see, H. L. Zetterberg, 'Complaint Actions', *Acta Sociológica*, Vol. II, No. 4, 1957, p. 179.

First, both Marris and Williamson[1]—and again we must emphasize that their work is of a different order to more popular versions of managerial theory—make the point that a 'reasonable' or 'acceptable' fulfilment of the shareholder interest is a pre-condition to the achievement of corporate leaders' own specifically personal and organizational satisfactions.

Secondly, to observe, like Crosland,[2] that most large shareholders (i.e. insurance companies, pension funds, investment and unit trusts) are 'purely passive' investors, because they are more concerned with *investment* than *control*, is not entirely satisfactory. In practice, institutional investors are not anxious to relinquish their voting rights[3] and Crosland himself has demonstrated the limitations of distinguishing between these two analytically separable motives for investing by writing that institutional investors 'seek representation on a board only if this is necessary to protect their investment'. Indeed, his argument that insurance companies 'abandon their passive role only when, as in the Docker dispute in B.S.A., a crisis in the firm's affairs threatens the security of their investment; and the sensation which this incident caused shows how rare such intervention is', is open to another interpretation.

One might equally well conclude that the rarity of such occurrences indicates that such intervention is not often necessary because, in the generality of cases, such shareholders are satisfied that their interests are reasonably well served. In this connection it is appropriate to make a third point for, as Williamson[4] notes, the evidence suggests that what shareholders regard as an 'acceptable' profit represents only a modest attainment by managements. In Britain, it is true, we have very little empirical data to indicate what this acceptable level might be, but a Stock Exchange survey[5]—which unfortunately excludes institutional investors—does suggest that only about 6% of shareholders buy shares for speculative purposes. The majority would seem to be interested in long run capital appreciation (43%) or in receiving a steady income (40%).

Thus, although in practice, few, if any, managements pursue

[1] cf. *The Economic Theory*, p. 55, *The Economics of Discretionary Behavior*, p. 37.
[2] *The Conservative Enemy*, p. 74.
[3] cf. the statement by the British Insurance Association, reported in *The Times*, May 28, 1962.
[4] *The Economics of Discretionary Behavior*, p. 36.
[5] *How does Britain Save?*, p. 28.

short-term policies of out-and-out profit maximization (1*a*), so that one cannot maintain that the shareholder interest is served in this sense, it is possible that a rather more realistic assumption (1*b*) might give support to the view that, by and large, their interests are reasonably well served. Indeed, one does not have to assume that we live in the most functional of all functionalist worlds to posit that shareholders probably place their investment in companies whose performance[1] is thought likely to meet their expectations.

Fourthly, of course, the point remains that not many investment advisers appear to recommend potential shareholder to seek out 'owner-controlled' rather than 'management-controlled' companies. Thus, if one regards profit-maximization and a preference for dividend distribution as synonymous with the shareholder interest it probably makes more sense to argue that this interest is not fully served by *either* management or owner-controlled companies.

Once again, then, on a comparative basis, there is much to be said for the view that the interests of shareholders are reasonably well served by the leaders of management-controlled companies. This is not to say, of course, that shareholders and management interests are identical: but, for our purposes, to ask whether they are identical is not a particularly illuminating question. It could be argued, for example, that the interests of lathe operators and maintenance men are not identical either. In this case, however, and in the case of managements and shareholders too, a definite overlapping of interests is observable when viewed from the standpoint of other members of society.

We must surely not forget that, in the case of shareholders, these other members of British society amount to about 95% of the population and even if we confine ourselves to the relationship of shareholders and managements at company, rather than society level, it is exceedingly difficult to argue that their interests are antithetical, and much more reasonable to assume, as we understand Marris and Williamson to do, that they are characterized by a good deal of overlap, which typically results in a policy compromise.

[1] Since nearly 90% of the personal holders of commercial and industrial stocks (and 99% of men) do know the value of their holdings, and since it is highly improbable that institutional investors are less well informed, it would seem that shareholders do have the requisite knowledge to support such a proposition, see *How Does Britain Save?*, pp. 27, 30.

More than this, however, there are grounds for supposing that all the evidence does not fully substantiate generally advanced assumptions of the type reported by Lintner at the beginning of this chapter. For example, statistical tests reveal no significant differences between the distribution ratios of those 'very large' owner and management-controlled companies (i.e. those with assets of £3 million or over) which Florence studied in *Ownership, Control and Success*.[1] This would seem to complement one of the more general findings to emerge from a recent empirical study of U.K. quoted companies,[2] namely, that large firms tend to constitute a class of their own, and show less than usual variability on a number of performance indices.

One might further add that though Williamson[3] has posited a positive relationship between the internal composition of the board (i.e. managerial representation) and the earnings retention ratio, he has been careful to note that the evidence for this is weak. A re-working of Florence's data seems to provide some indirect confirmation for his qualification.[4]

In addition to doubts which may exist about the proposition that high plough-back is related to 'management control', there may also be room for doubt about the equally, if not more, important assumption that fast-growing—and thus, often by implication, 'management-controlled'—companies are less

---

[1] We used Chi² to test the significance of the differences between the distribution ratios of Florence's 'Very Large' owner-controlled and other companies not so classified at three different dichotomized levels. In each case the differences were in the expected direction but in no case did they reach the 5% level of significance. The tests were conducted on 27 of Florence's 30 Very Large 'owner-controlled' companies (see, *Ownership, Control and Success*, Appendix B) and 66 of the 68 he did not consider to be owner-controlled (see those companies appearing in Appendix A.1 but not Appendix B).

[2] A. Singh and G. Whittington, in collaboration with H. T. Burley, *Growth, Profitability and Valutaion: A Study of United Kingdom Quoted Companies*, Cambridge, Dept. of Applied Economics, Occasional Paper 7, 1968.

[3] *The Economics of Discretionary Behavior*, p. 170.

[4] A correlation of only +0·02 was found between the percentage of votes held by the top twenty vote-holders and the distribution ratios of the Very Large companies for which Florence had data. Seven of the 98 companies studied by Florence were omitted from this correlation: four because the distribution ratios were not available, and three others either because the company had no profits, or because the largest twenty shareholders were not known, or because the directors held preference shares. Source: *Ownership, Control and Success*, Appendix A.1.

dependent on the capital market.[1] One study[2] found that 'Giant' corporations (those with assets of £8 million and over) which had high rates of growth were more, not less, likely to finance such growth by new share issues. Another analysis[3] points to the conclusion that firms with above average growth tend not only to retain an above average proportion of their profits but also, because they require so much more finance, to raise an above average proportion of this from outside sources.

Little's[4] finding, that neither size nor plough-back affect growth of earnings over time, since they appear to proceed in 'an almost random manner', is not, perhaps, such a damaging blow to the possibility of a theory of the firm as it appears at first sight. The *growth* of profitability, which concerned Little, is not the same as the *level* of profitability. In the latter case, as Singh and Whittington[5] have pointed out, there is evidence to suggest that above average levels of profitability may be maintained over time—and it is *this* which probably interests most shareholders. But of course, despite Little's inference from the random behaviour he describes—that this suggested either that 'good managements' do not exist, or, if they do, that they are short-lived—such a finding cannot amount to a proof that such non-random behaviour is solely a function of management/ownership type. Regrettably though, from our point of view, neither Little and Rayner nor Singh and Whittington directly report on the latter set of variables.

To clarify our position, we accept that the assumption that

[1] One might also note that as far as any relationship between 'management-control' and plough-back/dividend policy is concerned it may be unwise to rule out a possibility mentioned by Florence. That is, 'dividends may be kept low because managers, not owners, are in control; or managers may be in control in certain industries because low dividends and high plough-back have proved more successful there for survival and growth'. Furthermore, similar explanations might fit the positive correlations which Williamson found to exist between monopoly power and executive compensation and between the latter and management representation. See, *Ownership, Control and Success*, p. 190, and M. Silver, 'Managerial Discretion and Profit Maximising Behavior: Some Further Comments', *Journal of Industrial Economics*, Vol. 15, April, 1967, p. 162.

[2] R. F. Henderson, 'Comments on Company Finance', *Lloyds Bank Review*, Jan., 1959, p. 31.

[3] *Growth, Profitability and Valuation*, p. 67.

[4] cf. I. M. D. Little, 'Higgledy-Piggledy Growth', *Bulletin of the Oxford Institute of Statistics*, Nov., 1962, and the fuller report by Little and A. C. Rayner, *Higgledy-Piggledy Growth Again: An Investigation of the Predictability of Company Earnings and Dividends in the U.K.*, *1951–1961*, Oxford, 1966, pp. 62, 63–64.

[5] *Growth, Profitability and Valuation*, pp. 146–147.

modern corporate leaders are more likely to be interested in steady growth than in policies of out-and-out profit-maximization is a highly plausible one. Our major doubt is not therefore about this proposition but about those other propositions which are often associated with it, for example, that such behaviour is specifically a consequence of a separation of ownership and control. And since a brief review of the work of writers like Baumol, Marris and Williamson suggests not only certain similarities in approach but also that these writers have not yet produced any one generally accepted theory of the firm, and since, in addition to this, some economists still doubt the specifically managerial nature of some 'managerial' policies,[1] it would, perhaps, be foolhardy for a non-economist to go further than this.

There are signs, however, that future developments in the economic theory of the firm will take the form of producing more precise statements about the specific situations and limiting conditions for which particular theories are best suited. As this process continues we will be in a better position to assess the policy significance of that one factor which mainly concerns us here.

Meanwhile, it seems reasonable to suppose that, at any given point of time, the policy of a corporation may be affected by a variety of technological, market, political and other factors. It could even be, heretical though this now seems, that modern management techniques have provided corporate leaders with such (relatively) advanced measuring and costing methods[2] that they are more aware of profitability than their predecessors: if so, profit itself might be taken as an index of managerial excellence. This possibility is, in fact, specifically embodied in Williamson's theory.[3] We mention the point here only to emphasize that whereas it may be unwise to use the phrase 'profit maximization', which has so many misleading connotations and latent assumptions,[4] there is still much to be said

[1] cf. G. C. Allen, *Economic Fact and Fantasy*, Institute of Economic Affairs, Occasional Paper 14, 1967, p. 19.

[2] cf. P. A. Baran and P. M. Sweezy, *Monopoly Capital: An Essay on the American Economic and Social Order*, N.Y., 1966: see also p. 122ff.

[3] See his discussion of 'discretionary profit', *The Economics of Discretionary Behavior*, p. 36.

[4] cf. T. Scitovsky, 'A Note on Profit Maximisation and Its Implications', *Review of Economic Studies*, Winter, 1943, pp. 57–60.

for the view that 'managers' are interested in profit acquisition. This, in any case, is an important precondition to growth.[1]

There is also, of course, much to be said for the view that corporate leaders, being faced with a set of conflicting demands, will pursue policies which give the least offence to interested parties. In this context, one notes Florence's[2] observation that, in the period he studied, the varying proportions of equity profit ploughed back indicated that it was not the assets but the shareholders which had priority.

The above, we must repeat, is not to suggest that shareholders could not do better in some absolute sense. It is to suggest that those who decide corporate policy generally further their own economic, psychological and organizational satisfactions in such a way as to avoid take-over, loss of position, and even moral doubt.

Thus, by and large, one expects managements to seek a compromise solution which takes the form of attempting to balance the pursuit of growth, on the one hand, with fair treatment for shareholders on the other.[3] Fair treatment for shareholders would amount to a reliable form of investment being offered, rather than a gamble, and consequent benefits of average rather than excessively high, or low, rates of profit and growth. And this would appear to be what the larger companies do offer.[4] One assumes, also, that it is just this type of policy which is most attractive to the majority of institutional and private investors. It is possible that the managements of larger companies are more, rather than less, sensitive to the stock market[5] and clearly, from their point of view, there is good reason for such a compromise to be sought. There is still little inter-firm mobility at the highest levels and the top executive cannot readily afford to be tainted by failure.[6]

The above interpretation leaves open the question of how far managements' deference to the shareholder interest is of a strictly calculative or moral kind. In practice, it is very difficult to give an open or shut answer. Williamson,[7] who is inclined to

---

[1] cf. *Growth, Profitability, and Valuation*, chapter 7 and pp. 188–189.
[2] *Ownership, Control and Success*, p. 187.
[3] cf. J. Lintner, 'Distributions of Incomes of Corporations among Dividends, Retained Earnings and Taxes', *American Economic Review*, May, 1966, pp. 97–113.
[4] cf. *Growth, Profitability and Valuation*, pp. 19, 192–193.
[5] *ibid.*, p. 133. [6] cf. *The Economic Theory*, pp. 64, 67.
[7] *The Economics of Discretionary Behavior*, p. 3.

depict this relationship in calculative terms, has, however, observed that 'a casual examination of the history of mankind' indicates that 'where discretion exists it is apt to be exercised'. Subject to the reminder that not only would a similar examination disclose that 'Right' is apt to be associated with 'Might', and that in the present case shareholders have legal rights to begin with, and that in certain circumstances the many smaller ones may be effectively organized at little effective cost to themselves, we agree. On the other hand, our agreement is not whole-hearted. We also find some justification for the view that *some* element of moral concern for the shareholders' interests may enter into management's own definition of its role. Indeed, as we shall see in the following chapters, viewed in the context of society as a whole, there is reason to assume that managements, propertied or otherwise, may orient to shareholders as an important identification group.[1]

To develop this point we must now turn to a consideration of the modern director's social origins, the process of intra-corporate socialization he has undergone as a manager, and the position he occupies in society. In other words, we must consider those aspects of the problem which economic theorists of the firm have neglected. It is true, of course, that Marris[2] has given some consideration to these matters but he does not go far enough for our purposes, which are necessarily much more concerned with what he terms the 'external sociology' of the director's situation than he had cause to be.

Similarly, as far as the 'internal' sociology of the firm is concerned, we cannot confine ourselves, as Williamson[3] has done, to stressing that group functioning and organizational effectiveness depend upon a value consensus, and that this probably results from screening-selection procedures and the manager's intra-corporate socialization. We must go further than this, and ask questions about the *content* of this consensus which, in turn, means enquiring about the prescriptive aspects of the manager's role.

One of the very few works to attempt such a task, and then only briefly, is Dahrendorf's *Class and Class Conflict*. As will soon

[1] Our use of this term follows R. H. Turner, 'Rôle Taking, Rôle Standpoint, and Reference Group Behavior', *American Journal of Sociology*, 1954, Vol. 59, p. 323.
[2] *The Economic Theory*, pp. 54–56.
[3] *The Economics of Discretionary Behavior*, pp. 148–149, 153–157.

become apparent, however, though we have no doubt that Dahrendorf has conducted the right kind of analysis we suspect that, at least in the case of British society, some of his conclusions are open to question. But, for the moment, it is sufficient for us to repeat that, in our reading of them, at least two of the major recent contributions toward a managerial theory of the firm do not necessitate the assumption that non-propertied directors pursue policies which are radically at odds with the interests of shareholders.

One might further note that, if justified, this general observation (and also the possibility of corporate leaders accommodating their own interests to give some priority to those of shareholders) indicates a potential area of overlap between the theories of more sophisticated managerialist and 'Marxist' writers.

CHAPTER X

SOCIAL EXPERIENCE AND VALUES I

Pre-Corporate Socialization

'The number of workers who are capable of filling technical and
managerial positions must obviously be limited, and already a
high proportion of this number attains them. A vast majority of
successful managers and technicians have risen from the ranks.
The demand is still unsaturated and there is now little or no
impediment between bench and boardroom.'

O. W. ROSKILL, *Scope*, Feb., 1946

IN *Class and Class Conflict* Dahrendorf puts forward the view that
the crucial effect of the separation of ownership and control is
that it has produced two sets of roles, the incumbents of which
increasingly move apart in their outlook on and attitudes
toward society in general, and toward the enterprise in
particular. Their social background and experience place these
groups into different fields of reference. Hence, given the
premise that 'different reference groups make for different
values', Dahrendorf, like Sering before him, is led to suggest
that the group of professionally trained managers 'increasingly
develops its own functionally determined character traits and
modes of thought'.[1]

The thesis that the new men really have arrived has been
rehearsed so often, and Dahrendorf's treatment of the matter
is so succinct, that, momentarily, his analysis carries total
conviction. His assertion that, today, 'a majority of top management officials in industrial enterprises have acquired their
positions on the strength of some specialized education and
of university degrees'[2] is familiar to our ears. One is scarcely
given pause for thought when he notes, later on, that only about

---

[1] *Class and Class Conflict*, p. 46; citing P. Sering, *Jenseits des Kapitalismus*, Nurnberg,
1947, p. 205.
[2] *ibid.*

5% of British managers have been managers all their lives, and even that no less than two-thirds of them have been employed in manual labouring.[1]

Yet it can be seen from the evidence already presented that a substantial proportion of British managers—and even 'top management officials'—have not experienced a university or specialist education, or even professional training. Furthermore, the evidence we have about either inter- or intra-generational social mobility does not correlate very well with Dahrendorf's observations.

Though mainly concerned with managers, rather than directors, Clements' 1958 study of Manchester still probably provides the most thorough examination of intra-generational mobility. He found that about half of his sample had begun 'at the bottom' and that about a third of them had actually started work on the shop floor.[2] At first sight these figures appear to indicate that access to management positions is relatively 'open' but a further consideration of those men in the latter group indicates that such a conclusion should be advanced with extreme caution.

Clements tells us that, on average, these men started work when they were 14. But despite the fact that they started work earlier than any other type of manager, and despite the fact that they had worked eight years longer, they became managers four years later at the age of 37.[3] In short, they spent over 20 years at work before they even reached the fringe of lower management. Only 4% of them were directors and, as Clements put it, 'the small proportion in top management shows that their chances of getting into the top ranks of management are very limited'.[4] It seems unlikely that this situation has undergone any radical change[5] and one would, in any case, expect

[1] ibid., p. 278 fn., citing G. Thomas, *Labour Mobility in Great Britain, 1945-49: An Enquiry Carried Out for the Ministry of Labour and National Service*, Report No. 134, n.d. (This report employs a definition of 'manager' which includes chargehands and gangers: cf. the quite different implications of A. I. Harris and R. Clausen, *Labour Mobility in Great Britain: Government Social Survey for the Ministry of Labour*, H.M.S.O., 1966, table 52.)

[2] *Managers*, chapters VII, VIII: cf. Clark, *The Industrial Manager*, p. 74; Acton Society Trust, *Management Succession*, p. 10.

[3] ibid., Appendix II, table 7.   [4] ibid., pp. 75, 79.

[5] In Clark's later survey of the same area about 7% of those first employed as apprentices or in manual work were directors: only 18% of directors had begun in this way. *The Industrial Manager*, cf. tables 5.2, 5.5.

H

any increases in social mobility since the war to have resulted from inter- rather than intra-generational movements. Thus, unless one takes very special definitions of 'intellectual capacity' and 'initiative', and unless one makes unrealistic assumptions about their social class distribution, there is little to be said for Lord Shawcross' view that:

'whilst obviously there isn't room at the top for everyone, the man who starts at the bottom has a real prospect of working his way to the top if he has the intellectual capacity—and the initiative to use it.'[1]

Of course, most of the writers who suggest that a managerial revolution is under way in Britain have not argued that it will be heralded by increased mobility from shop floor to boardroom. Instead, assuming that the 1944 Education Act will have channelled off the best of a new generation of manual workers, they look to the rise of the ex-grammar school boy. Quite clearly, the expansion of grammar school places must have affected the educational composition of contemporary managers and Clark's[2] finding that 62% of managers aged under 40 had been to grammar school, compared to only 44% of those aged 55 or over, does provide evidence to suggest that at least some companies have decided to tap what a 1954 F.B.I. pamphlet[3] called this 'important source of talent'.

Here again, however, caution must be exercised in interpreting the significance of this process because directors collectively, and to a lesser extent senior managers too, are still substantially characterized by pre-corporate experiences and affiiliations which do not square with the technocratic-meritocratic image. To take the most obvious example, it appears that six or more out of every ten directors, and probably about five out of every ten senior managers, had fathers in social classes I or II, and Clark's study indicates (as an inspection of class chances to gain a grammar school education might also suggest) that the proportion of managers from such classes may be increasing, rather than decreasing.[4] Furthermore,

[1] *The Director*, Jan., 1965; see also, L. F. Urwick, *Is Management A Profession?* (published by Urwick, Orr and Partners), 1954, p. 22.
[2] *The Industrial Manager*, p. 32.
[3] *Public School and Grammar School Boys in Industry*, Dec., 1954, p. 2.
[4] *The Industrial Manager*, pp. 68, 70; cf. A. Little and J. Westergaard, 'The Trend of Class Differentials in Educational Opportunity in England and Wales', *British Journal of Sociology*, Vol. XI, No. 4, Dec., 1964. (79% of Northern City directors originated in these classes.)

not only do a substantial proportion of directors come from the higher social strata but an equally substantial proportion of them, probably over half their number, even in 1966, had fathers who were in some form of business or industrial management. (See Table 10.1). This is not to suggest that nepotism is widespread (though there is reason to believe that the mode of access into modern companies is less bureaucratized than sometimes assumed);[1] it is to suggest that a certain continuity

TABLE 10.1

The Business Origins of Businessmen

Father's Occupation	65 Directors and Senior Managers in Northern City 1962 %		Copeman's Study of over 1,000 Directors 1955 %	
Director—same company	(7)	11 ⎫	19 ⎫	
Director—other company	(6)	9 ⎬ 52%	9 ⎬ 51%	
Small Businessman	(11)	17 ⎪	16 ⎪	
Industrial Manager	(10)	15 ⎭	7 ⎭	
Non-Industrial Manager	(5)	8 ⎫	22	
Professional	(10)	15 ⎬		
White Collar	(4)	6 ⎫		
Skilled Manual	(10)	15 ⎬	8	
Unskilled Manual	(2)	3 ⎭		

Source: G. H. Copeman, *Leaders of British Industry*, Table 14.2. (Both studies asked for father's occupation at the time the director started work: the relevant information was not given by 16% of Copeman's respondents.) In 1966, 62% of the Institute of Directors' members had fathers who were in business, see *The Director*, April, 1966, p. 85.

of business culture may be facilitated by the transference of attitudes from one generation to another.

That directors often have a certain similarity of social experience, even before their working lives commence, is confirmed by a further consideration of their educational background. Thus, of the minority of directors who are graduates, probably at least half obtained their degrees at Oxford and Cambridge (see Table 10.2). In practice, of course, one would expect the proportion of directors who are graduates to increase, though it does not necessarily follow that the Oxbridge representation will decline. At least one writer[2]

[1] cf. *Managers*, p. 29; *The Director*, April, 1966, p. 85; *The Industrial Manager*, p. 112, table 5.34.

[2] M. Abrams, 'The Elite of Tomorrow', *The Observer*, September 4, 1960.

has estimated that these graduates will account for the bulk
of future additions. Such figures do much to underline
Clements'[1] comment 'that as the social scale is ascended,
chances of getting on the board greatly improve, from being
practically negligible at the bottom to being extremely good
at the top.'

There is even more justification for this view if we consider
another index of social origin, public school education. Even
if allowance is made for differences between the findings of
different studies[2] there is still strong evidence to suggest, not

TABLE 10.2

Graduate Directors

	% of Directors who are Graduates	% of Graduate Directors from Oxford or Cambridge
1. Clark (1966)	37	44
2. Copeman (1955)	36	56
3. Guttsman (1963)	46	73
4. Northern City (1962)	47	61

Sources:
1. *The Industrial Manager*, table 3.18, p. 44.
2. *Leaders of British Industry*, p. 100.
3. *The British Political Elite*, table 3, p. 336.
4. Of all the interviewees in Northern City (i.e. the 38 directors above plus
27 senior managers) 35% were graduates and of these 60% had been to
Oxbridge.

only that ex-public school boys are grossly over-represented
in the boardroom, but also that the management hierarchy
itself is stratified in terms of public school education. (See
Table 10.3).[3]

The data indicates that as we move up the corporate hierarchy the proportion of those with public school education
increases from approximately two out of ten for managers, to
four out of ten senior managers, to about five out of ten directors.
The Institute of Directors' 1965 survey even suggests that the

[1] *Managers*, p. 54.
[2] e.g. 'public school' is not consistently defined in the studies cited in Table 10.3;
The Director's 1965 and 1966 surveys employed different classifications. (Clark
(*The Industrial Manager*, p. 36) suggests his much lower figures reflect a (North
Western) regional variation.)
[3] For the possible effects of this on communications, see A. J. M. Sykes and
J. Bates, 'A Study of Conflict between Formal Company Policy and the Interests
of Informal Groups', *Sociological Review*, Vol. 3, No. 10, Nov., 1962.

proportion of public school educated directors is increasing,
for whereas 62% of all directors were found to have received
such an education the percentage for the youngest age group,
those aged 25–35, was 75%.[1] This could be a consequence of
the increased proportion of public school boys going into

TABLE 10.3

*Stratification by Public School Education
Within the Management Hierarchy*

	Directors	Senior Managers	All Managers
	%	%	%
1. Copeman (1955)	58	—	—
2. Acton Society (1956)	—	33	19
3. Clements (1958)	—	45	26
4. Northern City (1962)	63	44	—
5. Farrow (1963)	64	—	—
6. Institute of Directors (1965)	62	—	—
7. Institute of Directors (1966)	44	—	—
8. Clark (1966)	26	22	12
9. Heller (1967)			

Sources:
1. *Leaders of British Industry*, p. 101.
2. *Management Succession*, table 3, p. 4 (the 33% figure is for 'Top Management',
   defined as 'the general works manager, and, in a *very* large works, the works
   manager').
3. *Managers*, Appendix II, table 28.
4. Senior managers had similar titles to the Acton 'top managers' (see 2).
5. N. Farrow, 'How Old is Too Old?', *Business*, Nov., 1963, p. 60. (This study,
   confined to the largest 100 companies (measured by net assets), is only
   concerned with 'chief executives'. Glennerster and Pryke attempted to repeat
   this analysis for 1938, finding 57% of chief executives had then been to public
   school. See, H. Glennerster and R. Pryke, *The Public Schools*, Young Fabian
   Pamphlet, No. 7, Nov., 1964, p. 19.)
6. *The Director*, Jan., 1965, table 4, p. 90.
7. *The Director*, April, 1966, p. 85.
8. *The Industrial Manager*, table 3.8, p. 34.
9. R. Heller, 'British Top Directors', *Management Today*, March, 1967.

industry since the war,[2] or it might be explained by a tendency
for ex-public school boys to be promoted earlier than their
colleagues. What mainly concerns us here, however, is that
there is little reason to believe that the proportion of directors
with such an education is significantly decreasing.

Over all, then, we find that directors are predominately
recruited from the top two social classes and that a substantial

[1] *The Director*, Jan., 1965.   [2] *Management Succession*, pp. 14, 90.

proportion of them had fathers who were themselves in business; probably about half of them have been to a public school and where they have been to university at all there is a strong tendency for them to have been to Oxford or Cambridge.

It is not, of course, surprising that members of the business elite, or any other elite, should come from the higher social strata, nor is it remarkable that they should have a large number of members who attended the traditional elite educational institutions. But this is not to say that these facts are of no significance. We accept that taken one by one, or even collectively, they 'prove' nothing about the director's frame of reference and value structure. However, in our view, the general similarity of social origins and pre-corporate social experience which exists between the old and new generations makes it much more probable than improbable that in certain important respects, to turn Dahrendorf's argument upside-down, their reference groups will not differ, and, as he would assume, similar reference groups make for similar values.

To take another example it seems highly probable not only that a substantial proportion of directors come from families with business connections but that the majority of them were born into that section of British society which, above all others, is characterized by a high proportion of shareholders.[1] The fathers, friends and relatives of many of them are probably shareholders and, as we have seen, so most probably are they.

Such observations do not, of course, add up to any meaningful argument about the *control potential* of directorial voting power; nor do they amount to an indication that non-propertied directors—whose main income flow is not dependent on share ownership—will strive to maximize shareholder profit. They do suggest, however, and this hypothesis is best expressed in a negative form, that it is improbable that directors as an occupational group will not be politically conservative and satisfied with the *status quo* and that they will not have some sense of what is just and fair for shareholders.

In short, given the generally acceptable premise that whereas corporations may not meaningfully be said to have goals,

---

[1] The AB group—which is broadly comparable to the Registrar-General's social classes I and II, where most directors have their origins—accounts for 13% of the population and 43% of the holders of industrial and commercial shares. *How Does Britain Save?*, pp. 16–17.

mechanisms do exist within them for inculcating values and norms in new role incumbents, and given also another general assumption, namely, that some part of an actor's value orientation may derive from his initial and subsequent location in the social structure, one might well expect the directorial neophyte to come into contact with values of the above type when he enters the boardroom. More than this, however, one might even expect a substantial proportion of directors to share such values even before they enter the corporation. This line of argument has some bearing upon the matter of whether one can consider 'the managers' to constitute a 'new class' and we will discuss this question later.

So far, however, we have confined ourselves to a consideration of the director's probable values and frame of reference *before* he enters the corporation. But despite quite a high incidence of geographical mobility,[1] inter-corporate mobility[2] tends to be low, and in the firm, as in other organizations, the attainment of high office depends in part on the individual accepting the organization's values and objectives as his own. Thus, the process of socialization undergone *within* the corporation is an equally, if not more important factor in the development of the director's value orientation. It is, therefore, to a consideration of the probable significance of this process that we now turn.

In doing so we will be consciously attempting to offset the contemporary emphasis upon the likelihood that managers redefine their role to fit their own personal and economic interests. As is made clear in our discussion of managerial economics, we do not question that such redefinition occurs but we do feel that to present a balanced picture of the modern director some attention must be given to those factors leading to conformity in role performance, as well as to those which lead to innovation. Similarly, and for the same reason, we will deliberately underplay the significance of those unintended consequences of bureaucratic organization which have received

---

[1] cf. *1961 Census, Migration Tables*, table 16, *Occupation Tables*, table 18; for America, see J. Ladinsky, 'Occupational Determinants of Geographic Mobility Among Professional Workers', *American Sociological Review*, Vol. 32, No. 2, April, 1967, pp. 253–264.

[2] cf. *Leaders of British Industry*, pp. 107–108; *The Industrial Manager*, p. 86; *The Director*, April, 1966, p. 85; I. S. Pool, 'The Head of Company: Conceptions of Role and Identity'. *Behavioral Science*, Vol. 9, No. 2, April, 1964, p. 150.

so much attention in work on organization theory. We will, for example, be less concerned with the possibility of dysfunctional sub-unit identifications developing than with identification with the organization *in toto*. The works of Baumol, Marris, Williamson and other managerial theorists of the firm all imply that even this latter identification may be dysfunctional for profit maximization. As we shall see, however, and as their theories also imply, it is not necessarily in conflict with the pursuit of operational efficiency and profit acquisition. Both may figure prominently in the work values of the non-propertied director.

CHAPTER XI

SOCIAL EXPERIENCE AND VALUES II

Socialization within the Corporation

'The general method of maintaining an informal executive organisation is so to operate and to select and promote executives that a general condition of compatibility of personnel is maintained. Perhaps often, and certainly occasionally, men cannot be promoted or selected, or even must be relieved, because they cannot function, because they 'do not fit', where there is no question of formal competence. The question of 'fitness' involves such matters as education, experience, age, sex, personal distinctions, prestige, race, nationality, faith, politics, sectional antecedents; and such very specific personal traits as manners, speech, personal appearance, etc.'

CHESTER BARNARD, *The Functions of the Executive*

IT is popularly believed that the bureaucratization of the large corporation has led to the emergence of a new type of manager, the Organization Man. However, this view has often been advanced with more confidence than clarity and even if we leave aside questions about who the Organization Man is[1] and whether he really is more likely to be found in the large organization,[2] it still remains questionable that his emergence has any significance for the occurrence or otherwise of a separation of ownership and control.

Indeed, if it be maintained that, for the Organization Man, conformity *is* success, then the crucial questions to ask are, conformity with what, and are there not differences between the models of behaviour conformed to in different institutional spheres? Clearly the answer to this second question must be that such differences do exist and that the behavioural models to which self-approximation is sought are related to the

[1] See, W. H. Whyte, *The Organisation Man*, London, 1957, p. 3.
[2] See, L. W. Porter, 'Where is the Organisation Man?', *Harvard Business Review*, Nov.–Dec., 1963, pp. 53–61.

particular norms and values which exist in particular organizations and institutions. This, of course, is no more than a commonplace observation but it is one which has some relevance to the notion that a new stratum of managers is emerging which has its own distinctive attitudes and frames of reference. There are two reasons for this.

Firstly, it draws attention to the fact that the manager does not enter into a cultural void when he first takes up his position in the lower levels of the management hierarchy. Definitions of what Mills,[1] in America, has called the 'sound man' or of what Lewis and Stewart,[2] in Britain, have called the 'reliable man' already exist. They constitute prescriptive role definitions of the 'good manager' which probably enter into the selection process itself and present behavioural and attitudinal models to which those already in management will tend to approximate if they desire to be successful. Such definitions of 'reliability', 'character' and so on therefore provide us with some clues about what it is that the manager is expected to conform to and for this reason we will return to a fuller consideration of them later on.

There is, however, a second set of observations which flow directly from the commonplace assumption with which we began and which it is equally important to consider in relation to the notion that the 'new managers' have distinctive attitudes and characteristics. These concern the fact that the modern corporation is an economic institution. To some extent this very obvious fact has tended to be lost sight of in the discovery that the modern manager may act in accordance with a complex system of social and psychological costs and rewards. Yet there is good reason to believe that the progressive rationalization of the large corporation has increased, rather than decreased, the extent to which the manager's performance is assessed by essentially economic criteria.

The introduction of the computer, the development of better costing techniques, critical path analysis and operational research, all mean that departmental, product and company performance can now be more readily measured. Today, the individual manager's performance may be subject to analysis by the personal record card, regular reports by superordinates,

[1] *The Power Elite*, N.Y., 1959, p. 141.
[2] *The Boss: The Life and Times of the British Businessman*, London, 1963, p. 83.

and even assessment by consultants. In the future it seems certain that the use of such techniques will increase.[1] In historical perspective, then, the manager is becoming supremely accountable to the corporation. His promotion potential is increasingly likely to be assessed in terms of his past performance and his performance itself to be measured in economic terms.

Now even if, as Earley[2] has suggested, the above techniques are particularly well developed in the 'management controlled' corporations, it does not follow that the 'new managers' will necessarily come to regard the attainment of profit, efficiency and those other objectives, the pursuit of which such techniques facilitate, as anything more than pre-conditions to the attainment of their own ulterior ends. Nevertheless, even if we assume that the manager begins by regarding his compliance with organizational goals as no more than a means to his own ulterior ends, the possibility cannot be ruled out that he will, in time, come to regard them as terminal values. Indeed, we think it probable that such a process of 'inverted ritualism' does occur and that it should be possible to find attitudinal and possibly behavioural differences between managers with greater and lesser periods of exposure to the essentially economic cues with which they are confronted in the corporation.

We accept, of course, that those interests and satisfactions which can lead corporate leaders (i.e. directors) to institute policies which are not synonymous with profit maximization may also be present in the lower levels of the management hierarchy. For example, it is possible that those who occupy

[1] Assuming business rationalization reached the point where managers were typically set output norms, it is of course possible that, being treated like industrial workers, they would react in a similar way by restricting their output and resorting to 'fiddles'. Berliner's work provides some suggestive evidence that this may have happened in Russia—but any political inferences to be drawn from this are probably of limited value since the British equivalent of the Russian 'premium' is likely to be the share option. On Russian managers see, J. S. Berliner, *Factory and Manager in the U.S.S.R.*, Harvard, 1957.

[2] J. S. Earley, 'Business Budgeting and the Theory of the Firm', *Journal of Industrial Economics*, Nov., 1960, p. 39. For similar views see also, J. S. Earley, 'Recent Developments in Cost Accounting and the "Marginal Analysis",' *Journal of Political Economy*, Vol. LXIII, June, 1955, pp. 227–242; J. S. Earley, 'Marginal Policies of "Excellently Managed" Companies', *American Economic Review*, Vol. XLVI, March 1956, pp. 44–70; W. L. Baldwin, 'The Motives of Managers, Environmental Restraints and the Theory of Managerial Enterprise', *The Quarterly Journal of Economics*, Vol. LXXVIII, May, 1964, No. 2, pp. 238–256; P. A. Baran and P. M. Sweezy, 'Monopoly Capital', *Monthly Review*, Vol. XIV, Nos. 3 and 4, July–August, 1964, pp. 140–145.

positions in various management specialisms may develop sub-unit ideologies which set up strains toward the over-fulfilment of their role in the context of the organization as a whole.[1] However, recent advances in performance measurement would seem to add credence to the classical (but now almost unorthodox) view that managers are unlikely to be promoted for selling goods that cannot be produced, for producing those that cannot be sold, or for pursuing other well-documented forms of self and departmental aggrandisement.

In short, then, managers at all levels of the executive hierarchy are likely to be more closely involved with the process of profit-making, if not profit-receiving, as the rationalization of the large corporation continues. Indeed, it is open to question whether even the modern trend to decentralize authority will necessarily result in lower level managers having more discretion to pursue their own ulterior ends. Paradoxically, far from leading to a sub-unit level displacement of overall organizational goals, decentralization itself might provide corporate leaders with an additional stimulus to regard organizational sub-units (e.g. individual factories) as microcosms of the organization as a whole. If this were in fact the case, then since profitability provides the most suitable (since universalistic) measure of performance, one might well predict that not only the refinement of performance measurement techniques but, in its own way, decentralization too, will in future be important factors in sensitizing managers to the essentially *economic* nature of the corporation's cost and reward system[2].

It is no doubt true that as Thompson[3] has observed the modern corporation is a prolific generator of anxiety and insecurity. Indeed one might expect that corporation managers would be characterized by some degree of psychological

[1] cf. P. Selznick, *T.V.A. and the Grass Roots*, Berkeley, 1949.

[2] There is some evidence to suggest that decentralization is not necessarily tied to greater profitability. Dearden, for example, has argued that it may lead to an increase in hidden costs such as those associated with an increase in the number of finance specialists and that costly battles may develop between them and the heads of decentralized units about how much profit really was or was not made. However, this does not necessarily invalidate our hypothesis that decentralization may sensitize these managers to profit as such—it is this, after all, that the haggling is likely to be about. See, J. Dearden, 'Mirage of Profit Decentralisation', *Harvard Business Review*, Vol. 40, No. 6, Nov., 1962, pp. 140–148.

[3] V. A. Thompson, *Modern Organisation*, p. 24.

uncertainty. One might even argue that modern corporation directors are anomic, since not only do the corporation's various publics expect different things of them,[1] but many of the objectives they claim to set themselves are often not clearly defined, or are not finite ones. But whatever the case about this may be—and one might argue that the director's publics are more characterized by conflicting wants than by differing expectations about his conduct—we find it very difficult indeed to conclude that many large corporation *managers* can be in much doubt that, in future, their directorial potential will be increasingly assessed on the basis of their past economic performance.

Furthermore, if, as we assume, there are pressures which make it probable that managers will come to regard efficiency and profitability as terminal values, it seems highly improbable that they will 'de-internalize' these upon attaining boardroom status, or, one might add, that they will get that far if they do so.

The above is, of course, a very formal statement of the possible outcome of the manager's socialization within the enterprise. It has been deliberately presented as such to off-set that current tendency in the literature which invites the Paretian parody that the managers are a new breed of status-conscious 'sheep' who have taken over from the old entre-preneurs, or profit-hungry 'wolves'. Our point is merely that there is good reason to believe that efficiency and profit are an important part of the life organization of the modern manager and that in the contemporary and increasingly rationalized management hierarchy, personal success and inefficiency are unlikely to go together. Indeed the latter would probably be more readily tolerated in the old style family firm where personal ties and obligations can intervene in the formulation of policies. The above should not, however, be taken to imply that achievement has, or necessarily ever will, completely supersede ascriptive criteria as the basis for managerial success or, indeed, that a commitment to profitability and efficiency is always a sufficient qualification for directorial office.

Inevitably, certain 'personal' factors, like those referred to by Barnard, may also play a part. At the highest levels, com-petence is almost certainly not the sole factor to determine

[1] See Goldthorpe's argument, briefly cited in Marris, *The Economic Theory*, pp. 52–53.

promotion and 'other questions which have to do with the whole personality of the individual are likely to form the major subject for discussion. Is he dependable? Is he loyal? What is his wife like?'[1] Typically, we may assume that 'loyalty' and 'dependability' will be defined by those already at the apex of any given organization and that the reliable/sound/ dependable man will be a man who shares the characteristics, attitudes and values of those already in senior positions. These are not, of course, very bold assumptions to make but having made them explicit we are immediately made aware of the fact that the above definitions of 'fitness' for office *pre-exist* the entry of any given manager into the corporation. And since there are built-in pressures toward their perpetuation, any attempt to explain them away as 'anachronistic', or as some form of 'cultural lag', must be less than satisfactory. Thus, if, as many writers have assumed, the development of a new and distinctive managerial stratum is under way, we must not forget that such prescriptive role definitions constitute the organizational environment from which it must emerge.

This point has some significance for any consideration of the manager's relationship to his superordinates. Dahrendorf[2] may, for example, be right to argue that as far as the manager's relationship to his peers and subordinates is concerned (who, as he states, constitute 'the two important reference groups which the manager shares with the capitalist'), 'to be successful means to be liked, and to be liked means, in many ways, to be alike'. But as far as the manager's (i.e. non-directorial executive's) relationship to his *superordinates* is concerned, the above assumptions might lead us to rather different conclusions. Namely, that to be liked means to be successful, and to be successful means, in many ways, to become alike. Of course, super-ordinate-subordinate socio-cultural approximation may not always be consciously taken account of when decisions about selection and promotion are made. Furthermore, in practice, one would usually expect the role played by such factors to be expressed in a rather general manner.

We would consider the survey[3] finding that 65% of firms gave 'acceptability' as a major reason for employing Arts

[1] E. Gross, *Work and Society*, N.Y., 1958, p. 78.
[2] *Class and Class Conflict*, pp. 46–47.
[3] A. Collin *et al.*, *The Arts Graduate in Industry*, Acton Society Trust, 1962, p. 27.

graduates, the fact that Northern City businessmen often dismissed the use of executive selection tests on the grounds that 'I know a good man when I see one' and even the time-honoured belief that 'leaders are born, not made'—and thus also managers—to be examples of this. In fact it is worth noting that the British Institute of Mangement, which one might have expected to be a forerunner of professionalized management, was bedevilled in its early stages by a split between those who thought management could be taught and those who were convinced that leaders are born not made.[1]

In this context, then, it is perhaps appropriate to report the replies given by Northern City businessmen when we asked them what, in their opinion, made a 'good manager'. (See Table 11.1.)

This question unleashed a flood-tide of ill-defined and some-times contradictory responses. However, the answers given did make one thing quite clear, that 'character', 'personality' and social skills and personal characteristics in general were considered to be much more important than technical skills. By far the largest category of response contained references to 'leadership' or some supposed aspect of this, like 'being firm but fair' or 'commanding respect'. Only 16 responses mentioned a need for technical knowledge or qualifications and a further 18 put forward the view, without prompting, that technical knowledge was less important than personality or ability with people.

It is possible, of course, that the lack of emphasis placed upon specialized knowledge might constitute an acknowledgement by these businessmen that 'trained incapacity' does exist in business and that those so affected are unlikely to have directorial potential. To raise this possibility may, however, be no more than to rephrase the proposition that the good businessman should be a good all-rounder in the better, since neutral, language of organization theory. Thus, the question arises of whether the social skills and personality traits these businessmen thought so important were no more than those which are generally thought to characterize members of the upper middle class in general and the recipients of a public school and/or Oxbridge education in particular. If this were in fact the case it would not of course necessarily follow that businessmen simply prefer to recruit and promote ex-public

[1] 'Learning Not to Manage', *The Economist*, August 16, 1958.

TABLE 11.1

Classification of Responses to the Question
'What Makes a Good Manager?'

Character and Personality

(a) Leadership
'Must be firm but fair' (19)
'The gift of leadership' (18)
'Equable temperament', 'patience' and 'tenacity' (13)
'Being honest and straightforward', 'integrity'
and 'commanding respect' (9)
'Self-confidence' (6) 65

(b) Dynamism   80
'Ambition', 'enthusiasm' and 'drive' (9)
'Intuition' and 'vision' (3)
'Not accepting the second best' (3) 15

Social Skills
'Understanding people' (15)
'Ability to persuade others' (12)
'Acceptability' (10)
'Being a good judge of men' (3) 40

Specific Organizational Skills
'Ability to make decisions' (16)
'Knowing when to delegate' (4)
'Ability to co-ordinate' (4) 24

Technical Knowledge and Qualifications
'Technical knowledge' (9)
'Shop floor experience' (5)
'Training in management' (2) 16

Technical Knowledge of Secondary Importance
'Technical knowledge less important than
personality' or 'than ability with people' 18

Analytical Skills
'Ability to see the wood from the trees' (8)
'Logical mind', 'intelligence' (6) 14

Other Responses   13

Total number of responses   205

Total number of respondents   65

school boys and Oxbridge graduates. Actual experience in
these institutions might well be less important than the
appearance that one has had that experience. As one Northern
City director put it 'we don't particularly look for the ex-public
school boy—but we like the public school type'.

Studies of the role expectations of potential managers might
throw some light on the above, for we suspect that many
graduates present themselves to large corporation recruitment
officers with just these sorts of assumptions in mind. Regrettably,
however, we know of no British studies of this type so we will
confine ourselves to the proposition that directors do look for
qualities akin to those commonly thought to be developed by
such institutions. This, in any case, seems to have been true
of those in Northern City and the high proportion of businessmen with such educational experience and social origins
nationally, and also of course the proportions of senior businessmen with qualifications in science and technology, or even a
minimum acquaintance with formal management education,
would seem to indicate that, in this respect at least, Northern
City businessmen were not atypical.

In short, there are still very real difficulties in arguing that
eligibility for management positions, especially the most senior
ones, is now solely determined by achievement as opposed to
ascriptive criteria. As we argued in the preceding section, this
does not necessarily imply that nepotism is widespread, only
that certain socio-cultural factors are still important. It seems
possible, for example, that even where qualifications are held
by managers it is not merely the possession of the qualification
itself, with all that this implies about the possessor's specialized
knowledge and competence, which determines fitness to occupy
a particular position. The belief that the process of gaining the
qualification has itself conferred a diffuse, and desirable, quality
upon the possessor may also be important.[1] This would obviously
appear to be the case with those directors whose sole 'qualification' is an Oxbridge Arts degree but it is quite possible that
it holds true for those with other qualifications too. For
example, Clark[2] found in 1966 that 45% of 'top managers'

[1] For a general statement of this view see, J. A. Banks, 'The Structure of
Industrial Enterprise in Industrial Society', *Sociological Review Monograph*, No. 8,
1964, pp. 48–49.
[2] *The Industrial Manager*, table 3.15, p. 41 and table 3.11, p. 38.

I

who held 'appropriate' graduate qualifications (i.e. in science, technology, economics, law) had gained them at Oxbridge, compared to 23% of all managers so qualified. Unfortunately, it is not made clear in this study how far such differences might be attributable to the different age distributions of those in these two groups but Clements'[1] earlier study and the recent work of Hutton and Gerstl[2] does suggest that even those with engineering degrees are not necessarily as upwardly mobile as often thought, and those with Oxbridge degrees again appear to have been more successful.

We do not question that outstanding competence in a relevant field is a strong factor in the attainment of boardroom status. We would suggest, however, that promotion probably comes earlier and more readily to those thought to possess certain diffuse and intangible qualities. If this is indeed the case, then given that those attitudes, values and 'qualities' which are thought to be desirable will be deemed to be so by those who already occupy the highest positions, and given also that in the case of business these people will typically be directors, whose social composition has remained remarkably stable over the past half-century, we must be careful not to jump to the conclusion that the qualified 'professional' managers of the future will have distinctively different normative orientations, or that they will initially be selected, or ultimately promoted, on solely technical criteria.

In fact, of course, whether there is preferential treatment or not, the sources of recruitment to managerial positions are such that one would not, in the majority of cases, expect new managers to experience any fundamental 'culture shock' upon going into business.[3] Furthermore if we can once again assume that Northern City businessmen are not atypical, there seems little reason to assume that the minority of directors who begin on the shop floor will have much difficulty in assimilating directorial values and behaviour patterns. Those few we met in Northern City appeared to have adapted themselves very well indeed and, if anything, they tended to over-play their role. Indeed two things stood out in the interviews we had with them. First, the pleasure they derived from talking about their

[1] *Managers*, p. 89.

[2] *Engineers: The Anatomy of a Profession*, London, 1966, tables 2, 12 and 24.

[3] cf. M. Rosenberg, *Occupation and Values*, Glencoe., 1957.

lowly social origins and second the fact that it was they, above all others, who talked at length about their responsibilities to shareholders.

Thus, the above discussion of the possible significance of the manager's pre- and intra-corporate socialization suggests the following conclusions. First, that the majority of directors have social origins in the higher social strata: many of them share a common process of socialization in the elite educational institutions. This suggests that they may come to the corporation with a common value orientation and it is unlikely that this will be hostile to shareholders.

Those directors who do not share this common background undergo a process of socialization within the corporation itself. Here, the manager learns to measure 'success' in terms of economic costs and rewards: he learns that fulfilment of his personal goals can only be achieved by fulfilment of the corporation's own goals. It seems unlikely that the manager will 'unlearn' this behaviour pattern upon becoming a director. The increasing rationality of the modern corporation means that the individual director is more likely to be selected on the basis of past (economic) performance, and less on ascriptive criteria.

However, it is probably wrong to completely ignore the ascriptive elements in selection and promotion. Directorial primary groups have their own values, attitudes and behaviour patterns and it seems improbable that they will select new colleagues who are not compatible with these. The problems of adjustment for up-from-the-bottom managers are probably small. In economic terms, they have been promoted because of their success in improving efficiency and profits: in social terms, they are likely to be highly adaptable men to climb the corporation ladder at all. The boardroom is just one (last) stage in a lifetime of engagement with, and withdrawal from, a series of social strata.

Once the hitherto manager has gained his directorship, bought his shares, and perhaps even sent his son to public school,[1] then, in many important respects, he is indistinguishable from the propertied director. Given his experience within the corporation we find it most difficult to argue that even the

[1] One survey found that over a third of directors' children go to public schools, see 'The Director Observed Away from the Desk', *The Director*, May, 1966, p. 272.

up-from-the-bottom manager will differ radically from the propertied director in either economic policies or social values.

It would seem, then, that once we take account of the fact that the corporation itself is composed of individuals whose attitudes, values and behaviours pre-exist the entry of any given manager, it becomes questionable whether one can realistically hope to explain the latter's own attitudes, values and behaviour as if they were no more than a straight fulfilment of his (allegedly) professional goals.

One must accept, of course, that differences are likely to be found between managers with different sorts of professional training and indeed between those with such training, on the one hand, and those with no formal training at all, on the other. But if one is interested in predicting directorial values and behaviour it must be recognized that whatever a manager's professional identification groups may have been to begin with, by the time he becomes a director his conception of his own role, the role of management in general, and the role of the corporation in society will have been mediated through the social experiences undergone and the roles which he has been expected to play within the corporation itself.

Indeed, there is reason to believe that, with the possible exception of personnel and training, a fairly substantial amount of mobility takes place out of the different management specialisms, it being probable that almost three out of ten managers, and a higher proportion of directors, have changed from one function to another during their careers. There is also reason to believe that those in technical and development positions are more likely to be outwardly (i.e. cross-functionally) mobile than those in any other type of work.[1] This suggests that, unless those with technical training reach the boardroom early on in their careers, they are unlikely to retain a markedly 'technocratic' orientation when they do.

Thus, it becomes problematic whether directors who are science graduates should be primarily considered as 'ex-scientists' or as 'ex-managers'.[2] To a large extent, however, the latter must surely be the case, for we find it difficult to assume

[1] See Clark's findings and his summary of the Acton Society's (rather different) and Clements' (essentially similar) ones in *The Industrial Manager*, pp. 102–108.

[2] Conversely, it remains an open question how far those scientists and others whose first appointment is at boardroom level exercise influence outside their specialist sphere.

that such individuals will have remained unaffected by the norms and values perpetuated by those other, already established, managers with whom they will have interacted throughout their business careers. In any case, and as the Northern City interviews suggest, it seems improbable that many directors consider the possession of specialized technical knowledge to be a sufficient, or even necessary, condition for the attainment of boardroom status.

There seems, then, to be good reason to question Dahrendorf's argument that the social background and experience of propertied and non-propertied directors has placed these groups into different fields of reference. His statement that the members of these two groups 'increasingly move apart in their outlook on and attitudes toward society in general and toward the enterprise in particular'[1] would also probably benefit from qualification. As we have attempted to argue, in the case of British business there is no lack of pressure pushing in the opposite direction. Indeed, since he concludes[2] his analysis of ownership and control by telling us that—

'Despite many differences there are without doubt considerable similarities in the positions, roles, and attitudes of both the capitalist and the manager. . . . Moreover, there are numerous personal and social ties between owners and managers in all industrial societies. If anything, the unpropertied managers are more active in political affairs, both as individuals and through their associations and lobbies.'

—we might well conclude that Dahrendorf's own analysis contains a possible self-contradiction.

Whether or not such a conclusion is justified partly depends, however, upon whether one is primarily concerned with the work-related differences or similarities of 'managers' and 'capitalists', or whether one is more closely concerned with the relationship between the members of these two groups and the occupants of other elite positions—and also, of course, upon whether or not one considers 'managers' and 'capitalists' to belong to the same class in any given society. Accordingly, it is to a consideration of the class membership of British propertied and non-propertied directors that we now turn. As we shall soon see, however, the use of the terms 'manager' and 'capitalist' in this context may itself be problematic.

[1] *Class and Class Conflict*, p. 46.   [2] *ibid.*, p. 47.

CHAPTER XII

ARE 'THE MANAGERS' A NEW CLASS?

As we have already pointed out, the debate about the consequences of a separation of ownership and control has taken
place on at least two levels. The first of these, which has been
almost totally neglected by sociologists, has been concerned
with the possible consequences of a separation of ownership
and control for directorial and company performance. The
second, to which sociologists have in fact contributed (e.g.
Bendix, Dahrendorf, Kolko), has been concerned with the
question of the 'new managers' class location. It is this matter
which we intend to briefly consider here. Upon examination,
however, the precise questions at issue when class is discussed
appear to be no clearer than is the case with arguments about
directorial and company performance. Thus, we feel it
incumbent upon us to begin by stating just what we are and
are not interested in.

We are not concerned here with the question of whether
managers in general, that is not only those in industry but
those in the civil service, trade unions and so on, are all
members of the same class, or indeed with the argument that,
together, they constitute a new ruling class. As we argued in
our earlier consideration of Burnham (see Chapter II) such a
view is unlikely to stand up to serious consideration.

Nor are we concerned with testing the hypothesis that the
ruling class of industry is *ipso facto* the ruling class of society.
Indeed if we are concerned with the question of ruling classes
at all it is only in the sense that this term has been used by
Dahrendorf. What interests us here is, given that 'the managers'
have authority, whether the source of that authority and the
interests it is made to serve are so radically different from that
which is the case with 'owner-managers' that it is now desirable
to consider propertied and non-propertied directors as the
members of two disparate classes.

This particular problem is of course only one special case of the problem of whether any two formerly discrete groups have merged into one or, conversely, of whether any formerly united group has split into two or more new ones. Thus, since Lockwood and Goldthorpe[1] have already developed a framework of analysis for the relationship between socio-economic groups within a system of class stratification (in their case the alleged embourgeoisement of manual workers) we think it may be useful to analyse our particular problem from their general standpoint. This requires that we distinguish between the economic, normative and relational aspects of class stratification and then proceed to a consideration of the sociological implications of the view that 'the managers' are indeed a new class in terms of each of these dimensions. This line of thinking would seem to suggest the following propositions:

(i) That the 'new managers' have a different form and size of income to 'owner-managers';

(ii) That these same managers have different social perspectives and different norms of behaviour;

(iii) That being different from 'owner-managers' in (i) their economic position and (ii) their normative orientation, these managers are not accepted by the former on terms of social equality in formal and informal interaction.

When approached in these terms it is of course a relatively simple matter to demonstrate that the contemporary 'manager' is different from his historical counterpart. But unless it can be assumed—and we do not think it can—that the entrepreneurial class has been an historically stable one which, with the coming of the large corporation, has itself undergone little or no change in value orientation, social relationships to other groups, or even economic position, there can be little point in arguing that the 'new managers' are a new class simply because they differ from nineteenth-century entrepreneurs.

Clearly, the Ferranti's and Pilkington's of today are no more like to John Bright than Arnold Weinstock is to an early mill manager and the number of modern owner-managers of

[1] J. H. Goldthorpe and D. Lockwood, 'Affluence and the British Class Structure', *Sciological Review*, July, 1963, pp. 133–163.

large corporations who are entrepreneurs, in the sense that they founded their firms, must be very small indeed. If then, as we think probable, the old owner-managers have been largely superseded by a new group of propertied directors with different social relationships, different values and a different opportunity structure, there seems no good reason to compare the class situation of the new managerial stratum with that of the former instead of the latter group. It is not our intention here to argue the case against an historical approach: indeed we think it a limitation of many managerial theories that they lack any empirically based attempt to provide one. We merely wish to emphasize that in order to argue that managers are a distinctive class, it is necessary to compare them with the contemporary version of the entrepreneurial class—and not with an historical one, which may itself have undergone changes. If this is not done, then it is not possible to assess the significance of the managers' (essentially managerial) and the owner-managers' (essentially propertied) characteristics for the two groups relational, normative and even economic location within the present class structure.

At first sight, of course, it may appear that even in contemporary society economic differences do exist between propertied and non-propertied directors and given that, at bottom, class is economically determined it might be concluded that on these grounds alone one would be justified in speaking of the existence of a new managerial class. There are, however, additional factors which suggest that such a view may be an oversimplification. To begin with—even if we confine ourselves to this one (economic) aspect, it is rarely the case that even 'non-propertied' directors are in fact 'non-propertied'; they differ from 'propertied' directors only in the extent of their share ownership. Indeed, were we to exclude those directors who are heirs, these so-called 'non-propertied' directors would probably be found to constitute one of the largest (non-institutional) shareholding groups. As such, and whether this constitutes an immediate determinant of their organizational behaviour or not, they share with propertied directors an interest in the perpetuation of the private mode of production.

Furthermore, not only are non-propertied directors closely aligned with the interests of propertied directors but, *de jure*, their responsibilities are defined in terms of serving the shareholder interest.[1] The source of their authority *qua* directors stems from the powers entrusted to them by shareholders.[2]

Now, by itself, the fact that a particular group is wealthy or has power does not imply that its members share common interests with those of other wealthy and powerful groups. It certainly cannot be taken to imply that both groups are members of the same class. For example, it is possible that the source and form of wealth may differ and the two groups may exercise power over completely different spheres. It is partly because Dahrendorf has made this point so clearly that his work has been such a major contribution to the study of elites and ruling classes. But whereas *Class and Class Conflict* provides a useful theoretical framework for research it is no substitute for empirical enquiry in a particular society.

In British society it is arguable that the wealth and power of both propertied and non-propertied directors confers an interest in the perpetuation of private enterprise and of private property. The life chances and style of life of the non-propertied corporation director are closely related to those of the propertied director. Both are clearly dependent upon *private* property which, in 1966, provided 67% of directors of companies of £3 million capital and over with (pre-tax) incomes of £10,000 or better[3]—such rewards are much less readily available in the public sector. Furthermore, the more successfully the non-propertied director performs his work role the more likely he is to approximate to the economic position of the propertied director.

To clarify our thinking, however, we may posit that there are at least three possible relationships which any large corporation director may have to shareholders and propertied directors. First he may be part of the shareholder membership group. In this case the director will be 'propertied' and there are few problems which need concern us here about his motivation, economic interest and normative orientation. But if the director is not part of the shareholding membership group— in the sense that he does not have a substantial shareholding—

---

[1] To be strictly accurate the shareholders do not 'own' the company or the assets, they own the shares and these confer certain rights upon them. And again, to be strictly accurate the directors are the servants not of the shareholders, but of the company—though cf. p. 22, note 6.

[2] cf. Dahrendorf, *Class and Class Conflict*, pp. 43–44.

[3] *The Director*, April, 1966, p. 84: *P.I.B. Report*, No. 107, March 1969.

then, this does not mean that he has no relationship to the members and interests of that group. There are at least two further possibilities. These are that he may merely take the interests of that group into account, that is accommodate his policies to its interests, or, that he may identify himself and his company with shareholders and their interests. In short, then, the notional director may (*a*) be part of the shareholding *membership group*, or (*b*) take that group as an *interaction group*, or (*c*) take that group as an *identification group*.

For our purposes, we take the terms interaction group and identification group to be the end points of a continuum which ranges from the situation in which an actor merely takes the existence of a group into account in order to accomplish his own purposes, to the situation in which he takes that group to be a source of his major perspectives and values. In the latter case, given 'absolute' identification, the actor takes the role of a member and adopts the member's standpoint as his own and it becomes feasible to analyse his behaviour as if he were indeed a member of that group. We believe that in his relationship to shareholders and propertied directors the non-propertied director approximates more closely to the latter situation than many contemporary theorists would suggest. The reasons why we take this view will perhaps become clearer if we consider the normative and relational aspects of his position.

We have already argued that in terms of his pre-corporate and corporate socialization the non-propertied director is unlikely to have a general value orientation which is radically different from that of the propertied director. In terms of social experience and value orientation we would expect both propertied and non-propertied directors to have much in common. There can be no doubt, for example, that these two groups have much more in common with each other than either of them have with employees. Nor can there be much doubt that both of these groups depend for their power, life chances and life style upon the continuation of a business system based on private property. We know of no evidence, for example, which suggests that non-propertied directors are any more favourably disposed to nationalization than propertied directors.

That non-propertied directors often oppose nationalization on the grounds of efficiency may be irrelevant. In contemporary society it is no longer practical—i.e. politically efficacious—to justify private enterprise on grounds of inalienable property rights, and we think it highly probable that a systematic analysis would show that *most* large corporate directors (propertied and non-propertied) tend to adopt the argument that private enterprise is more efficient. We are not, on the other hand, aware that any of them have argued the case against the continued existence of a privately financed economy.

There is one other obvious point which should be made here, namely, that the distinction between 'propertied' and 'non-propertied' directors is one that is probably irrelevant to most people in British society. The latter's customers, the general public, and probably even shop floor workers, may regard him in essentially the same way that they regard a propertied director. Indeed, if as some sectional managerialists[1] have done, one accepts that some 'professional managers' may tend to regard their workers as analogous to 'irritating pieces of machinery' it must also be remembered that this attitude is not necessarily a consequence of a separation of ownership and control. As early as 1835 we find a businessman musing that, in the perfect factory, machinery would 'supersede human labour altogether'.[2] And if, as some non-sectional managerialists appear to do, one assumes that, being economically disinterested, non-propertied directors are likely to be more employee-centred (or just plain moral) than capitalists or propertied directors, then it must also be recognized that, in addition to ethical factors—(e.g. Quakerism)[3]—geographical location,[4] availability of labour, and the ratio of capital to labour costs have probably been important determining factors relating to the absence or presence of paternalism, and contemporarily 'neo-paternalism',[5] in British industry.

Unless these and other factors (like the competitive situation,

[1] Marris, *The Economic Theory*, p. 60.

[2] Andrew Ure, *The Philosophy of Manufactures, or, An Exposition of the Scientific, Moral and Commercial Economy of the Factory System of Great Britain* (H. G. Bohn edit), London, 1861, p. 23.

[3] For a discussion of Quakerism in British business, see J. Child, 'Quaker Employers and Industrial Relations', *Sociological Review*, Vol. 12, No. 3, Nov., 1964, pp. 293–315.

[4] For a historical account of the combined effects of Quakerism and geographical isolation in one industry, see A. Raistrick, *Two Centuries of Industrial Welfare: The London (Quaker) Lead Co., 1692–1905*, London, 1938.

[5] See, I. M. McGivering, D. Matthews, and W. H. Scott, *Management in Britain*, Liverpool, 1960, pp. 83–127.

unionization, and the prevailing political climate) are taken into account, it is exceedingly difficult to make meaningful contrasts between earlier and modern capitalism, and equally difficult to clearly attribute the modern 'manager's' attitude to labour to his non-ownership of the means of production.

In fact, it seems probable that the only unquestionable generalization which can be made in this context is that, today, to a greater extent than in all earlier periods, the top management is, both in and out of the factory, more socially distant from workers. This is so, not because ownership is separated from control, but because the progressive concentration of economic units has led to the development of large-scale organization. We have already seen that the great majority of directors do not have working class origins and most of them have not worked on the shop floor but with the advent of large-scale organization management's relationships with labour have been even further delimited. Today—and we assume this process to have developed as far, if not further, in the 'management' rather than 'owner-controlled' corporation—relationships with labour have been hived off into specialist departments and, in many instances, the director is effectively insulated from contact with direct production workers by intervening authority levels in the management (and union) hierarchy.

To return to our main point, however, it seems most inadvisable to argue that non-propertied and propertied directors are members of different classes solely because they own shares to a greater or lesser degree. We would expect the normative orientation of those two groups to shareholders, to government, employees and so on to be similar, and in terms of the relational aspect of their position we have no strong evidence to suggest that 'managers' are not accepted by 'owner-managers'. Indeed, there is some evidence to show that the directors of major industrial companies are interdigitated, not only with one another, but also with the senior members of other property owning institutions.[1]

For the most part, however, our knowledge of interaction between directors is based on the work of 'Marxist' writers.

[1] See, T. Lupton and S. Wilson, 'The Social Background and Connections of "Top Decision Makers", *Manchester School of Economic and Social Studies*, Jan., 1959. (It should be noted, however, that Lupton's study included few directors of large industrial companies and we know of no data which qualitatively or quantitatively compares to that now being amassed for manual workers.)

They have tended to use facts about directors' formal interaction (based on multiple directorships) and informal interaction (based for example on common club memberships) to indicate which directors 'control'. Quite obviously this cannot be done. Simply because Lord Chandos once sat on the boards of Alliance Insurance, ICI and AEI, it does not follow that he 'controlled' all, or any one of them. Indeed, the fact that two individuals share a common club membership does not necessarily mean that they interact, and even if they interact, this does not necessarily imply that they do so on terms of friendship.

However, what concerns us here, and what to some extent has concerned these writers too, is not whether any *particular* director interacts with another—and therefore possibly 'controls' him—but the fact that the 'social' interaction of propertied and non-propertied directors generally seems to take place in the same circles. In short, it is unlikely that in relational terms we can regard owner-managers and managers as members of two mutually exclusive classes. There is, in fact, very little evidence to suggest that non-propertied directors are ostracized by propertied directors and what meagre evidence that is available would seem to suggest the opposite.

Historically, then, it seems wiser to consider the separation of ownership and control as part of a progressive division of labour within capitalist society. In the century since the joint stock company was introduced the hired manager has gained in status. His power has increased along with that of the corporation. His social relations with shareholders and propertied directors are unquestionably more likely to be on terms of social equality. But, *de jure*, his function is still to serve the shareholder interest and, in practice, there is little reason to suppose that his outlook is much different from that of propertied directors. Certainly we think it doubtful that he has developed a distinctive professional or technocratic normative orientation. The norms which govern his conduct derive in part from the shareholder interest and in normative, relational, and to some degree economic terms his position approximates to that of the propertied director. Managerialists have written of a 'divorce' or 'separation' of ownership and control. In this context we find it more fitting to write of a 'marriage of convenience'.

In historical perspective there is probably sufficient evidence to support the argument that the entrepreneurial and managerial strata have converged, rather than moved apart. Furthermore, any assertion that the contemporary manager belongs to a different class to the contemporary owner-manager can probably only be substantiated if class is rigidly defined in economic terms. But even here the difference would seem to be one of degree.

A recognition of differences between the form, rather than the source, of the economic rewards enjoyed by these two groups may, as we indicated in our discussion of managerial economics, be a pre-condition to the development of 'realistic' micro-economic theories. As far as the matter of class is concerned, however, the proposition that non-propertied directors (i.e. the 'new managers') are a discretely different class—to say nothing of being a value free elite—would seem to become untenable once we consider the relational and normative aspects of class stratification.

In this matter, of course, as in so many others, our argument is open to further empirical validation (or invalidation) but it seems to us preferable to regard large corporation directors as part of an amorphous but none the less real business class than to have to explain their probable normative and relational integration with that class in terms of 'false consciousness'. A defining characteristic of both propertied and non-propertied directors is that their status, their prestige, their security, and not least their wealth are all directly dependent upon the continued existence of the large private enterprise corporation and, in British society, we would attach more importance to these obvious and readily observable facts than to the differing extent to which propertied and non-propertied directors own shares.

CHAPTER XIII

SOME CONCLUDING COMMENTS

I N the preceding chapter we discussed whether propertied and non-propertied directors belong to the same class. Our conclusion, that they do, is, with certain reservations, akin to a view widely advanced by 'Marxist' writers, like Wright Mills, Sweezy, and Kolko in America, and by the 'New Left' in Britain.

Now, we have already noted some reservations about the work of 'Marxist' theorists, in passing, in the text. At this point, however, it may be appropriate to clarify our position. First, though we accept that a consideration of class position and social origin has significance for the normative orientation of directors, we question the significance of collective class ownership for the decisions of any given director in any given corporation. These two levels of analysis are best kept separate. Secondly, for the reasons already given, we think that 'Marxist' writers have sometimes been too ready to attribute a 'control' potential to interlocking directorships. (At the same time, though, some other writers may have been too eager to dismiss the significance of certain 'guinea-pig' directors. If the latter exist, as they certainly do, one should surely ask why the values, connections or styles of life of these particular individuals are so valued. Undoubtedly, they often constitute rather incongruous symbols for a new managerial class.)[1] Thirdly, following Marris,[2] we doubt the immediate significance of stock-option schemes for profit-maximization policies.[3]

Our attempt to avoid the limitations of a mechanistic type of analysis has resulted in little space being devoted to either the potential role of the financial institutions or the take-over

[1] Cf. C. A. R. Crosland, *The Conservative Enemy*, pp. 80, 95.
[2] *The Economic Theory*, pp. 70–78.
[3] For an illustration of all three points see, G. Kolko, *Wealth and Power in America*, chapter 4.

bid. However, there is no criticism of the 'Marxists' implied here. In general terms, we find the work of 'Marxist' writers strongest when they deal with the macro-sociological implications of the concentration of corporate power and wealth, weakest when they consider micro-economic implications—the opposite of this being true of 'sectional' managerial writers (excluding James Burnham). As should be clear from our scant references to them so far, we consider 'non-sectional' theories to lack conviction on both counts.

Of course, given the basic similarity between our own treatment and that proposed by some 'Marxists', the reader may legitimately ask why we have discussed the matter of class at all. One answer is that we find substantial room for doubt in the interpretation of this matter put forward by Dahrendorf. His treatment of this matter, though constituting just one small part of *Class and Class Conflict*, is crucial for his general thesis and—outside Marxist circles—it has been extremely influential. There is, however, another answer to this question. This relates to the fact that, though class is of course too crude a tool by which to predict individual behaviour, any analysis in class terms immediately forces one to ask questions about the director's location in society.

With the partial exception of Marris (and of course Burnham), these are questions which most managerial theorists have neglected. Partly as a consequence of this, and partly too as a consequence of the use of that highly unfortunate phrase— 'the *separation* of ownership and *control*'—a rather mechanistic mode of analysis has generally been adopted. We find, for example, that most writers have made two fundamental, and theoretically significant steps in the formulation of problems for enquiry. Typically, the first of these steps has been concerned with the distribution of power between shareholders on the one hand and active management on the other. The problem has been seen to be rooted in the fact that two functions, A (ownership) and B (management), which were originally performed by one actor AB_1 have now become the functions of two discrete actors A_2 (the shareholder) and B_2 (the manager). Such a formulation does have the advantage that it immediately highlights the fact that, today, A_2 is seldom seen to interfere in the work of B_2 (low attendance at A.GsM.'., etc.) and that A_2 might find spontaneous intervention difficult in any case (greater diffusion of shareholding). But this type of formulation rests on the assumption that (i) A_2 and B_2 are discrete entities and, in practice, has tended toward (ii) neglecting the possibility that A_2 and B_2 have expectations of each other's conduct. Our enquiries into directorial share ownership suggest that the first assumption (i) is open to doubt and our discussion of directorial socialization, and also of class, further suggests that, as far as (ii) is concerned, there is need for a much fuller consideration of the role of social values and expectations than has yet appeared in the literature.

In more popular versions, of course, the above first stage of problem formulation has led to the conclusion that 'the managers' are autonomous. Even in strictly academic treatments, however, it has tended to lead to a second step in problem formulation which has taken the form of attempting to predict corporate policy from the seemingly unexceptional premise that managers, not being 'owner-controlled', act as they are motivated to act. We mention this point here, not because we wish to question the desirability of an 'action approach' in industrial sociology, or in sociology generally, but because, on the contrary, we think it a criticism of most managerial theory that it does not take such an approach far enough.[1]

In general terms, 'the manager', in sharp contrast to the industrial worker,[2] has been portrayed in the literature as the supreme *actor* (in the sense of supreme decision-maker) but typically managerial theories of the firm have taken as their starting point the manager, already established as policy maker, within the corporation. Such a starting point for analysis does of course facilitate the retention of a classical assumption of economic science, namely, that, other things being equal, the behaviour of the firm can be treated as a manifestation of the interests and satisfactions of the individual (i.e. 'the capitalist', 'the manager') who 'controls' it.

[1] On 'action' in economics see A. G. Papandreou, 'Some Basic Problems in the Theory of the Firm', in B. F. Haley (ed.), *A Survey of Contemporary Economics*, Vol. II, Illinois, 1952, p. 183.

[2] This point is strongly suggested when one compares the work of those economists who have followed Gordon to the theoretical perspectives until recently adopted by sociologists to study industrial workers' behaviour. For an account of the latter, see J. H. Goldthorpe, 'Attitudes and Behaviour of Car Assembly Workers: A Deviant Case and a Theoretical Critique', *British Journal of Sociology*, Vol. XVII, No. 3, Sept., 1966.

K

Unfortunately, however, any consideration of what the manager 'brings with him' to the corporation has generally been limited to the plausible, but incomplete assumption that his major objective will be economic gain.

Such an assumption quite clearly has a high face validity but, equally clearly, even if we allow for the possiblity that the manager is also interested in power, prestige and so on,[1] it does not follow that we can fully understand the significance of this dominant feature of his orientation to work in the absence of a further consideration of its other components. The manager also brings to his work certain notions about the structure and proper functioning of society, about what is 'fair' and 'just', and it seems reasonable to assume that these derive, in some part at least, from his extra-corporate social interactions and experiences. In short, he is not only a Psychological Man (the man with motives of managerial theory) but also a Social Man, that is a man whose motives (more properly termed by Williamson 'immediate determinants of behavior') operate within a given value structure.

His behaviour, and particularly the strategies he adopts in relation to the interests of other groups (e.g. shareholders) cannot be interpreted as a straight fulfilment of his own personal objectives unless the proviso is introduced that the 'selection' of these objectives in the first place, the priority given to some over others, and the relative intensity with which any given one of them will be pursued, may all be subject to certain internalized restraints which are part of the actor's own value system and which themselves may constitute ultimate determinants and limiting boundaries to his behaviour.

The source of such internalized restraints must clearly be sought outside the corporation and also in the expectations of managerial behaviour which are embodied in the corporation itself, for though the corporation clearly does not have a mind of its own, any more than it has its own goals, it does not confront the new manager with a *tabula rasa*. Nor can we assume that his own mind is free of values upon entry. These sorts of considerations have generally been neglected in managerial theory (except of course in the more moralistic and popular treatments of the non-sectional kind) because, as we have noted, the starting point for analysis is the manager *qua* policy maker,

[1] cf. Williamson, *The Economics of Discretionary Behavior*, pp. 28–31.

already established in the boardroom. In short, little attention has been given to the patterned regularity of social interaction, educational experience and social origin which, in the case of Britain, we posit to characterize directors before they enter the boardroom. Similarly, little attention has been given to those norms of conduct with which the director has been confronted within the corporation itself. Instead, it is his economic self-interest and rationality which are emphasized and he is represented as successfully pursuing self-rewarding objectives subject to the satisfaction of externally imposed constraints.

The point we wish to make here is that the exercise of social (in contrast to mechanical) power, and the nature of constraints to an actor's behaviour are more complex than many writers would seem to imply. A recognition that this is so may be a necessary pre-condition to the development of more 'realistic' analyses of directorial behaviour. To take a simple example, one cannot assume that shareholder's interests are not well served because they do not 'control', in the sense of intervening very often.[1] To cite an F.B.I. critique of the Labour party's *Industry and Society*—'it is in fact a fiction that the boards are responsible to no-one. It looks like the truth only because the shareholder's ultimate power of veto is rarely required to become active and openly determine the direction of the company's business'.[2] Indeed, to ask 'who controls?' may be to assume an over-simplified interpretation of decision making which leads one to equate the manifestation of power with power itself and to confuse power, authority, and influence.

Theoretically, if one assumes that modern corporations do not have to rely on external capital markets, that directors are not shareholders, and that the latter have great difficulty in organizing effectively, and in any case have limited knowledge, it becomes a major problem to explain why dividends are paid at all. In practice, we have no reason to confront ourselves with such an extreme and hypothetical case. Simply to state the problem does, however, raise the possibility that the director's treatment of shareholders may not merely be governed by calculative considerations about adverse criticism,

[1] cf. C. S. Beed, 'The Separation of Ownership and Control', *The Journal of Economic Studies*, Vol. 1, No. 2, pp. 29–46.

[2] *Nationalisation: A Report by the Federation of British Industries*, Nov., 1958, para. 117.

stockholder organization, potential take-over, or future capital requirements but also by some sense of justice or fairness which is a constituent part of the director's orientation to members of this group.

It is because we find this line of argument persuasive that we have concentrated upon a rather different range of factors to those which are generally given prominence in managerial theories. We have, of course, raised certain questions about the allegedly different motivation of propertied and non-propertied directors and we have also attempted to investigate the technocratic-professionalistic status of the modern British director. On the whole, however, we have avoided representing the director as a highly rational, very knowledgeable (and exceedingly successful) games player and we have also tried to avoid an undue emphasis upon the precise mechanics of interest articulation and interest aggregation. Instead, we have attempted to emphasize the possible significance of the socio-cultural milieu within which, whatever personal objectives he might favour, the director performs his role and which, in a meaningful sense, may be said to be part of the prescriptive element of his role definition itself.

We have seen, for example, that there is a substantial over-representation of directors from the highest social strata[1] (and notably of those whose fathers were in business), that there is also a substantial over-representation of those educated at the traditional elite institutions and that, though it is certainly true that most of them cannot be termed 'capitalists', directors collectively are clearly part of the wealthiest section of British society, and are among the largest (personal) share-holders.

Unless the reader began with the assumption that modern directors were truly the meritocratic-technocratic figures of more popular versions of managerial theory all this should be no more cause for surprise than the fact that nearly nine out of ten directors vote Conservative.[2] The social composition of directors is, of course, very much what one would expect given the historical development of the British class structure and

---

[1] For a comparison with American businessmen see S. M. Lipset and R. Bendix, *Social Mobility in Industrial Society*, Berkeley, 1959, pp. 134–135; W. L. Warner and J. C. Abegglen, *Occupational Mobility in American Business and Industry*, Minneapolis, 1955; M. Newcomer, *The Big Business Executive*, N.Y., 1955.

[2] See 'The Director Observed', *The Director*, April, 1966, p. 57.

educational system. But we must reiterate that whereas these and other observations may not be surprising it does not follow that they should be neglected altogether, or that one should necessarily conclude that they have no significance.

Clearly, the documentation of elite recruitment is not a substitute for a thoroughgoing analysis of social power. But in so far as it may shed some light upon the normative orientation of those who take decisions it constitutes one important line of investigation. And in our view such an investigation of British directors, which has in part been supplemented by a consideration of the probable norms and values with which the manager becomes acquainted in the corporation itself, points toward a theory of normative consensus. In short, the data we have cited and the arguments advanced point to the probability that in certain important respects both propertied and non-propertied large corporation directors share a common frame of reference.

We accept that the non-propertied director may derive satisfaction from increasing his corporation's share of the market and from pursuing various forms of growth policy which are not necessarily tantamount to maximization of the shareholder interest—but we suspect that similar 'managerial' policies might also be pursued by modern propertied directors.

As far as our general view has specific implications for the theory of the firm we would further posit that whether any given corporation will pursue one or other of these or allied objectives, and to what extent, will probably depend upon a multitude of factors like the competitive situation, the present state and history of labour relations, the general availability of capital, present and anticipated profit margins, the present share of the market, which market is most highly valued (for most corporations operate in more than one) and so on. In addition, we would emphasize that any consideration of the extent to which the modern corporation pursues specifically managerial policies must be prefaced with an explicit recognition that the large corporation has in part created, and must operate within, a different sort of economy, and a different sort of society, to that which formed the environment of the small nineteenth-century entrepreneur.

An enfranchised electorate, the increasing role of government in economic affairs, and not least, full employment, are all

factors which impose limiting conditions upon business policy—
just as oligopoly and the development of increasingly sophisticated techniques of measurement provide new opportunities.
It is most inadvisable to attempt to explain changes in particular
business policies without recognizing the significance of these
and other variables. Indeed, in our view, the plausibility of
managerialism is inversely related to the degree to which it
approximates to a one-factor theory of economic behaviour.

In general terms, we would expect those directors who
approximate most closely to the professionalistic ideal-type of
managerial theory to conduct their corporations more, not less,
profitably than the entrepreneur of classical economic theory
but we remain sceptical about the extent to which differences
exist between the profit utilization policies of modern 'owner'
and 'management-controlled' companies.[1] We think it probable
that the directors of both sorts of company will have an element
of moral concern for the interests of shareholders. It seems
improbable that this will lead *in either case* to policies which
can be strictly defined as shareholder-oriented profit maximization: [it is possible, however, that it will lead to giving
precedence over those personal and organizational satisfactions
which are part of the director's own specifically *managerial*
objectives, to a fulfilment of the shareholder's minimum
expectations.

In reaching this conclusion we have, of course, made use of a
number of terms like 'socialization', 'internalization', 'value
system', 'normative orientation' and 'consensus' and we are
well aware that it is all too easy for the sociologist who uses
such terms to put forward an oversocialized conception of

---

[1] We still lack empirically based studies about the relationship between type of
control structure and personnel and welfare policies. The most thorough analysis
of 'fringe benefits' in Britain (G. L. Reid and D. J. Robertson (eds.), *Fringe
Benefits, Labour Costs and Social Security*, London, 1965) makes no reference to this
particular variable. The only exception of which we are aware is the work of
McGivering. This provides some evidence for the view that 'family firms' tend
to be more traditionalistic than bureaucratic. But given that he considers only
one management function (personnel), that he considers only one type of 'owner-
control' (i.e. 'where a firm was controlled in its day-to-day activities by working
directors all or several of whom were members of the same family'), that all his
firms were in Liverpool and that (untypically) his family firms tended to be larger
than the others, it is doubtful whether McGivering himself would claim that his
work does more than raise many important questions: nor indeed does he do so.
See, I. McGivering, *Personnel Management in Large Manufacturing Firms in Liverpool*,
M.A. thesis, University of Liverpool, 1960, p. 8.

man.[1] This, however, has not been our intention and we would certainly not wish to justify the use of such terms, and consequently such a mode of analysis, upon the very poor grounds that this is what sociologists do. We have used them for two reasons. First, because in our view they help to make sense of the data at our disposal. Secondly, because they bring to light certain factors and processes which have been largely neglected by most of those writers we term 'managerialists'.

The extent to which the reader finds our first reason to be an acceptable one can only, of course, be decided by him on the basis of what we have, and equally importantly, have not written above. And given the emergence of a meritocratic-technocratic business elite, whose members had distinctive extra-corporate professional identification groups, which laid down codes of conduct which were seen to be adhered to, we have no doubt that our general thesis would have to be revised. Quite simply, however, we do not think this time has yet come. But to return to our second point, it should be remembered that even writers like Marris[2] and Williamson[3] have entered substantial qualifications about the empirical basis of their theories.

Marris indeed has gone so far as to state (quite rightly) that none of the commonly accepted notions about managerial motivation have been tested by methods which sociologists would regard as rigorous. (A possible exception here is the work of Haire, Ghiselli and Porter.[4] But the 'motives' they consider are probably of too high a level of abstraction to be of direct use to economic theorists of the firm). It is equally true that few, if any, sociologists could read Marris or Williamson without being tempted to quibble with the knowledgeability and rationality these writers impute to managers. The fact is, however, that this is the way in which most sociologists seem to react to any work in economics and it is to be regretted that so few of them have ventured into this field at all. This last assertion raises some significant questions for those concerned with the 'sociology of sociology' but it is not a matter which we

---

[1] cf. Dennis Wrong's important essay 'The Oversocialised Conception of Man in Modern Sociology', *American Sociological Review*, Vol. 26, 1961, pp. 183–193.

[2] *The Economic Theory*, p. 63.

[3] *The Economics of Discretionary Behavior*, pp. 167–168.

[4] M. Haire, E. E. Ghiselli and L. W. Porter, *Managerial Thinking: An International Study*, N.Y., 1966.

can pursue here. What, on the other hand, should concern us here is that as late as 1960, fifteen years after *Business Leadership in the Large Corporation* was first published, Gordon was able to write in his new preface that 'we still need a theory of the firm which takes account of these factors' (i.e. non-profit and organizational ones) and that the above two writers and others like them have made important steps in this direction.

Given this, and given also that the economic sociology of the firm is so much of a neglected subject and that its growth is so desirable, we have felt justified in leaving aside questions about knowledgeability and rationality in decision-making and we have attempted instead to build on the multi-disciplinary, but mainly economic and psychological, foundations of those theories which already exist.

Thus, we consider our emphasis upon the extra- and intra-corporate aspects of managerial socialization to provide some additional and complementary, rather than contradictory, evidence for those micro-economic theorists (and especially Marris) who have attempted to construct more 'realistic' theories of business behaviour. There already exists a large but mainly impressionistic literature about managerial motivation and there is even some work on the significance of child rearing practices, and the role of the Oedipus complex. With the notable exception of Dahrendorf, however, few managerialist writers have paid much attention to the director's pre- and extra-corporate social experience or to the prescriptive elements of his role *qua* manager within the corporation.

When, as in our case, an attempt is made to take such factors into account it becomes questionable whether the relative ownership or non-ownership of shares can justifiably be considered to be the crucial factor in predicting the value orientation and interests of 'propertied' and 'non-propertied' directors. The differences between them are best regarded as differences of degree rather than kind and in our view the compromise position of the present business elite—whose members survive and prosper by compromise—deserves a compromise label. Like Marris we would settle for 'Managerial Capitalism'.

Furthermore, though this has not been our main concern, we doubt whether the situation we find in British business necessitates the formulation of a third (managerial) macro-sociological theory to be interposed between those of the capitalist and socialist variety. We take no exception to the view that socialist economies are run by managers and we accept that the evidence we have reviewed also suggests that this holds true for the modern capitalist economy of Britain. As we stated at the outset, it is a nonsense to assume that the modern giant corporation is run by giant capitalists. But to make this sort of point may not be to say very much, since both socialist and capitalist 'managers' operate within given politico-cultural systems.

In short, the inferences we have made about the social experience and values of British directors suggest it is unlikely that they will not be identified with the fundamental tenets of the particular system (and more immediately of the corporation) in which they are employed. We do not doubt that they have certain immediate economic interests which are in conflict with the maximization of the shareholder's welfare. We do think, however, that in the long run moral, economic, and even legal considerations (and an as yet unascertainable mixture of all three) make it probable that they will satisfy shareholder expectations. There seems little reason to consider them, or the economic system they govern, as the manifestation of a 'post-capitalist' society. Indeed even diffusion of ownership might be taken to signify an expansion, rather than 'destruction', of capitalism[1]—though, as already noted, this is still far from 'diffused' in any ordinary sense.

However, the type of argument we have presented above does have one major weakness which it shares with all other theories of consensus, that is, it is difficult to test. As Dahl[2] has pointed out in another context, a theory of consensus cannot be proved or disproved without the examination of a series of concrete cases where key decisions are made. In fact, we have very little systematic evidence about such decisions and it will be remembered that one of our major themes has been that few writers on the ownership and control question, whether they be 'Marxist' or 'managerialist', have had such data either. But it is appropriate to note that some of the most widely publicized instances in which 'managers' have apparently put

[1] cf. Raymond Aron, *Eighteen Lectures on Industrial Society*, London, 1967, p. 183.
[2] R. A. Dahl, 'A Critique of the Ruling Elite Model', *American Political Science Review*, Vol. 52, 1958, p. 489.

their own pecuniary interests above those of shareholders have been cases where these directors were *themselves* large shareholders, that publicity has usually been focused upon their activities by fellow directors who were *not* large shareholders, and that the latter have typically revealed their disquiet to major institutional investors.

Regrettably, however, the fact is that though we now have a mounting number of studies about how the manager spends his day,[1] we still know less about the British director's social interaction and normative orientation than is the case in respect to other less prestigeful and less powerful occupational groups like coal miners and car workers. For this reason, if we are to conform to a rigorous and strictly scientific approach, we can go no further than to state that our consensus hypothesis seems to us to be a plausible one. Indeed, we would be the first to admit that one thing which stands out in the preceding chapters is that a great deal of further research is required into directorial behaviour, attitudes, and values, before *any* generally acceptable theory of the consequences of a separation of ownership and control can be safely arrived at.

The above reconsideration of managerial theories has, of course, largely neglected those of the 'non-sectional' type. One reason for this is that we consider sectional theories to have a higher face validity. Put simply, we think it more realistic to assume that businessmen will be more interested in pecuniary gain and the pursuit of other self-rewarding objectives than they will be in policies of the 'social service' variety. In addition, even allowing that policies of the latter type might sometimes be pursued, we suspect that they may also have been favoured by 'traditional capitalists', and it seems doubtful that they constitute a distinctive characteristic of modern (managerial) capitalism. More generally, we doubt the wisdom of assuming that the managers have 'introduced' non-profit goals—whether these be socially responsible or not.[2] Such a view, we suspect,

---

[1] cf. T. Burns, 'What Managers Do', *New Society*, December 16, 1964; R. Dubin, 'Business Behavior Behaviorally Viewed' in G. B. Strother (ed.), *Social Sciences Approaches to Business Behavior*, London, 1962; J. H. Horne and T. Lupton, 'The Work Activities of "Middle" Managers', *Journal of Management Studies*, Vol. 2, No. 1, Feb., 1965; L. Sayles, *Managerial Behavior*, N.Y., 1964, chapter 3; R. Stewart, *Managers and Their Jobs*, London, 1967.

[2] cf. R. A. Gordon, *Business Leadership in the Large Corporation*, Berkeley and Los Angeles, 1961, pp. xiii–xiv.

may owe more to the closer acquaintance of economists and others with the policies pursued by businessmen than to any empirically based historical or comparative analysis of 'owner' and 'management-controlled' companies. Indeed, in our view, it seems highly probable that businessmen themselves have difficulty in precisely separating out that part of their behaviour which might be termed 'socially responsible'[1]—and the fact that non-sectional theorists have not generally been able to provide us with specific hypotheses about which operational objectives distinguish the socially responsible businessman from his less altruistic colleagues suggests that they too have experienced difficulty in this matter. Like Bowen,[2] we would, of course, accept that a recognition of the manager's identification with 'his' firm, and his consequent concept of the corporation as an independent entity, is a necessary starting point for any consideration of contemporary business ideology. We are, however, more sceptical than Bowen would seem to be about whether such an identification may constitute a transitional step toward the allegedly 'new' and widely publicized concept of trusteeship. We find Halmos'[3] view, namely, that whatever motivates businessmen to appear socially responsible it is likely that such strategies will in turn affect their behaviour, to be equally problematic.

Just why we are so sceptical will become clearer in the following chapters which examine what social responsibility means to some British businessmen and attempts to test certain hypotheses generated by the preceding discussion against our Northern City data. To make one thing clear, however, our rather agnostic conclusion above—that in many respects there are insufficient facts to arrive at any hard conclusion—should not be taken to imply that we imagine the mere collection of such 'facts' will in itself provide us with an adequate theory. On the contrary, we would argue that as well as needing more facts—e.g. about the decision making process—there may also be a need to introduce new theoretical perspectives which, in turn, would lead to different questions being asked.

In particular, and our emphasis upon this in Chapters

[1] cf. *A Study of Industry's Contribution to Science, the Arts, Education and the National Welfare*, Economist Intelligence Unit, London, 1957, p. 11.

[2] H. R. Bowen, *Social Responsibilities of the Businessman*, N.Y., 1953, p. 88.

[3] P. Halmos, 'The Personal Service Society', *British Journal of Sociology*, Vol. 18 No. 1, March, 1967, p. 25.

VI, IX, X, XI and XII should have already made this clear, we believe that much more attention should be given to the director's normative orientation which, in many ways, is an important mediating link between the 'managerial motives' and the directorial 'class interests' about which managerialists and 'Marxists' have already written so much. For this reason, then, in what follows we hope not only to ask questions about what 'social responsibility' means to businessmen but also to briefly consider some limited but potentially theoretically suggestive data about the extent to which the values of Northern City businessmen can be related to their organizational position, professional activity and pre- and intra-corporate socialization.

PART III
CONTEMPORARY BUSINESS IDEOLOGY

INTRODUCTION

As we saw in Part I it is not only possible to distinguish between 'Marxist' and 'managerialist' theories about the significance of a separation of ownership and control for business behaviour and ideology but to distinguish further between two schools of thought within the latter category. We termed these the 'sectional' and 'non-sectional' variants of managerial theory.

However, since we argued that a consideration of the non-propertied director's probable frame of reference and values suggests that the most tenable position to adopt on many issues is one that lies somewhere between the sectional managerialist and 'Marxist' points of view, the discussion provided in Part II largely neglected those ideas associated with the main body of non-sectional theory. Part III attempts to redress this imbalance by devoting much more attention to the notion that the modern businessman adheres to a business philosophy of 'social responsibility' or 'service'.

It is true of course that some writers on British business have occasionally noted that businessmen are apt to define their role in terms of fulfilling responsibilities to employees, customers, shareholders and diverse other groups as well[1] and it is also true that a few social scientists like Fox[2], Halmos[3], and McGivering[4] and his colleagues have ventured into the field of business ideology. Generally, however, their forays have been of short duration and the fact is that with the exception of Bendix' study of British business ideology in an earlier period and a

[1] cf. G. H. Copeman, *Leaders of British Industry*, p. 47; R. Lewis and R. Stewart, 'The Men at the Top', *Encounter*, Nov., 1958, p. 48.
[2] A. Fox, 'Managerial Ideology and Labour Relations', *British Journal of Industrial Relations*, Vol. IV, No. 3, 1966, pp. 366–378.
[3] P. Halmos, *The Personal Service Society*, Inaugural Lecture, University College, Cardiff, May, 1966.
[4] I. M. McGivering, D. Matthews and W. H. Scott, *Management in Britain: A General Characterisation*, Liverpool, 1960, pp. 91-101.

recent work by Child[1], which in many important respects succeeds in extending the former's type of analysis to the present day, the study of business ideology has been largely ignored by British social scientists.[2]

Part of the reason for this may be that British management journals, in contrast to American ones, have not been eager to hold forth on management's social responsibilities, to put forward new philosophies of management or to discuss the utility of different types of ideology for the perpetuation and organizational effectiveness of private industry in its present form.[3] With a few well-known exceptions like Sheldon,[4] Mond,[5] and more recently, Goyder,[6] British businessmen have rarely written books on this, or any other matter and since, again with a few well-known exceptions like Esso[7] and Johnson and Johnson (both American off-shoots), most British companies have not formulated their own credos,[8] it may be that British social scientists have been deterred by a lack of readily available and already systematized data.[9] But whatever the reason, the fact remains that the study of business ideology in general, and of social responsibility in particular, has been subject to very little systematic enquiry.[10]

[1] J. Child, *British Management Thought and Education: Their Interpretation of Industrial Relationships*, Ph.D. thesis, Cambridge, 1967, Part I. (Now published as *British Management Thought—A Critical Analysis*, London, 1969.)

[2] For two more popular accounts see R. Lewis and R. Stewart, *The Boss: The Life and Times of the British Business Man*, London, 1963, and chapters 4–9 of the P.E.P. report, *Attitudes in British Management*.

[3] For some exceptions, which are very few indeed compared with the proportion of such articles in the *Harvard Business Review*, see 'Has British Management a Philosophy?', *The Manager*, Sept., 1953; Norman Bamforth, 'Towards a Philosophy of Management', *Times Review of Industry*, Jan., 1956; I. I. Hird, 'The State of Management Theory: An Appraisal', *British Management Review*, Jan., 1957. (For an example of the kind of American work which considers the utility of different ideologies for business see Gerhard R. Andlinger, 'The Crucible of Our Business Creed', *Business Horizons*, Vol. 2, No. 3, 1959, pp. 34–43.)

[4] Oliver Sheldon, *The Philosophy of Management*, London, 1923.

[5] Sir Alfred Mond, *Industry and Politics*, London, 1927.

[6] George Goyder, *The Future of Private Enterprise*, Oxford, 1951, *The Responsible Company*, Oxford, 1961.

[7] The Esso Petroleum company's statement, *Where We Stand*, is reproduced in Roger Falk, *The Business of Management: Art or Craft?*, London, 1961, p. 89. For the Johnson and Johnson credo, see Figure 1.

[8] cf. the 51 credos of North American companies in Stewart Thompson, *Management Creeds and Philosophies*, A.M.A., Research Study No. 32, 1958.

[9] cf. the N.A.M. Economic Principles Commission's *The American Individual Enterprise System: Its Nature and Future*, 2 Vols., N.Y., 1946.

[10] cf. H. R. Bowen, *Social Responsibilities of the Businessman*, N.Y., 1953.

It may be that 'it is widely accepted that, in taking their decisions, directors of companies take account of certain social responsibilities as well as the objective of profit maximization, and that they have regard to the interests of a number of groups—employees, customers, the local community, the nation as a whole—as well as those of shareholders' but what concerns

FIGURE 1

The 'Credo' of the Johnson & Johnson Company

WE BELIEVE

that our first responsibility is to our customers.
Our products must always be good, and
we must strive to make them better at lower costs.
Our orders must be promptly and accurately filled.
Our dealers must make a fair profit.

Our second responsibility is to those who work with us—
the men and women in our factories and offices.
They must have a sense of security in their jobs.
Wages must be fair and adequate,
management just, hours short, and working conditions clean and orderly.
Workers should have an organised system for suggestions and complaints.
Foremen and department heads must be qualified and fair minded.
There must be an opportunity for advancement—for those qualified—
and each person must be considered an individual
standing on his own dignity and merit.

Our third responsibility is to our management.
Our executives must be persons of talent, education, experience and ability.
They must be persons of common sense and full understanding.

Our fourth responsibility is to the communities in which we live.
We must be good citizens—support good works and charity,
and bear our fair share of taxes.
We must maintain in good order the property we are privileged to use.
We must participate in promotion of civic improvement,
health, education and good government,
and acquaint the community with our activities.

Our fifth and last responsibility is to our stockholders.
Business must make a sound profit.
Reserves must be created, research must be carried on,
adventurous programmes developed, and mistakes made and paid for.
Bad times must be provided for, high taxes paid, new machines purchased,
new factories built, new products launched, and new sales plans developed.
We must experiment with new ideas.
When these things have been done
the stockholders should receive a fair return.
We are determined, with the help of God's grace, to fulfil these obligations
to the best of our ability.

L

us here is that we know of no hard evidence about what proportion of businessmen do or do not think in this way.[1]
Furthermore, we take it to be self-evident that a local study,
like the Northern City one, can provide us with little more than
suggestive evidence on this point.

It should be noted, then, that our main concern in Part III
will not be to provide an estimate of the proportion of British
boards of directors which are characterized by this type of
thinking. Instead, we will be largely concerned with a consideration of the extent to which it appears feasible to infer
the existence of socially responsible behaviour from the
acceptance by businessmen of the language of social responsibility, the extent to which it seems warranted to talk about
'the socially responsible ideology' at all, and the extent to
which *businessmen* consider social responsibility and allied
notions to differ from, or conflict with, those values and social
perspectives which are consistent with 'Marxist', and sectional
managerialist, rather than non-sectional theories of modern
directorial behaviour.

In short, we will be substantially concerned with what social
responsibility means to businessmen, for we take the view that
if the seemingly straightforward statement 'I am middle class'
is open to so many interpretations that it is a severely limited
predictor of behaviour, or even attitude, then there are very
good reasons indeed for not side-stepping the problem of what
businessmen mean when they talk about their diverse 'social
responsibilities'. For this reason, parts of Chapters XIV, XV and
XVII will be largely concerned with an attempt to shed some
light upon the above matters and with the partial exception of
Chapter XVI our main concern throughout will be to move
toward a better understanding of the businessman's frame of
reference.

Chapter XVI constitutes a discussion of the extent to which
the businessman's ideology (i.e. as it concerns us here, his
conception of his organizational role and that of his corporation
within society) is related to the position he occupies, his pre-
and intra-corporate socialization, his membership and partici-

---

[1] The above quotation specifies the field of enquiry for an on-going P.E.P.
research project: once published this should substantially add to our knowledge
in this much neglected area. For further details see, *Research Supported by the S.S.R.C.
1967*, Social Science Research Council, London, p. 76.

pation in 'professional' management bodies, his age, social origin and so on. And most of the hypotheses which we will attempt to test in this chapter flow directly from the discussion presented in Part II. As we noted at the outset the policy of presenting all such data in one section has been a deliberate one. To recapitulate, it was adopted both to draw attention to the large number of questions which, though they are to some extent resolvable by the type of research we have conducted, have not yet been subject to such empirical investigation and also, and this is by no means less important, to emphasize that the Northern City study was no more than one case study and that it should therefore be given this status unequivocably.

The Northern City study is not well suited to provide the basis for an intensive factorial analysis and it was not designed for this purpose but in order to further our knowledge of the businessman's frame of reference, this being a matter which has been largely neglected by the jump from 'motives' to behaviour in managerial theory. In short, then, the special position of Chapter XVI has resulted from an attempt on our part to structure the discussion in Part III in such a way that the reader will keep the above points in mind, for clearly, though we hope some of the data presented there will stimulate further empirical research, it cannot be maintained that, by itself, it provides the basis for a confirmation or rejection of many of the ideas we discussed in Part II.

Following Chapter XVI, in the concluding chapter of Part III, we will take up the question of how far business ideology is explicable in terms of an interest 'theory' and the partly related question of whether the key values of modern British business are 'under attack'. But even in Chapter XVII a definite attempt will be made to relate a general interpretation of social responsibility to the experience we gained in the Northern City study.

Our reasons for proceeding in this way will become clearer later on but it should already be apparent that there are very large differences indeed between the scope of the enquiry we will report and that conducted by Sutton et al.[1] in America. In addition to this, however, there are also certain methodological differences and two of these merit mentioning here.

[1] F. X. Sutton, S. E. Harris, C. Kaysen and J. Tobin, *The American Business Creed*, Cambridge, Mass., 1956.

Sutton and his colleagues set out by collecting the public statements of businessmen and then proceeded to attempt to systematize and thus explain the data they had amassed. We, on the other hand, began by confronting Northern City businessmen with certain statements and asking them to choose between them.[1] Then, after they had made their choices, we interviewed each of them and asked why particular choices had been made.[2] This approach was adopted because we were not merely interested in gaining information about the statements favoured by businessmen but also, in addition to this, in encouraging them to explain to us in their own words just what such statements meant to them. Such information is, of course, an extremely useful bridge by which the researcher may move from documenting the existence of certain values and attitudes to explaining them. But such a procedure has a special importance for the study of those particular matters that concern us here because, as we will argue throughout, unless precautions are taken to establish just what an actor's public representation of self or of structure means to the actor himself, the practice of inferring behaviour from ideology (of which statements about business social responsibilities are only one special case) must always be regarded as a highly questionable one.

There is, however, a second and closely related difference between the research method employed in *The American Business Creed* and the Northern City study. We refer here to the fact that in our case study the actual construction of statements with which to confront businessmen necessitated that we formulated certain hypothetical types of business ideology before and not after the study itself was conducted. We hope that the advantages which stem from this will become clearer when we report the actual items used in Chapter XIV and consequently it is only necessary at this point to draw attention to several elementary assumptions which inform the nature and structure of Part III.

First, there is the assumption that whether an internally consistent and self-contained idea system exists is a matter for empirical verification; secondly, that it seems preferable to

[1] For the items used see Appendix III.
[2] A fuller account of the method employed is given in Appendix I, the interview schedule used is given in Appendix II.

assume that adherence to particular values or ideologies is, at a certain level, a matter of choice; thirdly, that this 'choice' is not wholly explicable in terms of concepts like 'function' or 'interest', and fourthly, that to understand the significance and explain the existence of given ideologies one must attempt to take into account the perception of socio-economic structure held by those who occupy the structurally defined positions in question. As stated, the above assumptions are all elementary ones but an attempt to take account of them has led us to adopt what, at least in some respects, is a rather different approach to the study of business ideology than is generally found in the literature.

CHAPTER XIV

BUSINESS IDEOLOGY IN NORTHERN CITY

Three Hypothetical Ideologies

The data collected in Northern City refers to the views of sixty-five directors and senior managers in fifteen of its largest companies. In order to gain some knowledge of the value structure and frames of reference of these directors[1] we took a series of statements about business and the role of the businessman which had particular reference to four topics. The topics presented were concerned with,

    (*a*) redundancy (see Appendix III, Group A);
    (*b*) the purpose and goals of industrial companies (see Group B);
    (*c*) giving information to employees (see Group C); and
    (*d*) the role of the businessman in public life (see Group D).

Each of the three statements within each group was designed to fit in with one of three broad conceptions about the role of business and the businessman. We termed these 'Laisser-Faire' (see items A2, B1, C2 and D3), 'Long-term-Company-Interest' (see items A1, B3, C3, D1) and 'Social Responsibility' (see items A3, B2, C1, D2). For heuristic purposes it was hypothesized that any one businessman would make all four of his choices in line with one, and only one, of these 'ideological sets'. For example, it was predicted that if he chose the Laisser-Faire item in Group A (A2), then he would proceed to choose similar items in the other three groups, (i.e. B1, C2, D3).

The salient differences between these three ideological sets may be put as follows. The Laisser-Faire set is conformable

---

[1] Here, as elsewhere, we will refer to both directors and senior managers as 'directors' or 'businessmen'. These terms are more convenient to use and the practice would seem to be legitimate in so far as we cannot find any significant differences between them. There were 38 directors and 27 senior managers.

to what Sutton *et al.* and other writers have referred to as the 'classical' ideology. It expressed the view that businessmen are primarily concerned with economic matters and that consideration of ethical issues and social consequences should be outside the ambit of policy making. Both the Long-Term-Company-Interest and the Social Responsibility sets differ from the Laisser-Faire items in this respect. They both emphasize that the businessman must be directly concerned with the social consequences of his actions.

The difference between the L.T.C.I. and S.R.[1] views is mainly one of motive. Thus, the distinction between them does not rest upon whether apparently socially responsible behaviour is favoured but upon the motives which lead to its acceptance. The S.R. set embodies a specifically moral element in the sense that the businessman is depicted as choosing between alternative policies on the basis of *ethical* rather than *practical* (i.e. predominately economic) considerations. The L.T.C.I. set, on the other hand, puts the view that policy formulation should take account of social and other aspects of the problem because this is the *practical* thing to do.

At this point, perhaps, it would be prudent to enter a disclaimer. It is quite clear that any social scientist who concerns himself with the ethics of others is likely to find himself on shifting sand. But unless one takes the view that morality is the manifestation of divine intervention or guidance there seems no good reason why we should not investigate its relation to alleged or actual changes in the structure of industry and society. This is all that we intend to do in our attempt to distinguish between the L.T.C.I. and S.R. ideologies. Thus, even though we have couched the S.R. statements in 'moral' terms we do not wish to imply that they are any more, or less, 'moral' than other statements. Nor do we wish to imply that the choices with which we confronted businessmen are the only possible ones.

Quite the contrary to this, it is our intention to attempt to assess whether, in fact, Northern City directors will accept the choices we offer them, which ones they will opt for and with which degree of consistency. If there is no clear pattern of choice, or if choices are made inconsistently (i.e. if they are

[1] In future the following abbreviations will generally be used: L.F. (Laisser-Faire), L.T.C.I. (Long-Term-Company-Interest), S.R. (Social Responsibility).

split between the three ideological sets), this will tell us something about the ideology of contemporary directors. In particular, we hope that it will tell us something about what social responsibility means to businessmen and whether in fact their views are conformable with the expectations of some of the writers whose work we reviewed in Part I. The imputation of moral choice is implicit in some of their work (e.g. Berle) and one of our objectives is to enquire into the businessman's perception of this choice.

Before we proceed to consider the results of this study there is one further and related preliminary point which we must make. This is that there are certain values implicit in some of the items—e.g. some of them even contain the word 'moral'. As a consequence of this some care had to be taken to avoid the inference, in other items, that those who agreed with them might, so to speak, be 'beating their employees'. This was a major problem with the L.F. items which we have attempted to 'soften' by including certain escape clauses. Thus we have included phrases about 'the country's economic position' (B1), suggested that redundancy is 'simply a risk which all those in industry have to bear' (A2), that employees 'do not want' information (C2), and that 'a manager has work enough to do' (D3). Similar clauses have been incorporated into the L.T.C.I. items. However, we think it doubtful that they invalidate the items used. It is the essence of an ideology that it is made up of just such statements.

The general orientation which we attempted to build into each ideological set is presented below:

Laisser-Faire. Managers should not concern themselves with social and moral consequences: if they did, the result would be economic disaster for us all (B1). The manager's place is with his firm, and he's enough work to do there without becoming a leading figure in the community (D3). Business exists for one purpose only, to satisfy a need at a profit (B1). Unemployment is a risk we all live with but it's no part of management's responsibility to make provision to safeguard their employees (A2). Nor is it desirable to provide employees with company information; they don't want it and its circulation might injure the company (C2).

Long-Term-Company-Interest. It's true that profit is the one absolute in business and it's a good thing for the nation that this is so. But in its own interest every firm must gain the sympathetic understanding and co-operation of all concerned (B3). This means that the public must accept us as thinking people. We should try to bring this about by taking every opportunity to put our views across (D1). It also means that we should convince the worker that we are concerned for his welfare and make him feel secure so that he will work better. This can be done by some form of redundancy provision (A1), and also by providing him with information. Giving information to employees can make them feel an important part of the team and make their co-operation more likely (C3).

Social Responsibility. A business conducted solely for the profit of shareholders is unethical. The firm is a social institution and its management is an arbiter with responsibilities to serve the social and economic needs of employees, customers, shareholders and the local and national communities (B2). In the case of the community, both the firm and its senior executives have a duty to make what contribution they can to public life (D2). Similarly, management has a moral responsibility to safeguard workers from redundancy (A3) and to provide them with full information about their own and their company's position (C1).

The Predominant Types of Choice

The results gained from the forced choice questionnaire demonstrate one fact quite clearly. This is that, at least in Northern City, very few businessmen favoured the L.F. or 'classical' ideology. Only 27, or 10% of the possible total of 260 choices (65 subjects with four choices each), were made in

TABLE 14.1

The Distribution of Choices Between the Three Ideological Sets

Ideological Set	% of Choices	No. of Choices
L.F.	10·4	27
L.T.C.I.	57·3	149
S.R.	32·3	84
	100	260

favour of the L.F. items. Furthermore, as can be seen in Table 14.1, there is little evidence to indicate that this was because a majority of businessmen chose the S.R. items. In fact only 32% of choices were made in this way and the majority, 57%, were made for the L.T.C.I. items.

A further measure of the predominance of L.T.C.I. choices is given in Table 14.2 which classifies the responses to the questionnaire in terms of set rejection. This shows that whereas 49 directors chose no items from the L.F. set and whereas

19 chose no items from the S.R. set, not one director managed to avoid making some choices from the L.T.C.I. set.

Given these results there is some evidence to indicate that the general value orientation of these directors was much closer to that presented by the items in the L.T.C.I. set than in either the S.R. or L.F. However, to proceed immediately to speculate at length about the proportion of businessmen who opted for each of the three types of items might be to lose an

TABLE 14.2

The Number of Respondents who did not Choose any Items from the Different Ideological Sets

Ideological Set	No. of Respondents Making No Choices from the Set	Total No. of Respondents
L.F.	49	65
L.T.C.I.	0	65
S.R.	19	65

opportunity. A study of this kind has an equally fruitful contribution to make if it explores how far the discrete ideological sets which we postulated to exist are in fact perceived as discrete entities by businessmen. Our method of investigation is tailored to the study of this question and also the related one of what meaning businessmen attach to particular statements.

In an attempt to shed some light upon these questions we will, therefore, turn to a consideration of the consistency of response.

The Consistency of Response

As can be seen from Table 14.3, 9 of the 65 businessmen made all of their choices from one ideological set and 40 of them made three of their choices from one set. *Prima facie*, this second figure might be taken as a reasonable indication that the three hypothetically discrete ideological sets which we constructed were, in practice, perceived as discrete entities by businessmen.

However, since the majority of those making consistent choices tended to do so from within the L.T.C.I. set, this raises the question of the relative 'distance' between this set and the other two. It also begs the question of whether this is the only kind of consistency of response which may be said to exist.

And quite clearly it is not. For example, if a certain proportion of businessmen were to choose the S.R. items from Groups A and B and the L.T.C.I. items from Groups C and D this too would have to be recognized as a consistent pattern of response.

Such patterns of response do exist. There are four groups of businessmen with 10, 9, 8 and 7 members respectively, each of which has its own response pattern.[1] It would be unwise to attach too much significance to the actual details of each of these sub-patterns of response but it would be equally unwise to ignore the fact that each of them is made up exclusively of L.T.C.I. items, or L.T.C.I. and S.R. items combined. This

TABLE 14.3

The Number of Businessmen making Choices from within any One Ideological Set as a Measure of Consistency of Response

Ideological Set	Measure of Consistency Employed	
	Four items chosen from one set	Three items chosen from one set
	(N)	(N)
L.F.	0	3
L.T.C.I.	9	26
S.R.	0	11
Observed No. of Consistent Choices	9	40
Possible No. of Consistent Choices	65	65

is in line with the overall pattern of response. Thus, we find that no directors made their choices exclusively from the L.F. and S.R. sets and that only 10 of them made their choices exclusively from the L.F. and L.T.C.I. sets—but 40 of the 65, or 62% of them, made their choices exclusively from the L.T.C.I. and S.R. sets combined. This indicates that, from the businessman's point of view, there was less 'distance' between the L.T.C.I. and S.R. sets than there was between the S.R. and L.F., or indeed the L.F. and L.T.C.I.

This question of the extent to which the L.T.C.I. ar S.R. sets of items were each regarded by directors as mutually exclusive alternatives is of some significance for any assessment of managerial theory. As we saw in Part I there is a division within managerialism as a whole between those we termed

[1] Assuming that choices were made randomly, patterns that emerge more than 4·03 times are significant at the 5% level.

sectional and non-sectional managerialists. And if the latter are to be regarded as the representatives of a reasonably distinct variant of managerial theory it must be admitted that one of their distinctive characteristics is that they impute an ethical choice to the businessman. They imply that he does recognize a choice between acting in terms of the values presented in the L.T.C.I. and S.R. sets of items and that he formulates his policies in accordance with the criteria associated with the latter. Quite clearly we cannot 'prove' or 'disprove' such assumptions in a study of this kind. We can, however, hope to shed some light upon the matter and perhaps, in the light of our new knowledge of directorial values and orientations in Northern City, complement some of the ideas put forward in our previous sections on social experience and values.

In order to do so we intend to begin by considering the values, social experience and the choices made by the directors of one particular company, Zed Ltd.

CHAPTER XV

QUESTIONS OF MEANING AND ETHICS

Zed Ltd as a Deviant Case

Zed Ltd has progressively increased its share of the market over the past few years. Despite this, however, Zed is not viewed with much enthusiasm as a potential employer by most employees. Wages and conditions of work are no more, and probably less, attractive to unskilled workers (who constitute the bulk of its labour force) than at other local factories.

Given these facts Zed appears to be a rather ordinary company which happens to be well managed. Yet the distribution of choices made by its directors was different from that made by all 65 directors combined. The latter's distributtion of choices between the ideological sets was as follows: L.F. 10% (Zed nil), L.T.C.I. 57% (Zed 38%) and S.R. 32% (Zed 62%). Furthermore, as can be seen from Table 15.1,

TABLE 15.1

Differences between Companies in the Choice of L.F., L.T.C.I., and S.R. Items

Company	Businessmen Interviewed (N)	Choices Per. Co. (N)	Choices Made for Each Type of Item %		
			L.F.	L.T.C.I.	S.R.
Aye Ltd	13	52	14	52	34
Bee Bros	6	24	17	62	21
Dee & Co	5	20	10	60	30
Gee Ltd	5	20	10	65	25
U-Products	5	20	0	45	55
Zed Ltd	6	24	0	38	62
	40	160			

Note: The companies included above have been confined to those in which we interviewed five or more businessmen.

with the partial exception of U-Products (of which we will say more later) Zed's pattern of response is different from that found in other companies.

If, then, we wish to ask how far the S.R. and L.T.C.I. items are perceived as real alternatives, or indeed what social responsibility means to businessmen, there seems to be a good case for beginning our analysis with a rather fuller consideration of the Zed company and its directors.

One of the most interesting things about Zed's directors is that though in terms of social origin and career history they appear to be six discrete individuals, in other respects they constitute a tightly knit and homogeneous primary group. So much was this the case that there were not only strong similarities between the actual choices they made but there was also a high degree of unanimity in the comments they made about issues which the interviewer raised as asides. To all intents and purposes they spoke as one man. And it did not take long to discover that that man was John Brown, the chairman and managing director.

Their replies were often prefaced by the phrase 'as John says' and with an almost predictable regularity they reiterated the views of John Brown. It is not possible to explain this pattern of response as the product of collusion, nor indeed is such an explanation necessary. This became apparent once we realized that several of John Brown's colleagues were not so much *businessmen* who had been won over by his dynamism and management expertise but personal friends and acquaintances who had been persuaded to leave other fields of work in order to join him. In this respect their position was much closer to that of 'retainer' than 'bureaucrat'. To some degree they had been recruited *because* they shared certain beliefs and values and as a consequence of this, to use a shop floor analogy, they were not just 'mates' but 'mates and friends'.

They interacted within a complex network of common social, political and even religious affiliations and to a large degree participation within this network presupposed the acceptance of a John Brown ethic. In many respects, then, Zed's directors were radically different from those we interviewed in other companies. And within Northern City business as a whole they constituted a deviant sub-culture. They considered themselves to be a minority, and judging from their unsolicited comments it would not be going too far to say that they felt they were a persecuted minority. Several of them suggested that their idealism, their religious and above all their (in business terms unorthodox) political affiiliations caused them to be shunned by other directors—and indeed one or two directors we interviewed in other companies did regard them with a certain wry humour.

Zed's directors all believed it important not to alienate work from non-work and desired to carry over their 'personal' social-religious-political values into the work situation itself. Yet this attempt to live as 'whole men'—a phrase they often used—involved them in the performance of several discrete roles which were perceived to be in conflict both by non-work associates and also by work associates in the business community. The fact that their work and non-work roles were regarded by others in this way was well known to Zed's directors and indeed, to some extent, they perceived this conflict themselves.

Now given the general lines of the argument we put forward in Part II (especially the emphasis upon 'fit' and socialization) one would not expect such conflict to arise very often. Its existence at Zed, however, led to the company's directors occupying the position of marginal men. They shared certain ideals and normative standards with former associates in trade union and political life. But their own involvement in the business system bred suspicion and scepticism even amongst those with whom such ideas were shared. And the fact that their non-work associates held such views in turn contributed to the directors being received with a similar scepticism and suspicion in business circles. Located in a directorial membership group, which they did not fully accept as an identification group, they felt themselves to be partially rejected both by their own non-work identification group (because of their membership group) and also by their work membership group (because of their non-work identification group). Full assimilation back into their non-work reference group was thought to impose heavy demands—as one of them put it, 'do they want me to work on the shop floor?' But it was thought that equally heavy demands had to be met in order to placate the business community. Thus, it was believed that 'you can't balance the Big City influence' and the interviewer was told that, at Zed, this led to a situation where—because of the directors' non-work affiliations—'we have to be more successful than other firms'.

It is possible, of course, that J.B. and his colleagues exaggerated their dilemma. Nevertheless, the belief that they were *conspired against* (by 'the City'), and were thought to be *conspiring* (by their non-work associates), meant that at the very least they had placed themselves in a conflict situation. As a result of this we can see that, for them, any conflict of interest between shareholders and employees was not merely an 'external' conflict but one which was internalized and felt as a conflict between their 'social-moral-political self' on the one hand, and their 'business self' on the other.

This became apparent in the discussions we had with Zed's directors about the reasons which underlay their choice of items in the forced choice questionnaire. However, it would be quite wrong to over-simplify the reasons which led them to make particular choices. For example, with the exception of J.B., none of them appeared to experience much difficulty in actually choosing an item: they knew what they believed, and the issues raised were familiar to them. But, to say that they had no great difficulty in making choices is not to say that the choices did not confront them with certain difficulties. On the contrary, it is only to say that they had evolved a strategy by which these difficulties could be overcome.

The traditional ways in which businessmen have overcome the conflict between societal and business mores has either been to refuse to accept that there is a conflict, or to compartmentalize.[1] Yet Zed's directors were quite clearly aware that there could be conflicts between societal and business values, and their desire to live as 'whole men' made compartmentalization difficult.

We have already noted that this group could hardly be described as 'bureaucrats'. It is perhaps surprising then that the actual strategy which they adopted to resolve their difficulties was what is often considered to be a typically bureaucratic one. It was, in fact, a variant of 'passing the buck'.

Thus, when asked to justify the choices that they had made— almost invariably for the S.R. items—these directors tended to say, quite simply, 'well, this is what I believe'. And the fact

---

[1] cf. Thurman Arnold, *The Folklore of Capitalism*, Yale, 1950, p. 331.

that what they said to be desirable was not reflected in company policy—as, for example, in making provision for redundancy—seemed to cause them limited concern: indeed they themselves sometimes pointed out that the policies they advocated were not in line with company practice.

The acceptance of this seemingly obvious conflict between the desired and actual situations was facilitated by two inter-related factors. The first was that they did not accept full responsibility for the company's policy, since they refused to consider themselves as fully competent businessmen. The second was related to the fact that J.B. occupied a very special position in the group and, as far as we could judge, took most of the major decisions himself.

It would appear, then, that in making choices from the questionnaire, J.B.'s colleagues had adopted the same strategy that they employed in the day-to-day conduct of the business. As one of them put it 'I just do what I think's right and leave it to J.B. to correct—otherwise we'd never make a profit'. This strategy—paralleled in the choice of the S.R. options in the questionnaire—allowed them to remain true to their ideals. And because of the very special position which J.B. held in the group his subsequent 'correction' of decisions—and his expected choice of L.T.C.I. rather than S.R. items in the questionnaire—did little to tarnish their own conception of themselves as 'whole men'. Nor indeed did this method of resolving their own problems lead to any diminution in J.B.'s status.

Within the group J.B.'s judgment was regarded as infallible. If he did not make the right decision it was because it was inevitable. J.B. was never wrong: it was simply that sometimes even he could not balance the odds imposed by the 'Big City influence'. J.B. was the final judge of what was 'practical' and practicality was defined, not by him, and certainly not by other members of the group but by pressures external to it. J.B. was doing his best in an adverse situation and the external pressures which sometimes forced him to take undesirable decisions were clearly an important factor in maintaining the solidarity of the directorial primary group.

In the case of Zed, then, we have a directorial primary group which in many respects constitutes a sub-culture within Northern City business. Its directors do recognize a clear alternative between the L.T.C.I. and S.R. options and even though they do not feel that their firm is entirely characterized by 'socially responsible' policies they have devised a strategy which allows them to maintain their preference for such policies and indeed to opt for them on the questionnaire more regularly than the directors of any other company. The particular strategy they resorted to is of some interest in its own right, but the matter of prime concern to us here is that they did recognize L.T.C.I. and S.R. items to be *alternatives*. This will be demonstrated even more clearly if we now briefly consider the way in which J.B. decided between these two sets of items on the questionnaire.

When confronted with the choices he had actually made in the questionnaire, J.B.—as his colleagues expected—moved his pen sagely to and fro between the L.T.C.I. and S.R. items. After a pause he would then begin to explain his choice. Twice he began by using an almost identical formulation: 'as a person I believe . . ., as a businessman I think . . ., as a person who is a businesssman I must choose . . .'. This form of argument intrigued the interviewer who (since J.B. had stated both that he 'loved' his employees and that his firm had to be more successful than most) asked him how these two things could be reconciled. 'The answer', he said, 'is that you oughtn't to be born'.

Now clearly, Zed Ltd has provided us with some intriguing material but we intend to resist the temptation to write at greater length about the structure, functions and values of its directorial primary group. In many respects, as we have seen, this particular 'elite' primary group resorts to the same type of strategics as those employed by more familiar 'aboriginal' ones. But this, of course, is not the point. Zed's significance is that it is governed by individuals some of whom, to quote their own words, don't appear to be 'made for business at all'.[1] The question therefore arises whether businessmen in other companies who had different (and more orthodox) histories and different (and more orthodox) socio-political affiliations perceived the choices with which we confronted them to have the same meaning as that attached to them by Zed's directors.

---

[1] As one said of public relations: 'if it involved telling a hall full of school kids that there were good prospects for them at Zed—oh no, I couldn't do that— I sometimes wonder whether I'm made for business at all'.

On the basis of our interviews with other directors we can only conclude that the answer to this question is that they did not.

More Orthodox Companies

It was quite common for the interviewer to be greeted with some such phrase as 'you know this is all very interesting, I've never thought about things like this before' and far from being mere pleasantries, such remarks were often substantiated by the ensuing conversation. Directors often had difficulty in seeing any difference between the L.T.C.I. and S.R. statements and

TABLE 15.2

Distribution of Choices by Subject Group

	Subject Group			
	A	*B*	*C*	*D*
Ideological Set	*(Redundancy)*	*(Purpose)*	*(Information)*	*(Public Life)*
L.F.	10	0	4	13
L.T.C.I.	30	52	53	14
S.R.	25	13	8	38
Total No. of Choices	65	65	65	65

some of their reasons for opting for S.R. items were more closely related to the 'letter' than the 'spirit' of the statements concerned.

Thus, if we look at Table 15.2 we find that those subject groups in which S.R. items were most likely to be chosen were A and D. *Prima facie*, this might be taken to indicate that businessmen believed that managements had a 'moral responsibility' (A3) to make provision for redundant workers—as opposed to believing that such provision was desirable on the 'practical' grounds that 'the secure contented employee . . . will work better' (A1)—and that they believed it was 'the duty' of senior executives to fulfil their business's social responsibilities by contributing their skills and knowledge to community life (D2)—as opposed to believing that it was desirable to be publicly active on the 'practical' grounds that this would improve the public image of their business (D1).

However, a closer look at the items concerned (i.e. A1, A3 and D1, D2)[1] suggests that such an interpretation is not the only possible one. Neither of the S.R. items concerned (A3 and D2) constitute simple statements which the respondent could accept or reject: both of them are 'double-barrelled'.

The most obvious case of this is D2 which posits (a) that 'every business has a social responsibility to the community' and (b) that 'it is the duty of senior executives to fulfil this by contributing their skills and knowledge to public life'. We were aware of the nature of this item at the pilot stage: we retained it because it seemed an admirable tool by which to assess how far the individual businessman felt obligated to the corporation in his non-work activities and social life. However, the double-barrelled nature of item A3 was not apparent to us at the pilot stage. Yet this item did appear to consist of two discrete propositions in the eyes of many businessmen.

Thus although all 25 of those who opted for this item quite clearly believed that 'management has a moral responsibility *to guard against redundancy*', 17 of them said they had chosen this item because—unlike A1—it did not necessarily imply 'some form of redundancy *payment*'. To complicate matters still further it should be noted that of the 30 who opted for A1 none came from companies which had any established form of redundancy payment system for (manual) workers. The view generally expressed about redundancy provision for workers was that 'it will come'[2] and except for Zed's directors, and one other, we met no strong feeling that the interviewee's own company should have taken the initiative and already introduced such a scheme.

It would seem, then, that the difference we built into the three ideological sets were not always readily perceived by businessmen and that the reasons underlying the choice of S.R. items in the two groups from which they were chosen most often (A and D),[3] were, to say the least, not always the expected ones.

As we have already pointed out, the perceived 'distance'

[1] See Appendix III.

[2] The interviews were conducted before the introduction of legislation to secure financial compensation in such cases.

[3] Thirty of the 38 opting for item D2 dissociated themselves from the second sentence which implied they had a duty to perform in public life because they were *businessmen*.

between the L.F. and the L.T.C.I. or S.R. sets was much greater than that between the L.T.C.I. and S.R. ones. Businessmen generally had no problems at all about recognizing that the L.F. statements were radically different. Some made the comment that a particular L.F. item was 'pure laisser-faire', or 'real nineteenth-century stuff'. When it came to justifying the choices made between the L.T.C.I. and S.R. items, however, no such clear distinction was evident. This perhaps is best illustrated by a brief reference to the case of U-Products.

U-Products is the regional branch of one of the largest British companies. Furthermore, it is one of those companies which has sometimes been cited as an example of the 'managerial revolution'—and indeed of the emergence of a social responsibility ethic. Only one of the six businessmen we interviewed in this firm was a main board director but all of them had worked in the company's other offices and factories and in some cases had done so overseas. In this sense, then, they could well be described as 'managerial spiralists'.[1]

As we saw in Table 15.1, the directors of U-Products were second only to those of Zed Ltd in their choice of S.R. items. There can be no doubt that the actual phrase 'social responsibility' was part of their vocabulary before we met them. Nor can there be any doubt that they were sincere in their belief that U-Products was a socially responsible company. It is thus worthy of our attention that with the exception of one man (perhaps significantly an ex-trade union official) their conception of social responsibility differed radically from that held at Zed.

As far as we could judge they had generally chosen the social responsibility items because they believed themselves and their company to be socially responsible but—and this would seem to be of the utmost importance—they did not think in terms of a distinction between (a) policies designed to serve the long-term interests of the company and (b) policies which are formulated on the basis of an ethical framework. As far as they were concerned S.R. was in no way an *ethical* alternative to L.T.C.I. policies. For them, *'socially responsible' policies were in keeping*

---

[1] Though one was associated with a large shareholding, another the nephew of a main board director. On 'managerial spiralists' see William Watson, 'The Managerial Spiralist', *Twentieth Century*, May, 1960, pp 413–418.

with the pursuit of the company's long-term interests and the pursuit of the company's long-term interests was in keeping with implementing management's social responsibilities.

We can perhaps illustrate this general inability to distinguish between the L.T.C.I. and S.R. sets if we briefly consider some specific cases. For example, one businessman at U-Products had chosen the S.R. item on redundancy (A3): asked to explain his choice, he replied, 'today, if you don't act responsibly toward your employees you won't have any shareholders. If you don't have any shareholders well . . .'. Another, who had chosen the same item, explained that he thought it was right because 'if you help a man he'll come back to you'. Yet another, who chose the S.R. item on purpose (B2), emphasized that 'in future all companies are going to have to act along these lines if they're to keep standing still'. In each of these cases the actual item which fitted best to the reason given for choosing the S.R. item was not the S.R. one but the L.T.C.I. Yet there is little possibility that U-Products directors thought they were contradicting themselves. Indeed, their case provides no more than a specific example of the general tendency we found in all companies—again, except for Zed— to interpret S.R. choices in terms of the (hypothetically different) meaning which we had built into the L.T.C.I. items.

We are, of course, fully prepared to accept that our data has very great limitations. It is based upon the responses of only 65 businessmen to only 12 statements. All the directors are from one locality and our contact time with them was limited to approximately one hour in each case. There can be no doubt that much fuller investigation is called for, which either uses much more refined techniques of questionnaire construction and analysis, and/or the kind of intensive observation and informal rapport achieved by Dalton.[1] Despite this, however, the general inability of Northern City businessmen to see the L.T.C.I. and S.R. sets as *alternatives* and their tendency to explain the S.R. choices they had made in terms of the views expressed in the L.T.C.I. items seems to us to be of some importance. It raises questions about the meaning of 'social responsibility' to businessmen, and indeed about business ethics in contemporary Britain.

---

[1] M. Dalton, *Men Who Manage: Fusion of Feeling and Theory in Administration*, N.Y. and London, 1959.

The Ethical and the Efficacious

So far we have emphasized that Northern City businessmen had difficulty in distinguishing between the S.R. and L.T.C.I. items and that they often explained choices for the former in terms of the latter. In this section we wish to explore the possible reasons for this a little more fully.

We believe that one of the major reasons for the pattern of behaviour we have described is that it really is extremely difficult for businessmen to separate policies which are in the interests of the company from those which are socially responsible. For example, in one company, Bee Bros, businessmen talked at length about their firm's 'enlightened' labour policies. Several of them went out of their way to point out that the company made a practice of 'carrying' a section of the labour force when work was short. Now, when we had first gone to Bee Bros to gain background material we had found out that part of the company's work was seasonal. It seemed to us, then, that given a general scarcity of labour and taking into account the cost of recruiting and retraining new workers it was probable that Bee's practice of carrying workers over the off-season was economically advantageous. We put this to those directors who had argued that this particular practice was evidence of the company's desire to fulfil its social responsibilities to labour. It was quite clear that none of them had thought about the matter in this way. When forced to do so their general line of argument was, to quote one of them: 'Well, the employees don't complain, you know, but to be honest I suppose we do it because it's the sensible thing to do'.

In another case, at Kay & Co., the managing director gave an example of the way in which his company acted socially responsibly to the local community. He explained that they had just gone to considerable expense to cut down the air pollution from one of their chimneys. This policy, he said, was in line with his choice of item D2. But, as one of his colleagues informed us, there had been 'a devil of a fuss' about air pollution and the action to prevent it had only followed an extensive campaign by local residents.

In yet another case, at Aye Ltd, we found that a senior manager we interviewed held a part-time position with a local authority. Because this arrangement was so unusual we made a point of asking about the reasons behind it. The individual concerned replied he had

'a vague sort of feeling that it was thought it might be useful to the company but I can assure you that it isn't and I'm not sure exactly why it was done. In fact, I don't think the Board do either.'[1]

One of his colleagues who occupied a rather uncomfortable position—another respondent informed us that he had just been 'promoted downwards'—was rather more cynical and raised some important questions. 'Is it', he asked, 'any more "responsible" than providing accommodation for union meetings, or making nothing out of canteen facilities?'

In Aye's case we might perhaps explain the reluctance to come to a conclusion about the motives involved as evidence of a suspicion that they were not 'good' ones. But this would be to miss the point which is that, generally speaking, directors found it hard to distinguish whether actual policies were designed to promote the long-term interests of the company *or* to fulfil a responsibility to some or other group. We think the fact that they found this difficult is not at all surprising.

This follows for one good reason. If a businessman really believed that there was a fundamental difference between advancing the long-term interests of his company and pursuing socially responsible policies he would have to recognize that he had placed himself in a virtually insoluble conflict situation. Instead of asking himself whether a particular policy was feasible or 'practical', or whether one course of action was economically preferable to another, he would be continually concerned with the problem of whether any particular course of action could be justified on ethical grounds. In practice this is not a situation in which many businessmen find themselves.

This is not, of course, to say that we think businessmen unethical or immoral. Nor is it to say that they have no concern for their fellow-men, or that they experience no difficulty in reaching decisions. There is no doubt that they do experience certain strains and that, at a certain level, they feel uncertain about their ethical situation. It is, for example, surely no

---

[1] Similar uncertainty characterized the practice of giving money to charity. When asked what criteria were employed in giving to charities many respondents could not give an answer. A few gave only to local institutions, some only to causes related to their firm or industry, others employed a rota system: cf. *A Study of Industry's Contribution to Science*, p. 11.

accident that they often believe that 'the trouble with industry is people'. The belief that a good manager needs to be 'firm but fair' and have a 'strong personality' is to some degree evidence that they feel such qualities are necessary if the hard decisions—those which involve people—are to be taken at all. Nor is this to say that directors are not conscious that others often regard them with less deference than they would hope for. They are fully conscious that, in some quarters, business is thought to be 'sordid' and by no means as 'respectable' as the established professions. But to say that the decisions they have to take are not without difficulties or that they are sensitive about the public's image of business is not to say that they recognize the interests of business and society to be in conflict. If they believed this they would almost certainly not be in business at all.

Perhaps this point can be reinforced if we briefly consider a study of American businessmen. In 1961 the *Harvard Business Review* conducted a survey of its readers in an attempt to answer the question 'how ethical are businessmen?'[1] As part of this, businessmen were asked their opinion of a statement made by a management consultant, Theodore Levitt. Levitt had previously written several articles in which he criticized the advocates of socially responsible management and expressed concern that businessmen were taking social responsibility seriously. In his view:

'concern with management's social responsibilities (had) become more than a Philistine form of self-flattery . . . more than merely intoning the pious declarations of Christian brotherhood which some hotshot public relations man (had) pressed into the out-stretched hands of the company president . . . it (had) become a deadly serious occupation.'[2]

This, Levitt argued, was quite wrong. As he states elsewhere this, in his opinion, is not what business is about:

'the businessman exists for only one purpose, to create and deliver value satisfactions at a profit to himself. . . . If what is offered can be sold at a profit (not even necessarily a long-term profit) then

---

[1] 'How Ethical are Businessmen?', *Harvard Business Review*, July–August, 1961. p. 6.
[2] T. Levitt, 'The Dangers of Social Responsibility', *Harvard Business Review* Sept.–Oct., 1956, p. 41.

it is legitimate. . . . The cultural, spiritual, social and moral consequences of his actions are none of his occupational concern.'[1]

When American businessmen were confronted with this (last) statement 94% of them expressed disagreement. They did so on the grounds that 'for corporation executives to act in the interests of shareholders alone, and not also in the interests of employees and customers, is unethical.[2]

Now the above response can tell us very little about how widespread a socially responsible ideology is in America.[3] It can, however, tell us something about the meaning of social responsibility, since 99% of the respondents *also* agreed to the proposition that 'sound ethics is good business in the long run'. Thus we can see that for these American executives, too, there was no sharp contrast between the L.T.C.I. and S.R. frames of reference. The fact that businessmen may believe themselves to be 'socially responsible' should not then blind us to the fact that the policies which they claim to illustrate the enactment of their social responsibilities are often in no way out of keeping with the long-term interests of their company—and indeed are not thought to be by them.

At a more general level we would postulate that the self-selection inherent in the choice of a business career, the ability to stay in business and to attain a senior position, presupposes that no radical conflict is perceived between societal and business values, or indeed between the interests of sub-sections of the society and business itself. As far as we are aware this particular type of explanation for the existence of a socially responsible ideology is not commonly put forward. Instead, it has been explained either in terms of recent changes in the structure of industry (e.g. separation of ownership and control, and the growth of a professional management stratum) or

[1] T. Levitt, 'Are Advertising and Marketing Corrupting Society?', *Advertising Age*, Oct., 1958, p. 89. (Modified forms of this statement were used in items B1 and B2, see Appendix III.)

[2] See, 'How Ethical Are Businessmen?', p. 10.

[3] There are two reasons for this. First, 66% of the sample did not respond, secondly, the sample was based entirely on the readership of *Harvard Business Review*. In the post-war period this journal published a large number of articles about social responsibility, Christianity and business ethics. (It will be noted that the view expressed by 94% of the respondents is similar to that which we put to Northern City businessmen in item B2. It is quite clear, however, that their responses—in a forced choice situation—are not comparable to those of the American executives whose view the statement expressed.)

in terms of changes in the structure of society itself (e.g. the countervailing power of government and trade unions and the problems of retaining a work force when there is full employment).

Whereas we think the former type of explanation is, at best, premature there is clearly something to be said for the latter. However, the latter explanation is not entirely satisfactory when taken by itself. *Prima facie*, it may appear convincing to argue that the days are now past when the British counterpart of the head of General Motors can argue that 'what's good for General Motors is good for the United States'. But this type of observation, though it contains more than a grain of truth, is inadequate in so far as it reduces the businessman to some kind of automaton that responds to external events. To a large degree, of course, the businessman does—like other men— adapt to changes in the structure of society but—again like other men—the fact that he occupies a particular position in society presupposes, to some extent at least, that he has a common frame of reference and common values with others in similar positions. Our understanding of these common frames of reference and common values does not lead us to expect that the contemporary businessmen will conceive of the relationship between his company and society in terms of any deep-seated conflict.

So much is this the case that a public relations man has defended the head of General Motors by pointing out that what he *really* said was 'I've always thought that what was good for the country was good for General Motors, *and vice-versa*'.[1]

We believe that this particular instance exemplifies the kind of problem encountered when one attempts to explain business ideology 'from the outside'. For example, we suspect that most Northern City businessmen would find nothing exceptional about the above 'defence'—such thinking, far from being considered illogical, constitutes an inner dynamic of business ideology. Indeed, the acceptance of such a logic becomes almost inevitable for businessmen unless they believe themselves to be working for a sectional interest which is at odds with the welfare of society as a whole. And clearly, most do not.

[1] See the letter to *The Guardian*, January 27, 1966, from Robert Johnson, General Motors public relations manager.

CHAPTER XVI

TRADITIONALISM, PROFESSIONALISM, AND THE IDEOLOGY OF BUSINESSMEN

A Recapitulation

So far we have mainly confined ourselves to two major observations about the choices which Northern City businessmen made when they were confronted with the forced-choice questionnaire. The first of these was that businessmen were more likely to choose items from the L.T.C.I. than the S.R. or L.F. sets. This, like the fact that no respondent managed to make his choices without including at least one item from the L.T.C.I. set, suggested that the items in this set approximated most closely to the predominant business ideology in Northern City.

The second observation concerned the extent to which businessmen might be said to have made consistent choices. Here we found that whereas only nine businessmen could be said to have made consistent choices, in the sense that all the items chosen came from one of the postulated ideological sets, six out of ten of them had made choices which were consistent in the sense that they were selected exclusively from L.T.C.I. and S.R. items. This further suggested that there was less 'distance' between the S.R. and L.T.C.I. sets than between any two others. Additional support for this view was provided by the observation that businessmen often explained their choice of S.R. items in terms of the ideas expressed in the statements in the L.T.C.I. set.

It is possible, then, that the above might provide some confirmation for the general standpoint we have adopted so far. In short, by stressing the extent to which the businessman's ideology can be considered as a function of his social experience and his exposure to the corporation's cost and reward system,

we have been led to suggest that these may have the consequence
of leading him to define as non-problems those value alternatives
which armchair theorists, like the writer, see to reside in a
conflict between the ethical and the efficacious. The deviant
case of Zed Ltd would seem to add to the plausibility of this
interpretation.

It should be noted, however, that so far in Part III we have
mainly confined ourselves to writing about Northern City
business ideology as a whole. We have concentrated upon
questions of meaning and as far as possible we have avoided
attempts to compare the choices made by different categories
or sub-groups of Northern City businessmen. For these purposes
it has been sufficient to analyse responses to the forced-choice
questionnaire in terms of the proportion of choices made for
items in each of the three hypothetically different ideological
sets (as in Table 14.1). But this form of analysis is of limited
value to investigate differences between the ideological preferences of one or more categories of businessmen, which is the
matter with which this chapter is concerned.

A New Classification Scheme

For the present purpose a new classificatory scheme is required
which is based upon the patterns of response of businessmen
themselves and which allows us to compare the frequency
distribution of businessmen across particular categories. In
practice, however, the majority of businessmen made choices
which consisted entirely of L.T.C.I. and S.R. items. Thus,
though there is of course no perfect solution to this problem,
any new classificatory scheme must necessarily be developed
in the light of this and other features of the actual distribution
of responses. Following this line of reasoning, then, we have
adopted less stringent criteria for a businessman's inclusion in
the new category we term $L.T.C.I._1$ than for the new category
we term $S.R._1$, and less stringent criteria still for the new
category we term $L.F._1$.

Consequently, the new category $L.T.C.I._1$ includes all those
individuals who chose either four L.T.C.I. items or three
L.T.C.I. items plus one item from the old S.R. set ($N = 23$);
the new category $S.R._1$ includes all those individuals who chose
either three items from the old S.R. set plus one from the

L.T.C.I. set, or two items from each of these ($N = 26$); the new category L.F.$_1$ includes all individuals who chose one or more of the L.F. items ($N = 16$)—this was necessary since only three individuals had made as many as three L.F. choices and is partly justified by the fact that most interviewees had no doubt the L.F. items really were different.

Quite clearly, the above categories do not constitute 'pure types' since each of them shares certain elements in common with the other two. Such a circumstance is, however, no more than a reflection of the situation we found to exist in the responses of businessmen themselves. It should also be noted that the three new categories are based on all four of the choices made by such individuals. This basis of classification was adopted because, having seen the ease with which businessmen could redefine some of the items they had chosen in terms of those they had not chosen, and *vice-versa*, we had good reason to suppose that comparisons based on the choice of any one of three options in any one of the four subject groups could be highly misleading.

To make one thing quite clear, however, it is not the purpose of this chapter to continue our investigation into the important and (as we hope to have already convinced the reader) highly complex question of what social responsibility means to businessmen. Instead, we intend to proceed on the basis of treating the statements in each of the new categories quite literally as forms of words and to ask whether businessmen with different characteristics and social experiences are likely to differ in their inclination for certain of these rather than others.

We are of course dealing here with a small exploratory study and much fuller investigations are clearly necessary if any definitive conclusions are to be arrived at. Furthermore, we have no doubt that our method of analysis and the classificatory scheme we have developed could be improved upon. But given the absence of similar studies tne latter must stand or fall on the basis of the answers it can give to the sorts of questions we wish to ask. Before we ask these questions, however, there is one additional point to be made. This is that in the following analysis all sixty-five businessmen are included, irrespective of whether they be directors or senior managers, or whether they occupy line or non-line positions. As can be seen from Table

16.1 we found no significant differences between the ideological preferences[1] of businessmen in these broadly defined organizational positions.

TABLE 16.1

Ideological Preference and Organizational Position

	Directors		Senior Managers		All B/men in Line Positions		All B/men in Non-Line Positions		All Northern City B/men	
	(N)	%	(N)	%	(N)	%	(N)	%	(N)	%
L.F.1	(9)	24	(7)	26	(11)	31	(5)	17	(16)	25
L.T.C.I.1	(13)	34	(10)	37	(12)	33	(11)	38	(23)	35
S.R.1	(16)	42	(10)	37	(13)	36	(13)	45	(26)	40
	(38)		(27)		(36)		(29)		(65)	

Pre-corporate Social Experience and Ideological Preference

In Chapter X we argued that it was important that any consideration of business ideology should not neglect those factors associated with the social bases of business recruitment. Their importance was held to reside in the fact that recruitment to senior positions in industry is still far from 'open', so that the continuing stability in top management's social composition might be a factor in facilitating the transmission of 'old' business norms and values to those 'new' role incumbents, 'the managers', even if they were from lower social origins or had a more meritocratic/bureaucratic career structure. On the basis of these and allied propositions (especially those advanced in chapter 11) one would not expect to find significant differences between the ideological preferences of businessmen with 'traditional', as opposed to 'professional', pre-corporate experiences and characteristics. And evidence to support this line of thinking was forthcoming from the survey.

For example, no significant difference was found between the ideological preferences of businessmen who were the sons of directors and those who were not (see Table 16.2), nor between the ideological preferences of graduates and others

[1] We have used the term 'ideological preference' with the deliberate intention of reminding the reader that we are not dealing here with the sum total of the businessman's ideology—or even its 'quintessence'—however that may be measured —but with what we take to be an indication of his ideological standpoint in so far as this can be directly assessed from the forced-choice questionnaire.

(see Table 16.3). Indeed, if anything, the sons of directors (and also those who had fathers in business), and those originating in the higher social strata (i.e R.G.'s social classes I and II) tended to be slightly more, not less, likely to fall into the S.R.$_1$ category. Furthermore, the opposite of this tended to be true of the graduates.

TABLE 16.2

Father's Occupation and Businessmen's Ideological Preference

	Father a Director		Father not a Director	
	(N)	%	(N)	%
L.F.$_1$	(3)	23	(13)	25
L.T.C.I.$_1$	(3)	23	(20)	39
S.R.$_1$	(7)	54	(19)	36
	(13)		(52)	

Chi^2 = 1·49 n.s.

They appeared to incline more toward the L.F.$_1$ category and less toward S.R.$_1$ so that, with the possible exception of their slightly higher representation in L.T.C.I.$_1$, their distribution of ideological preferences does not square at all well with many commonly held assumptions about the ideological correlates of graduate status in business. It should be

TABLE 16.3

University Education and Ideological Preference

	Graduates		Non-Graduates	
	(N)	%	(N)	%
L.F.$_1$	(8)	35	(8)	19
L.T.C.I.$_1$	(9)	39	(14)	33
S.R.$_1$	(6)	26	(20)	48
	(23)		(42)	

Chi^2 = 3·36 n.s.

noted, however, that far from having experienced any extensive social mobility, all but one of the graduates had originated in the higher social strata. Also, if any conclusion is to be drawn about them as a whole it is only that they tended to be more cynical than their fellows—this being a possibility forcibly brought home to us in some half-dozen cases when we asked why L.F. items had been chosen from the forced-choice questionnaire.

Other comparisons we made between those businessmen who had experienced a public school, as opposed to state secondary, education, and between those who gained access to their first management position through an introduction rather than through more 'conventional' bureaucratic procedures, yielded similar non-significant differences to those reported above.[1] Thus, so far, we have not been able to find the sort of differences in ideological preference which much of the discussion about contemporary business might lead one to expect. However, we have not yet considered any such possible differences which may be associated with age.

Age, Length of Industrial Management Experience and Ideological Preference

If age is to be treated as a possible indication of the businessman's socio-cultural experience then one would not necessarily expect to find any clearly observable age-related trends as one moved from considering the ideological preferences of younger to older businessmen. This was found to be the case. On the other hand, one would expect to find certain cut-off points above and below which there were significant differences in the ideological preferences of businessmen in different age groups. In order to test this latter proposition we compared the ideological preferences of Northern City businessmen at the five points where the small numbers involved made such an exercise permissible. In only three cases (those where dichotomies were made at ±40, ±50 and ±55 years) were the signs of the resulting differences in the same direction but in the case of the dichotomy at ±50 years the difference was found to be a statistically significant one.

As can be seen from Table 16.4 B this last dichotomy does provide some support for the generally accepted assumption

[1] For a more detailed analysis of the matters dealt with in this chapter see the writer's *Ownership, Control and Ideology*, M.A. thesis, University of Hull, 1968, pp. 278–328. (Any possible ideological correlates of income and salary are not investigated here for the reason given in Appendix 1. However, ownership type of firm does not appear to be associated with any consistent differences in this respect: cf. Appendix 1 and Table 15.1, in which those firms likely to be termed 'management-controlled' are Aye Ltd, Bee Bros, Gee Ltd and U-Products.)

N

that older businessmen (in this case those born in the first decade of the century or earlier) are more likely to incline toward an L.F. type philosophy of business. But, in contrast to the expectations of some non-sectional managerial theorists, the percentage of older businessmen in the $S.R._1$ category does not suggest that they are any less given to talk of their

TABLE 16.4

Age, Length of Industrial Management Experience, and Ideological Preference

A. *Age Related Differences*

	B/Men Aged Less than 50 years		B/Men Aged 50 years or over	
	(N)	%	(N)	%
$L.F._1$	(8)	17	(8)	42
$L.T.C.I._1$	(21)	46	(2)	11
$S.R._1$	(17)	37	(9)	47
	(46)		(19)	

Chi^2 = 8·38   p = < ·05

B. *Trends Related to Length of Industrial Management Experience*

Length of Experience

	(a) 10 years or less		(b) 11–20 years		(c) 21–30 years		(d) 31 years or over	
	(N)	%	(N)	%	(N)	%	(N)	%
$L.F._1$	(2)	15	(4)	17	(5)	24	(5)	71
$L.T.C.I._1$	(2)	15	(12)	50	(9)	43	(0)	—
$S.R._1$	(9)	69	(8)	33	(7)	33	(2)	29
	(13)		(24)		(21)		(7)	

(a) v. (b) + (c) + (d)
Chi^2 = 5·87 n.s.

social responsibilities than younger men, of whom, as can again be seen from the table, the largest percentage (46%) fell into the $L.T.C.I._1$ category.

It is possible, however, that the age-related differences in ideological preference which the above table purports to test have been contaminated by other socio-cultural factors which are themselves partially related to age itself. Certain differences are discernible, for example, between the distributions of ideological preferences of those businessmen with greater or lesser periods of industrial management experience.

Thus, though it is difficult to come to any conclusion about the L.T.C.I.$_1$ category, it does appear that the percentage falling into S.R.$_1$ decreases with length of industrial management experience (see Table 16.4 B). And *prima facie*, those differences which exist in this respect between businessmen with 10 or less and more than 10 years' experience would seem to be theoretically, if not (quite) statistically, significant ones. The possible shift toward the 'efficacious', as indicated by the higher percentages in the L.F.$_1$ and L.T.C.I.$_1$ categories, and the move away from the 'ethical', as indicated by the decreased percentage in the S.R.$_1$ category, might even be taken to be a partial confirmation of the hypotheses we put forward in Chapters XI and XV about the correlates of occupational socialization in business. As we point out below, however, any such conclusion requires some qualification and for the moment we are mainly concerned to investigate to what extent the age-related differences reported can, in fact, be considered age-related ones.

A limited test of the relative importance of age and length of industrial management experience becomes possible if we dichotomize the ages of businessmen at the four points at which numbers permit and then observe the direction of differences between the percentage distributions of preferences for those businessmen with more or less than 10 years' experience of industrial management within each of the eight resulting categories. Although such a procedure clearly constitutes an imperfect 'test' it does indicate that the direction of the sign differences found in Table 16.4 B ((a) v. (b)+(c)+(d))—

i.e. L.F.$_1$ +   (where + = a higher percentage of those
    L.T.C.I.$_1$+   with longer experience of industrial manage-
    S.R.$_1$ −   ment in any given category)

holds good in seven out of eight instances even when an attempt is made to control for age. On the other hand, the signs of the differences between the distribution of ideological preferences of all businessmen aged over or under 35, 40, 45, and 50 years remain the same in only one out of eight instances, once length of industrial management experience is held at less than, or more than, 10 years.

Such a finding can do little more than sensitize future researchers in this field to the possible existence of an interesting problem area. But, tentatively, we are led to suggest that there may be a negative relationship between length of experience in the managerial role and an ideological preference for $S.R._1$, and a preference for the $L.F._1$ and $L.T.C.I._1$ categories. At the least, such a conclusion provides little support for those who predict the emergence of a new, non-sectionally oriented, managerial stratum. In short, it appears that even if those relatively new to business are more likely to fall into the $S.R._1$ category, their inclination to do so may decline with their length of experience in business itself.

As noted above, this latter possibility ties in with the general assumptions put forward in our earlier and more theoretical discussion of the manager's intra-corporate socialization. Ironically, though, the problem from our point of view is that it ties in almost too well. As Berlew and Hall[1] have argued, one would expect the first year's experience to be the crucial one for the development of the manager's organizational identity. After this, one would expect the relative 'goodness of fit' attained by any given manager to remain a more or less enduring one—and perhaps even that those who did not fit would eventually drop out. Thus, given that the Northern City businessmen are at the apex of their organizations and are thus, presumably like those at the apex of other types of organization, more likely to be characterized by 'normative' than 'calculative' involvement, and to have generally attained a good 'fit' already, it is pertinent to establish any further distinguishing characteristics of the thirteen men with less than 10 years' experience. In particular, it is important to note that five of them had previously been engaged in some form of non-industrial administration or other employment.

This suggests that the ideological preferences reported above are not solely the result of the absence or presence of a long exposure to business norms and values but that they may also be a function of the orientations which some businessmen have developed in their former (non-business) careers. Thus, the possibility that businessmen with different career experiences

---

[1] cf. D. E. Berlew and D. T. Hall, 'The Socialisation of Managers: Effects of Expectations on Performance', *Administrative Science Quarterly*, Sept., 1966, pp. 207–223.

may already have different norms and values when they enter business leads one to ask further questions about the extent to which such differences may also pertain between those who perform different organizationally defined roles. Some light might be shed upon this question if we now return to the rather crude distinction we made earlier (see Table 16.1) between those who occupy line and non-line positions.

Differences Between Non-Line Specialists

A further breakdown of those in the non-line category suggests that at least one group, those in personnel, had a distinctively different distribution of ideological preferences. As can be seen in Table 16.5, nine of the ten personnel specialists we met in Northern City fell into the $S.R._1$ category.

TABLE 16.5

The Ideological Preferences of Non-line Specialists

Non-Line Specialism

	Personnel	Sales	Finance	Technical
$L.F._1$	0	2	1	2
$L.T.C.I._1$	1	3	5	2
$S.R._1$	9	3	0	1
	10	8	6	5

The contrast between those in personnel on the one hand, and those in finance on the other, may be a reflection of the people, and particularly employee-centred, and balance-sheet-centred, outlooks which are often held to characterize those in these two positions. It could also, of course, be an indication that personnel managers go into business with different sorts of expectations in the first place. In short, they may still have a lingering attachment to certain aspects of the old position of industrial social worker,[1] and be more concerned with performing a 'social service' than other businessmen.

This is a plausible argument but it is a double-edged one because if it is accepted that those in personnel are so different from other businessmen it becomes difficult to avoid the conclusion that most businessmen are *not* characterized by a similar sense of social responsibility. There is, however, one further

[1] cf. M. M. Niven, 'The Beginnings of the Institute', *Personnel Management*, March, 1957, p. 29.

point to be made about personnel specialists in general, and those in Northern City in particular. This is, that if one must talk about professionalism in business at all, those in personnel probably approximate most closely to the notion of 'the professional manager'.

In Northern City these were the people who were most likely to read management literature, to participate in the affairs of management bodies, and to hold professional memberships. It is possible therefore that their highly atypical distribution of ideological preferences may be partially related to this. Accordingly, it is to a more precise consideration of the possible relationship between certain indices of professionalism and the ideological preferences of Northern City businessmen that we now turn.

Professionalism and Ideological Preference

As we pointed out in Chapter VIII very few Northern City businessmen could be said to be professionals in the sense of their being familiar with an established body of knowledge. Only just over one-third of them (37%) had received any formal training for management and even fewer, only four out of the sixty-five, had received any such training prior to taking up their first position. Only 37% of them were members of professional management bodies and a clear half of them (57%) had never participated in any way in any professional management activities at all. Their knowledge of management literature was often non-existent, 46% being unable to name the title of one book in the field of management, and only 20% claiming to be familiar with the name of Elton Mayo. In fact, less than a third of them (31%) even claimed to think of themselves as 'professionals'.

Despite the above, however, questions remain about whether those who had the 'professional characteristics' detailed above had different ideological preferences to other businessmen and, in particular, whether such differences confirm the hypothesis that the 'professional manager' is more inclined to find statements about business's social responsibilities attractive. In practice, this does seem to be the case.

Table 16.6, for example, shows that those who had participated in the affairs of management bodies were more likely to

fall into the S.R.$_1$ category, and much less likely to fall into
L.F.$_1$ than other businessmen. Thus, given this statistical
association—the direction of which is confirmed by similar
but much weaker and non-significant associations between
other possible indices of professionalism, like the experience
of some management training, and a knowledge of management
literature—it becomes appropriate to establish which Northern
City businessmen had, in fact, participated.

TABLE 16.6

Participation in the Activities of Professional Management
Bodies and Ideological Preference

	B/Men who have Participated		B/Men who have Not Participated	
	(N)	%	(N)	%
L.F.$_1$	(1)	3	(15)	41
L.T.C.I.$_1$	(10)	36	(13)	35
S.R.$_1$	(17)	61	(9)	24
	(28)		(37)	

$\text{Chi}^2 = 14 \cdot 12 \quad p = \; < \cdot 001$

We have attempted to answer this question in Table 16.7
where businessmen with those characteristics which approximate to those of 'the professional manager' are compared to
businessmen with more 'traditional' characteristics. And,
overall, evidence is forthcoming to support the view that those
with professional characteristics were more likely to participate.
However, it is necessary to enter some qualifications about this
general finding.

First, the differences reported for graduates and non-
graduates are in the 'wrong' direction: the former being significantly less, not more, likely to have participated in professional
activities. Since eight of the twenty-three graduates were the
sons of directors this is not perhaps surprising, for the latter—
presumably because they are the least likely to feel it necessary—
are the least likely to participate. However, two-thirds (10)
of the remaining graduates did not participate either. This
observation, in conjunction with our earlier report of the
distribution of graduates' ideological preferences (see Table
16.3), further underlines the need for a much fuller investigation

than has yet been conducted into the behavioural and attitudinal correlates of graduate status in industry.

The second qualification which must be entered here about Table 16.7 concerns the extent of the difference it suggests to exist between those in line and non-line positions. We have

TABLE 16.7

The Percentage of Businessmen with Different Characteristics who did and did not Participate

	Characteristics of Businessmen	% Who Participated	% Who Did Not	
Social Origin	Father a Director* (N = 13)	15	85	p< ·05
	Not	50	50	
	Father in Business* (N = 34)	38	62	n.s.
	Not	48	52	
	Father in R.G. I or II* (N = 48)	44	56	n.s.
	Not	41	59	
Education	Public School* (N = 36)	44	56	n.s.
	Not	41	59	
	University (N = 23)	26	74	p< ·05
	Not*	52	48	
Access to First Position	Bureaucratic (N = 48)	44	56	n.s.
	Traditionalistic*	41	59	
Present Position	Director* (N = 38)	40	60	n.s.
	Senior Manager	48	52	
	Line* (N = 36)	28	72	p< ·01
	Non-Line	62	38	
Age	Less than 50 years (N = 46)	46	54	n.s.
	Over 50 years*	37	63	
Experience of Ind. Mgt.	Less than 10 years (N = 13)	46	54	n.s.
	Over 10 years*	42	58	
	All (N = 65)	43	57	

Note: The hypothesis tested is that those businessmen having, or commonly thought to have, traditional characteristics* will be less likely to participate.

already noted that those employed in the personnel function of management had a markedly different distribution of ideological preferences and that they were much more likely to participate in professional activities. And since all ten of them claimed to participate in such activities the table over-estimates those differences which generally pertain between businessmen in line and non-line positions. When we exclude them from this comparison, even though the difference reported remains in the same direction, its magnitude is decreased, and it ceases to be a statistically significant one. In this sense one of the most important conclusions to be drawn from the line/non-line comparison reported in Table 16.7 is not that the latter are more likely to participate, though as we have seen this may be true, but that once again we have found that those concerned with the personnel function are different—even from others in non-line positions.[1]

Thirdly, it must be stressed that with the exception of those in personnel positions, and also of course 'non-graduates', we were unable to find any group of Northern City businessmen

TABLE 16.8

Participation, Length of Industrial Management Experience
and Ideological Preference

| | B/Men Participating | | | | B/Men Not Participating | | | |
| | < 10 years Ind. Mgt. Exp. | | > 10 years Ind. Mgt. Exp. | | < 10 years Ind. Mgt. Exp. | | > 10 years Ind Mgt. Exp. | |
	(N)	%	(N)	%	(N)	%	(N)	%
L.F.$_1$	(0)	—	(1)	4	(2)	29	(13)	43
L.T.C.I.$_1$	(1)	17	(9)	41	(1)	14	(12)	40
S.R.$_1$	(5)	83	(12)	55	(4)	57	(5)	17
	(6)		(22)		(7)		(30)	

in which more than 50% of those included *did* participate. The 'professionals', even loosely defined, were clearly in the minority.

Of course, having gone this far to document which business-men with which characteristics fell into which ideological categories, one is tempted to go further and attempt an elementary form of multivariate analysis. In particular one would like to know whether participation, perhaps the best index of business professionalism we have (see Table 16.6), or the theoretically interesting possibility of length of industrial management experience (see Table 16.4 B) is more closely related to the distribution of ideological preferences. This question is taken up in Table 16.8 which suggests that the relation-

---

[1] Compared to others in non-line positions those in personnel are significantly more likely to participate; Fisher (one-tailed) p < ·01.

ship between these two factors may be of an additive nature.

Thus, we find that the highest percentage of cases in the L.F.$_1$ category is of those with more than 10 years' experience of industrial management who did not participate: none of those with less than 10 years' experience who did participate appearing in this category at all. By contrast, the lowest percentage in the S.R.$_1$ category is of those with more than 10 years' experience who did not participate: the highest percentage in this category being of those with less than this period of experience who did participate. However, this relationship does not appear to hold good for the percentages in the L.T.C.I.$_1$ category. Those with longer periods of experience were more likely to fall into L.T.C.I.$_1$ whether they participated or not. But to write of 'percentages' in this context is highly misleading and given the very small cell frequencies which result from tables such as the above we do not feel justified in proceeding with any further analysis of this type.

The Northern City study was in any case primarily conducted in order to assess the extent to which it is legitimate to make inferences about business behaviour from those statements which some businessmen are apt to make about their social responsibilities. And despite some of the data cited in this chapter, which suggests that certain differences do exist between the ideological preferences of businessmen with different characteristics, we are still inclined to hold to the view put forward earlier in Chapters XIV and XV, namely, that for most businessmen the 'distance' between the S.R. and L.T.C.I. frames of reference is a very short one.

Such a conclusion is given further credence by the results of other (exclusively American) studies.[1] In Guzzardi's study,[2] for example, executives were asked—'does the question of your own ethical conduct come up in your business?'—over 70% replied, only 'once in a while (31%) or 'almost never' (41%). When asked—'have you any general comment about the relationship between ethical conduct and business life?'— 30% replied that 'ethical conduct and business life are identical', or that it 'improved business'. Guzzardi's basis of classification is by no means clear but the replies given by the majority of

---

[1] cf. the *Harvard Business Review* study, 'How Ethical Are Businessmen?' (reported in Chapter XV above); W. Guzzardi, *The Young Executives*, N.Y., 1964.
[2] *ibid.*, p. 194.

respondents do seem to support his claim that the executive
'generally . . . seems happy with the ethical condition of the
business world'— this being very much in line with the underlying assumptions of Northern City businessmen.

There are, however, three further observations that support
the above assertation. First, when our interviewees were
asked whether they thought their own responses were reasonably
typical of other businessmen in the same firm only six replied
that they doubted this. Given that those with 'professional'
characteristics were fairly evenly spread across the firms,
this hardly suggests that those differences in ideological
preference which we have reported were perceived to be
radical ones by businessmen themselves. Secondly, when we
asked an open-ended question about 'the greatest need of
industry today' only *one* respondent mentioned the need for
socially responsible managements. Since the time prior to this
question being put had largely been spent looking at a questionnaire consisting of statements about social responsibility, and
in asking businessmen what they meant by social responsibility,
it is difficult to avoid the conclusion that either these businessmen thought most managements socially responsible enough
already, or that the issues raised were not ones with which they
were generally preoccupied outside the interview situation.

In our view both the above propositions are well founded.
Either one of them goes some way to explain why the L.T.C.I.
items were chosen more often than the S.R. ones. But this
brings us to a third and related point. In short, neither the
new L.T.C.I.$_1$ or S.R.$_1$ categories are 'pure types'. As explained
earlier, the new classificatory scheme had to be introduced for
the very reason that it was not possible to find a single case in
which a businessman chose an S.R. item without also choosing
one or more from the old L.T.C.I. set—the majority having
patterns of response made up from *both* these types of item.

Having made the above points, however, it must be accepted
that this chapter has suggested that certain differences may
exist between the ideological preferences of Northern City
businessmen with 'professional' and 'traditional' characteristics.
This raises two questions: (*a*) what is the nature and extent
of these differences, and (*b*) what factors may be responsible
for their existence?

As far as the first of these questions is concerned it should be noted that though businessmen with professional characteristics were less likely to fall into the $L.F._1$ category they were *not* markedly less likely to fall into $L.T.C.I._1$. This observation, in conjunction with the fact that, even though the highest percentages of $S.R._1$ preferences were of businessmen with professional characteristics, some groups of businessmen with traditional characteristics also had a high percentage of $S.R._1$ preferences, suggests that the ideological correlates of traditionalism and professionalism may not be as straightforward as sometimes thought.

Indeed, it must not be overlooked that the special position of those concerned with the personnel function of management has not only had the consequence of exaggerating the difference between those employed in line and non-line positions, the percentage of the latter in the $S.R._1$ category being reduced from 45% to 22% when they are excluded (cf. Table 16.1) but, as noted above, that this group is also partly responsible for the very high percentage of those businessmen who participated in professional management activities in the $S.R._1$ category too. This provides yet another reason for exercising caution in interpreting the relationship between certain indices of business professionalism on the one hand and an inclination to accept statements about social responsibility on the other, in so far as the percentage of cases in the $S.R._1$ category is an indication of this. However, the fact remains that the more formal statistical analysis conducted in this chapter does show that those businessmen who participated are more likely to fall into the $S.R._1$ category than others. And this gives rise to question (*b*).

Of course, one reason for this might be that some businessmen really are proselytized to a socially responsible type of philosophy by idealistic teachers of management and management writers. In fact, there is some evidence that British management teachers do consider managerial responsibility an important matter.[1] But in our view it is most unlikely that Northern City businessmen had been 'converted' in this way. Despite this, however, we believe that a consideration of those functions

---

[1] cf. J. Child, *British Management Thought and Education*, Ph.D. thesis, Cambridge, 1967, p. 491: but see the quite different implications of an American study, E. H. Schein, 'Attitude Change During Management Education', *Administrative Science Quarterly*, March, 1967, p. 611, tables 1 and 2.

served by professional management activities, over and above the dissemination of technical skills, can provide some clues to the general relationship between the S.R.$_1$ ideological preferences and reported interaction in (or at least a minimal acquaintance with) professional management circles.

One such function is almost certainly that professional management activities provide an opportunity for businessmen to solicit prestige at a local (cross-company), regional, or national level. Some circumstantial evidence for this assertion was provided by those local and regional meetings and conferences which we attended in and around Northern City. It was, for example, particularly noticeable that there was a limited number of businessmen in the region who sat on the platform at such meetings and whose opinion was generally sought by the chairman of conferences, those reading papers, and other leaders of discussion. The comments and speeches of these people were apt to be liberally interspersed with the current clichés of management folklore—'the job of management is of course to manage'; 'management *is* leadership'; 'by "communications" I mean communications *up* as well as *down*'; 'at XYZ we're all members of the same team'; or (this being the writer's favourite) 'let us begin with the assumption that the worker is a *man*'.

In addition to this, these businessmen often made statements like 'now, I believe that we have three (or four, or more) responsibilities', or, 'there are three partners to industry'. In short, the opinions they expressed were often conformable to those presented in the S.R. items included in the forced-choice questionnaire. This being so it is possible that for some Northern City businessmen—though by no means all, for in the interviews some of those who did not participate in such activities went out of their way to belittle the managerial ability of those who did—these prestigeful figures provided ideal role conceptions to which proximity was sought.

After all, the language of social responsibility—especially the talk of 'partners', and broadly defined 'responsibilities'—is particularly well suited to giving the impression that those who use it are able to stand above the day-to-day problems with which they are confronted, and to grasp the major relations of Industry, Labour and State. In this sense, one might argue that such formulations are often displays of role-distance and that they constitute the ideological equivalent of the tidy desk.[1] Thus, it might be that a connection exists in the minds of some businessmen between the notion of business statesmanship on the one hand and the language of social responsibility on the other. If so, the latter may be as much the manifestation of a desire for prestige as it is the token of a newly emerging morality, for, at one and the same time, the businessman who speaks of his 'social responsibilities' may seek to enhance not only his own prestige but also that of his 'profession'. Child, who arrives at an essentially similar conclusion, has also noted, on the basis of a survey of the management literature, that 'a general expression of "social responsibility" is quite willingly made, but this is relatively non-committal . . . (implying) . . . that priority ha(s) now to be given to finding better technical methods of management— to "getting on with the job".'[2]

We believe that the latter interpretation is also supported by the Northern City study. Just why we take this view will become clearer if, assuming that those businessmen who talk in terms of social responsibility must be trying to say *something*, we ask why so many of them considered our two hypothetical L.T.C.I. and S.R. frames of reference to be complementary, rather than contradictory, and if we also ask what an (albeit partial) acceptance of the latter can tell us about the businessman's own perception of the conflict situation in which he is placed, and indeed about the nature of that conflict situation itself. These matters constitute the basis of Chapter XVII. There, in contrast to the predominately short-range nature of the discussion in this chapter we intend to provide a much more general interpretation of social responsibility and, in so far as this must be linked to those notions which we associate with L.T.C.I., of contemporary business ideology.

At one level, of course, the 'explanation' of social responsibility as a business ideology is a relatively simple matter. One can, for example, readily put forward a superficially convincing argument which begins by pointing to the existence of a given structural configuration (in this case the relations of the corporation to the economic system, and of the latter to society), proceeds to adumbrate certain structurally defined strains

---

[1] cf. E. Goffman, *Encounters*, Indianapolis, 1961, pp. 105-132.
[2] *British Management Thought and Education*, pp. 227, 377-378.

(in this case those associated with the concentration and differential distribution of power, and thus a quest for legitimacy and compliance) and concludes by postulating that these strains, or structurally defined 'problems', can be seen to be 'solved' by the notion of social responsibility. However, in so far that any such argument leaves out of account the actual self-conceptions of the actors involved, relying upon the concept of 'interests' to link ideas and social structure, it must be accepted that, by itself, it is indeed a superficial one. Thus, though propositions similar to the above will be put forward in the following chapter an attempt will also be made to take some account of the meaning of their own ideas to businessmen.

It should already be apparent, then, that the discussion provided will take place on two levels. It is hoped, however, that it will illuminate for the reader the understanding of social responsibility which we gained in Northern City, complement and add credence to those points which have already been made and, not least important, suggest how, in the case of business ideology, a study of the meaning of their own ideas to businessmen may be wedded to the concepts of 'interest' and 'conflict' which have for so long been considered appropriate to the sociological analysis of ideology as such.

CHAPTER XVII

OF CONFLICT AND ORGANICISM, MATERIALISM, AND SOCIAL RESPONSIBILITY

THE sociological analysis of ideology is beset with difficulties, the study of business ideology being no exception. Thus, given that we now intend to provide a much broader interpretation of social responsibility it is imperative that we define the term business ideology a little more precisely. In doing so we will not only delimit our field of enquiry, we will also make explicit, and thus hope to avoid, certain methodological and theoretical difficulties.

Partly to limit the nature of our discussion and partly for other reasons which will become obvious as we proceed, we take the view here that business ideologies are about power and that they consist of those patterned and selective self and structural representations put forward by businessmen which pertain to its distribution. Such a view has something in common with those put forward by Bendix and Sutton *et al.* The former defined management ideologies as 'all those ideas which are espoused by or for those who exercise authority in economic enterprises, and which seek to explain and justify that authority'.[1] The latter took ideology to be 'any system of beliefs publicly expressed with the manifest purpose of influencing the sentiments and actions of others'.[2]

Despite some obvious similarities there are, however, several differences between the definition which we have proposed and those put forward by the above writers. Some of these differences are of a formal nature only. For example, we have stressed that business ideologies do not consist of just so many individual opinions but that these opinions—which we prefer to call 'self

[1] *Work and Authority*, p. 2.
[2] *The American Business Creed*, p. 2.

and structural representations'[1]—are patterned. We have also stressed that they are 'selective', which underlines the important assumption that the businessman opts for certain ideas out of what is, to all intents and purposes, an almost infinite universe of ideas available. We have gone out of our way to make these assumptions explicit because they make it quite clear why we used a forced-choice questionnaire in the case study and why we devoted some time to investigating the 'consistency' of responses to this in Chapter XIV.

There are, however, some important differences between the other two definitions cited above and that which we have proposed. One of these is closely related to certain methodological problems and it concerns the fact that these other definitions do not delimit the term business ideology to the ideology of businessmen.

In Bendix' case the problems arising from this are not acute ones because his is a comparative analysis of the inter-relationship of social class, bureaucracy and ideology in the course of industrialization and his major concern is therefore the extent to which industrialization can be seen to have certain cross-cultural ideological correlates.[2] On the other hand, however, such a definition does raise major problems for the theory advanced by Sutton and his colleagues because they attempt to explain American business ideology of the 1940's in terms of a predominately socio-psychological analysis of the role strains experienced by businessmen. As other writers[3] have already pointed out such a procedure must be suspect when, as in their case, the ideology or 'creeds' considered consist of statements not put forward exclusively by businessmen themselves.

Similar reservations must also be expressed about attempts to equate the ideology of businessmen with apparently representative historical shifts in the literature of management or to

[1] In the case of social responsibility we refer by 'self representations' to the notion that the businessman is a disinterested administrator, or arbiter: by 'structural representations' we refer to the pluralistic conception of company structure and to the notion that the goals of industrial companies are multiple ones, the company being depicted as serving the multiplicity of interest groups which give it its existence. It follows from this of course that we are concerned here with much larger issues than those which typically arise when 'social responsibility' is treated as synonymous with 'Christian stewardship'.

[2] *Work and Authority*, preface, pp. xvii-xx.

[3] D. Rogers and I. E. Berg, 'Occupation and Ideology; The Case of the Small Businessman', *Human Organisation*, Vol. 20, No. 3, p. 108.

equate the former with the opinions of major business theorists, whether they be businessmen or not. Indeed, the author of a recent work of this type in Britain has felt bound to state it was possible that what he termed 'British management thought' was 'never in fact whole-heartedly accepted by most practising managers'.[1]

Before we return to the above definitions—for we think they raise certain theoretical problems too—there is, however, one further comment which is appropriate to make here about another methodological difficulty encountered in the study of business ideology. We refer of course to the fact that even if the term business ideology is confined to the ideology of businessmen we are still confronted with the problem of deciding just what the universe of business ideology may be.

Sutton *et al.* attempted to solve this problem by collecting a very large number of statements made by businessmen, apparently claiming representativeness for these on the basis of the sheer number collected.[2] But in addition to some obvious criticisms which could be levelled at this it is questionable whether it is legitimate to assume that those businessmen who have made recorded public statements are representative of those—probably the great majority—who have not. Our own attempt to avoid this difficulty took the form of one small local study which enabled us to choose businessmen rather than allowing those who had made public statements to 'sample themselves'.

It is as a result of this that we have so far avoided references to the opinions of businessmen outside Northern City and why, in the latter parts of this section, we have tried to make references to them only in order to illustrate propositions which emerge from the case study itself. Of course, it cannot be claimed that Northern City businessmen are necessarily representative of British businessmen in general but this obviously limited local study does have the advantage of making its own limitations clear to the reader. There can be no doubt, for example, about whose ideology we are referring to. This is not true to the same extent of the study provided by

[1] A possibility which, as far as a formal knowledge of 'human relations' is concerned, is given some measure of support by the Northern City study: see J. Child, *British Management Thought*, chapter 7.
[2] *The American Business Creed*, pp. 10–11.

Sutton and his colleagues. Their heavily annotated presentation of opinions about business and labour, the businessmen and his customers, the functioning of competition, government and business, economic fluctuations and so on[1] derive—i.e. when they do stem from statements made by businessmen—from the opinions of many businessmen and this being so it places us at one remove from the way in which any given businessman defines his role and that of his corporation within society. As we shall see, this practice is partly responsible for another deficiency in their work.

However, we are not concerned here to provide a critique of *The American Business Creed* but, accepting it as a major contribution, to avoid some of the difficulties its authors encountered. In the above context, this means recognizing that their work was ill-suited to tackle the highly complex question of meaning which is a matter that all such studies of ideology must be concerned with at some level. To clarify the points we have made so far, then, we are not claiming that business ideology must always be treated as synonymous with the ideology of businessmen, only that for our present purposes we intend to define it in this way.[2] Similarly, we do not deny that it may be useful to assume that business ideology is a 'front' behind which businessmen shelter or seek to further their interests but we are suggesting that it may also represent attempts which have been made by them to define their role and that of the corporation in a meaningful way. Both these observations lead us back to the definitions with which we began.

It can be seen, for example, that Bendix' and our own reference to 'authority' and 'power' and also Bendix' and Sutton's reference to the fact that ideologies 'justify' or have the purpose of 'influencing', all imply, to some extent following Manheim,[3] that such ideas may be interpreted as maintaining or furthering the effectiveness of a given system (or the position

[1] *ibid.*, especially chapters 6–10.

[2] For instance, it is possible to regard Berle's work as representative of some aspects of modern business ideology when the term is not delimited to the ideology of businessmen themselves.

[3] We refer to Mannheim's distinction between 'ideologies, i.e. those complexes of ideas which direct activity toward the maintenance of the existing order, and utopias—or those complexes of ideas which tend to generate activities toward changes of the prevailing order'. See Wirth's preface to *Ideology and Utopia: An Introduction to the Sociology of Knowledge*, London, 1960, p. xxiii.

of those who govern it) and even that they do so in the face of latent or manifest, intra- or inter-system conflict. Consequently, since business ideologies themselves do not have a 'purpose'[1] but are espoused by those who occupy certain structurally defined positions, who may well be said to have interests, both of a strictly economic kind and in the perpetuation of a given authority structure, it is not a far step from any of the above definitions to that conceptual trilogy of power, interests and conflict which is the hallmark of the traditional approach to the study of ideology.

Sutton *et al*. would of course dissociate themselves from these inferences but, like Rogers and Berg, we find their insistent rejection of what they term 'the interest theory of ideology'[2] to be at odds with their own use of the concept of role-strain. It is in any case arguable that their tendency to explore the nature of business ideology in terms of its consistencies or otherwise as a symbol meaning system only forestalls the ultimate question—why *this* symbol meaning system? Or, as we would prefer to put it, why *these* self and structural representations? Once this point is reached, then as far as the matter of business ideology is concerned, one tends to be thrown back upon that historically ubiquitous trilogy of concepts we noted above, all of which lead one to seek explanations in terms of the pressures generated by the structure of business and society.

As Birnbaum[3] has noted, such an approach

'leaves open a number of questions to which no answers of a conclusive sort have yet been found: in particular, the question of the precise relationship and (inter-relationship) of ideas and social structure, and the vexed question of interests.'

However, provided that to make use of the notion of 'interest' does not of itself commit one to the untenable position that *all* ideas held by businessmen stem from their private economic advantage and provided that it does not reduce one to merely asserting that 'men act as they are motivated to act'—and in contrast to Sutton *et al*. we are less inclined to accept that either conclusion necessarily follows—we see no reason to reject it

---

[1] Which is not to imply that social action can be understood without accepting that ideas may be important in their own right.

[2] *The American Business Creed*, pp. 12–13 and chapter 15, especially pp. 303–304.

[3] N. Birnbaum, 'The Sociological Study of Ideology (1940–1960): A Trend Report and Bibliography', *Current Sociology*, Vol. 9, No. 2, 1960, p. 91.

altogether. Indeed, if we are prepared to make the assumption that the different 'members' of the director's role-set (e.g. employees, customers, shareholders) do have different economic interests, to further posit that as a consequence of this he finds himself in a conflict situation, then, in conjunction with a recognition of the fact that the major economic units of today are joint stock companies, this may even provide us with a useful starting point for a much more general interpretation of certain aspects of modern business ideology than we have presented so far. For example, it might lead us to put forward the following sort of argument:

1. That the 1856 legislation which facilitated the development of the joint stock companies was introduced fairly and squarely in terms of the economic philosophy of *Laisser-faire*.[1]

2. That today, what were then fondly referred to as 'these little republics' are far from little, sometimes being referred to, and not at all fondly, as 'states within states': their size alone makes it difficult for those who direct them to gain credence for the view that their own power is constrained by competition or consumer sovereignty.

3. The above, taken in conjunction with a recognition of the emergence of powerful trade unions, an enfranchized and industrially experienced workforce, full employment and increased participation by government in economic affairs might suggest that businessmen would be likely to claim that they serve the interests of customers, employees, government and so on—in short, to claim to be socially responsible. In this sense the latter may be no more than a sign of managements adjusting themselves to a changed situation and recognizing that 'their contacts with society must be wider than those merely of buying and selling.'[2]

4. The organizational problems of co-ordination and soliciting compliance are likely to have led to a recognition that 'what is required is that the social sentiments of groups be regarded, not as hurdles to surmount, but as an integral part of the objective for which the organisation is working.'[3] In this sense the ideology of 'social responsibility' might be expected to take the form of the ideology of 'human relations', writ large.

5. When seen in the above light it seems improbable that Tube Investment shareholders had any cause to worry when their

---

[1] In the words of Robert Lowe (then Vice-President of the Board of Trade) who introduced the Bill—my 'object at present is not to urge the adoption of limited liability. I am arguing in favour of human liberty—that people may be permitted to deal how and with whom they choose, without the officious interference of the state'. *Hansard's Parliamentary Debates*, CXL (1855), p. 134.

[2] Gunnar Myrdal, 'The Relation Between Social Theory and Social Policy', *British Journal of Sociology*, Vol. 4, 1953, p. 214.

[3] T. N. Whitehead, *Leadership in a Free Society*, Harvard, 1947, pp. 85-6.

chairman (Mr Stedeford) told them at the 1951 A.G.M.—'the purpose of an industrial company . . . is to produce more and better goods at relatively lower prices; to strive to provide a good and secure living for its employees and to provide a good investment with a reasonable return to those who found the money for the enterprise' —as another chairman[1] pointed out 'it is only by having in mind the facts Mr. Stedeford puts forward that there is any worth-while return on capital.'

However, as we noted at the end of Chapter XVI, though we think that certain aspects of this type of argument[2] contain more than a grain of truth it is, at best, still a highly superficial one. Furthermore some of its inadequacies partly derive from the implicit use of notions like interest and conflict. Like the concept of 'function', that of 'interest' can serve to suggest seemingly inevitable causal relationships on the basis of surprisingly little historical data—and it is partly as consequence of this that the above type of argument often begs the question of how new and indeed how widespread the ideology of social responsibility may be.

Similarly, in so far as the above type of argument leads one to consider ideology as some sort of problem solving device and consequently to think in terms of 'attack' and 'defence' it manages, though implying conflict to exist between employees and management, customers and management and so on, to avoid specifying the precise type of conflict which prevails. If this is not specified one might well be led to explain contemporary business ideology in terms of the popular assumption that business itself is presently undergoing a crisis of 'legitimacy'— this being an assumption we would consider to be at odds with the facts.

This observation leads us to draw attention to one further characteristic of the above argument. Namely, that by making some major assumptions about historical changes in the relationship of business to society and by pointing to changes in the structure of enterprise itself it manages to provide an explana-

[1] The Chairman was Mr A. F. Hurst (of the Samuel Osborn & Co. steel company) who, like several others, wrote a letter to the *Financial Times* (December 20, 1953) commenting on Mr Stedeford's statement. Fuller details of reactions to the letter are provided by Copeman in his brief consideration of social responsibility and the position of the director. See *Leaders of British Industry*, p. 44.

[2] cf. Morrel Heald, 'Management's Responsibility to Society: The Growth of an Idea', *Business History Review*, Vol. XXXI, 1957, pp. 376–384; E. F. Cheit, in E. F. Cheit (ed.), *The Business Establishment*, N.Y. and London, 1964, chapter 5.

tion of modern business ideology without citing any concrete evidence about the role conceptions and structural representations of businessmen themselves. In other words it manages to side-step what we have referred to as the 'vexed question of meaning'.

Since we have already made it clear that in our view the analysis of ideology in terms of conflict, which focuses attention upon *interests*, should not be severed from an attempt to investigate the problem of meaning, which focuses attention upon *identity*, we will accordingly attempt to use the Northern City data to shed some light upon this problem below. Having done so, we will then conclude by presenting the reader with two analytically separate summaries of our understanding of contemporary business ideology. One we will refer to as 'the argument from interests'; the other as 'the argument from identity'. But before we reach this point it is appropriate that we provide a rather fuller consideration of the implications of regarding ideology as a defensive mechanism, for if ideology is to be considered as a 'defence' this begs the question—'then what is the attack?'

One answer to this question is that 'the attack' is represented by those pleas for workers' control, nationalization, and production for social use, which are put forward by some members of the political left—but today such battle cries are rarely heard and seem most unlikely to be accepted and implemented as matters of principle by those who are effectively organized politically.[1] It may be true that by the 1920's two generations of Fabian intellectuals had turned the sacred word 'profits' into an obscenity[2]—but a later generation has sought to do just the reverse for the words 'productivity' and 'efficiency'. Today, it is against these two criteria that private industry is largely evaluated, even by Labour governments. This does not of course imply that government has completely accepted the logic of an unrestrained private enterprise economy. Indeed in many important respects it has sought to delimit the socially undesirable consequences which may flow from determined policies of profit maximization. The above

[1] The Donovan Commission was unable to produce a majority recommendation for the appointment of 'workers' directors', see *Report of the Royal Cammission on Trade Unions and Employers' Associations*, Cmmd. 3423.

[2] R. Lewis and R. Stewart, *The Boss: The Life and Times of the British Business Man*, p. 52.

point is none the less an important one because a noticeable feature of the criticism to which business is most often exposed is that it does not take the form of a sustained politico-moral critique at all.[1]

Any debate over the natural rights of property is now long dead[2] and the focus of potentially effective political opinion upon the matter of system *functioning* (as evidenced by the current concern with efficiency and productivity) rather than upon the matter of system *legitimacy* has served to obfuscate the one distinctive feature of capitalist production, namely, its private ownership. Indeed, it even makes sense to term many of the criticisms to which business is most often exposed 'endo-capitalistic' ones.

Some of these, far from being directed at the nature of capitalism itself are directed instead at the absence of what is considered to be capitalist behaviour. Thus advertising expenditure is criticized because those so long accustomed to be told that private enterprise satisfies consumer demand and that the consumer is sovereign now find difficulty in accepting that the creation of demand is not at odds with its satisfaction at the lowest possible cost. And as with consumer sovereignty, so with competition and hence in part the creation of a Monopolies Commission, the eventual abolition of resale price maintenance, and the apparent public unease about 'take-overs'. The point we are attempting to make then is not that there is *no* hostility toward business today or that business and businessmen now enjoy a high status, for both of these things are probably untrue, but that what criticism there is of business is not typically concerned with the matter of system legitimacy but with system and, perhaps more significantly, sub-system functioning. The source of public and political disquiet would appear to be predominately related to the fact that the large corporation has broken some well-established rules.

The significance of the above observations, assuming them to

---

[1] cf. M. Ivens and D. Dunstan (eds.) *The Case for Capitalism*, London 1967, which is prefaced by the statement that 'capitalism in Britain has for many years, been intellectually on the defensive'. This work, jointly produced with Aims of Industry, attempts to set matters aright. (It represents one of the very few post-war books of this genre and in keeping with our comments about right wing political theory in Chapter V, it deals very superficially in both quantitative and qualitative terms with the significance of the separation of ownership and control.)

[2] cf. R. Schlatter, *Private Property: The History of an Idea*, London, 1951.

be valid ones, is that they put us on our guard against the temptation to exaggerate any recent changes in business ideology or, having assumed that these exist, positing that a new business ideology has resulted from any thorough-going and recent 'attack'.

In fact, it is appropriate to remember at this point that the Northern City study provided no convincing evidence either for the proposition that most businessmen had a strong inclination for the language of social responsibility or for the proposition that those who made such choices from the forced-choice questionnaire did so in such a way that 'the socially responsible ideology' could be considered as an independent and internally consistent idea system. Thus, even allowing for the limitations of our case study, this does suggest that if one pursues the type of argument sketched out above (see points 1–5) there may be a real danger of providing a seemingly water-tight explanation for a phenomenon which, statistically speaking, hardly exists. In this context it is also appropriate to note that several of the allegedly distinctive characteristics of 'the new ideology of social responsibility' are by no means of recent origin.

As Parsons[1] has noted, authority has always been institutionalized in collectivity—oriented terms within the organization, and even *laisser-faire* economic philosophy was, in practice, rooted in the assumption that the employer's regard to his self-interest would further the interests of all members of society. In this sense the idea of common purpose is probably not of recent origin and to perceive earlier industrialists through the eyes of Galsworthy's mine-owner in *Strife*—'it has been said that Capital and Labour have the same interests. Cant!'— may be misleading. In fact, it is arguable that the idea of self-interest and the emergence of the notion of self-help provided an important basis upon which employers and employees could be conceived as members of the same community.[2] And there is reason to suppose that it was not a far step from this to depicting the interests of labour and capital as identical.[3] It even seems questionable whether the notion that the businessman provides

[1] *The Social System*, London, 1952, pp. 318–319.
[2] *Work and Authority*, p. 115.
[3] A claim which, in 1867, a trade unionist claimed he had to listen to 'every day of the week'. See the evidence of William Allen of the A.S.E. to a Royal Commission of that year cited in L. G. Johnson, *The Social Evolution of Industrial Britain*, Liverpool, 1959, p. 112.

a service to the rest of humanity is a new development either[1] and as early as 1835 traces of that particular structural representation which is commonly associated with social responsibility are to be found in the work of Andrew Ure who wrote—

'the object of manufactures is to modify the productions of nature into articles of necessity, convenience or luxury, by the most economical and unerring means. . . . They have also three interests to subserve, that of the operative, the master and the state, and must seek their perfection in the due development and administration of each.'[2]

We have little doubt that an intensive historical analysis would bring to light many such similarities between the 'old' and the 'new' in business ideology.[3] However the above must not be misunderstood. For example, we accept Child's[4] conclusion that the representation of management as socially responsible and claims to professional status have been put forward with greater frequency at times when management has been subject to particular pressures and we do not doubt that Quakers in industry have made an important contribution to the representation of management as socially responsible in their own right.

The point we are attempting to make here is a rather different one, namely, that the idea of 'service', of 'social responsibility', and of common purpose have probably been more or less recurrent themes in British business ideology throughout this century,[5] and that we know of no evidence to

[1] Weber, for one, thought it an 'obvious truth' that it was not. In fact his account of the 'joy and pride' felt by Benjamin Franklin is remarkably similar to much, more recent, speculation about the satisfactions of non-propertied managers. See *The Protestant Ethic*, pp. 75–76.

[2] *The Philosophy of Manufactures*, p. 56; cf. Sir (then Mr) Ivan Stedeford's statement of 1951, pp. 213-214.

[3] Consider for example Sir Benjamin Browne in 1916—'Position, influence, money and property are not given to us for our own enjoyment and profit: they are talents to be used for the glory of God and the help of our fellow men' (cited in Child, *British Management Thought*, chapter 3) and Sir William Robson Brown in 1961—'management must consider its responsibilities as those of a new Aristocracy—not of wealth and privilege, but of trust and honour, with a high degree of *noblesse oblige* . . . let us humbly remember that the position we hold in society is not a privilege but a trust'. *Management and Society*, p. 9.

[4] *British Management Thought*, especially chapter 7.

[5] Compare, for example, the Quaker employers' conference (cited by Child above) in 1917; the writings of Lee, Sheldon, and Mond in the 1920's and 1930's; the 'credo' signed by 120 businessmen in 1942; the writings of Goyder

suggest that they ever were, or are now, specifically associated
with businessmen in those companies which are often considered
to be 'management-controlled'.[1]

As a result of the above observations we now hope to have
avoided at least some of the many pitfalls to which the student
of business ideology is exposed. One of these is to treat those
aspects of business ideology with which one is concerned as if
they constituted self-contained and internally consistent idea
systems.[2] Another is to assume that they represent new or
wholly contemporary developments (or, in the case of social
responsibility, that this is a consequence of a separation of
ownership and control). Yet another is to assume that, almost
by definition, business ideologies are about system legitimacy,
that they can accordingly be explained in terms of the distinctive features of the economic system being considered—in the
case of capitalism, private ownership—which, to make what
we consider a further questionable assumption, may therefore
be assumed to be subject to radical 'attack'.

---

in the 1950's and 1960's. See, John Lee, *Management: A Study of Industrial Organisa-
tion*, London, 1921; Oliver Sheldon, *The Philosophy of Management*, London, 1923;
Sir Alfred Mond, *Industry and Politics*, London, 1927; George Goyder, *The Future
of Private Enterprise*, Oxford, 1951, and *The Responsible Company*, Oxford, 1961.
The war-time 'credo', 'A National Policy for Industry', is cited in Joan Robinson's,
Economic Philosophy, London, 1962, p. 144.

[1] For example, we find Col W. H. Whitbread, chairman of Whitbread & Co.,
stating at the company's 1961 A.G.M. that 'your board take a view here that a
company is run for at least three elements—the shareholders, the staff and the
employees—and management has to take into consideration the happiness and
prosperity of all three'. But he also stated that 'a very small group of the Whitbread
family holds well over 50% of the voting power of the Company . . . this group is
dedicated to maintain control of the Company for at least one more generation'.

[2] This point has some significance for the analytical strategy adopted by Sutton
and his colleagues because it appears that in some respects the assumptions implicit
in their use of the concept of a symbol meaning system have led them to play an
exceedingly elaborate game of their own devising. Thus, having set out by informing
us that of the 'two strands of thinking in the creed' the managerial one is "not
sufficiently different nor sufficiently complete to stand as a separate creed', they
arrive at a position where they can write, 'the managerial creed is logically weak
in providing no mechanism by which managers who fail to live up to their broad
social responsibilities will lose power', and then proceed to tell us that 'ultimately
it has to fall back on the classical arguments of competition and consumer
sovereignty'. Given the authors' acceptance that 'ideologies are constrained by
logic only to a limited degree', their abstraction of certain statements made by
businessmen (and others) into 'strands of thinking' which then become treated
as self-contained idea systems—which are only written of as such to show that they
are *not*—is singularly unfortunate. See, *The American Business Creed*, pp. 33, 34,
358, 359, 360.

We can summarize our own views on those matters as follows: (a) the idea of social responsibility is not new to British business; (b) judged by the Northern City survey it is probably not widespread either;[1] (c) nor does this study provide much support for the view that, where endorsed, statements about social responsibility constitute a self-contained or independent idea system[2]; (d) there is little evidence to support the view that the distinctive feature of the capitalist system is now subject to a sustained and effective politico-moral attack.

Of course, in going out of our way to make the above premises explicit we are not in any sense going back upon our earlier statement that the notion of conflict may provide us with a useful tool by which to come to a closer understanding of some aspects of contemporary business ideology. On the contrary, the above was intended to pave the way for a more precise consideration of the significance of conflict for the ideology of businessmen than was possible before. In particular, it draws attention to the fact that the significance of the notion of 'social responsibility' is not so much that it either serves to, or is used in order to, overcome conflict but that, in many ways, like those notions associated with the 'human relations' school of thought,[3] it presupposes its absence. Furthermore, it should now be clear that the particular type of conflict such statements preclude is that which, in macro-terms, relates to system legitimacy and, in microcosm, takes the form of what Pugh has termed 'role-legitimation conflict'.[4] Indeed, it is possible that if we borrow Pugh's term 'role activation conflict' to refer to the nature of the conflict situation which pertains between the different 'members' of the director's role-set we will not only have described that conflict itself in more precise terms but we may also be in a better position to see why some businessmen find those structural representations associated with 'social responsibility' attractive.

Pugh developed these terms in a study of the different expectations pertaining to the role of inspectors in manufacturing industry. In the present case the retention of the term

---

[1] See Chapter XIV.
[2] See the discussion of 'consistency' in Chapters XIV and XV.
[3] See A. Touraine, 'Ambiguité de la Sociologie Industrielle Américaine', *Cahiers Internationaux de Sociologie*, Vol. 12, No. 1, pp. 131–146.
[4] D. S. Pugh, 'Role Activation Conflict: A Study of Industrial Inspection', *American Sociological Review*, Vol. 31, No. 6, 1966, pp. 835–842.

'member' to refer to categories of actors in the directorial role-set is rather awkward. But the advantage of taking role as the unit of analysis is that it provides a particularly useful bridge by which to move from a consideration of conflict to a consideration of role conceptions, or, in our usage here, 'identity'. Pugh uses the term 'role activation conflict' because he is concerned to distinguish between cases where there is dispute over *which facet of the role function* should be 'activated' in a particular situation and those cases where members of the role-set challenge the very legitimacy of each other's expectations about the focal role.[1]

Now to characterize that conflict which pertains between some members of the director's role-set in the above terms (say, suppliers and shareholders) is perhaps quite unexceptional. They may have conflicting interests in directorial role performance but it seems improbable that this will take the form of questioning the legitimacy of the directorial role itself. Suppliers, one presumes, who often represent other corporations anyway, are unlikely to deny the legitimacy of directors making a profit for shareholders; and shareholders themselves, and these too are sometimes other corporations, are unlikely to deny the legitimacy of suppliers making a profit either.

But even if one considers the relations between employees (or their trade union representatives) on the one hand and shareholders (or those who represent them) on the other, the same sort of generalization may again be in order. Thus, it seems doubtful that one can assume—or hope to understand contemporary union-management relations if one does—that the formal representatives of the employee interest now consistently challenge the right of management to manage, or the right of shareholders to participate in the rewards of profit-making.

The above, to make this quite explicit, is not to deny that the different interests of employees, customers, shareholders and so on place the director in a conflict situation (though as we argued in Part II we do think that the extent of shareholder-management conflict has sometimes been exaggerated). It is

[1] *ibid.*, p. 842. The general reader should note that the term 'activate' is used in keeping with the notion that these expectations are a constituent part of the focal role. However, if he finds this sort of formulation alien to him he can, in what follows, interpret the phrase 'to activate the expectations' to mean 'to meet, or fulfil, the expectations'.

to posit that neither the legitimacy of the directorial role or of capitalism itself is in question today.

The questions at issue are not, for example, *whether* employees should be given fair wages, or shareholders a reasonable return, or customers or suppliers a fair price. They concern the priorities with which these conflicting expectations should be met and are about what *is* 'fair' and what *is* 'reasonable' at given points in time.

Now quite clearly, were the director's intra-role conflict situation not as we posit it to be and were the expectations and thus conflicts, which pertain between the different members of his role-set, to be of an all-or-nothing kind, one important strategy would be denied him. That is, he could not solicit the compliance and tolerance of those parties to his role-set, whose expectations had not been fully met, by claiming that he was attempting to fulfil his obligations ('responsibilities') to all other members as well.

On the other hand, however, given that the conflict situation in which the director is placed is one of role-activation conflict, then not only is the above type of strategy available to him but it also becomes possible—and as Pugh has observed this is possible only in cases of role activation conflict—for him to lay claim to simultaneously activate the multiple expectations of all the members of his role-set. And here perhaps we have a clue to why Northern City businessmen had difficulty in clearly distinguishing between the L.T.C.I. and S.R. frames of reference. Indeed, given some further assumptions about the way *businessmen* perceive the structure of the corporation and its relationship to society, it becomes possible to glimpse how their promise simultaneously to activate the above expectations may be expressed *either* in terms of the language of social responsibility *or* in terms of what, on the face of it, is a rather different promise—'the promise of productivity'. To understand this, however, it is imperative that we first attempt to come to a closer understanding of the businessman's perception of his own role and that of the corporation, and the assumptions which he makes about its structure.

As we have already noted, it can sometimes be highly misleading to treat many differences between the 'old' and the 'new' in business ideology as if they were anything more than shifts in emphasis. Nevertheless it must be admitted that the notion that the various parties to industry have interdependent interests is one that is particularly suited to the collective rather than individual nature of work in the modern company and that such notions are likely to be highly attractive to modern directors who spend a large part of their time co-ordinating the efforts of others. In fact, we take this notion of interdependence to be central to the thinking of the modern businessman. One Northern City interviewee even drew a diagram to explain this to us. 'Now I'm here', he said, drawing a small circle, 'and here', drawing a larger circle around it which he then trisected, 'are the shareholders, the employees and the customers—the three main partners who, together with management, make all this (i.e. the company) possible. That's why we're a "social institution"—no profits, no shareholders—no shareholders, no wages—no wages, no workers—no workers, no product—no product, no customers—and round we go again. You can't have one without the other'. This, he explained, was why he chose the S.R. item on 'purpose'.

Of course a recognition of the fact that directors and senior managers are co-ordinators provides an important explanation for the practice whereby management and labour are often depicted as members of the same 'team'. It further suggests one important reason why Northern City businessmen stressed management's need for 'leadership' qualities and social skills (see Table 11.1). Similarly, it helps to explain the emphasis they placed upon the desirability for the 'common purpose' of industry to be recognized as such. This was a common response to an open-ended question we asked—'what would you say was the greatest need of industry today?'—which was sometimes alternatively expressed in terms of a need for increased productivity or a need to return to the purpose of the war years.[1]

More than this, however, the above quotation suggests (a) that like some writers of the 'human relations' school[2] businessmen may be inclined to the view that there is 'no item

---

[1] Traces of nostalgia for the sense of common purpose in war-time are scattered through management writing about the need for workers to make the long postponed Taylorian 'mental revolution': cf. Bamforth, 'Towards a Philosophy of Management', *Times Review of Industry*, Jan., 1956; Goyder, *The Responsible Company*, p. 92; Sir Frederick Hooper's review of Sir Walter Puckey's *Management Principles* (London, 1962) in the *Sunday Times*, April 1, 1962.

[2] cf. J. Monro Fraser, *Human Relations in a Full Employed Democracy*, London, 1960, p. 333.

224   OWNERSHIP, CONTROL AND IDEOLOGY

of industrial work which cannot be shown in terms of the needs of other people' and perhaps even more significantly (*b*) that from the businessman's point of view, it may well appear that the corporation is a great collectivity to which the interests of those other 'sub-collectivities' of labour, capital, and consumption converge.

We argued in Chapter XI that the businessman's social experience within the corporation is likely to lead him to define his own role and that of the corporation in essentially economic terms and this, in conjunction with the propositions that he may be inclined not only to stress co-operation rather than conflict (because he is a co-ordinator) but to actually perceive the company as a social organism, a 'social institution' (because it appears to him that it is the focal point to which the interests of labour, capital and so on converge), leads us to suggest a rather unorthodox explanation for why he may occasionally find terms like 'service' and 'social responsibility' attractive.

We term this explanation 'unorthodox' because, unlike many critics and advocates of social responsibility in business, we are not convinced that most businessmen are beset by doubts about what to do with the resources at their command. In the case of Northern City businessmen, for example, it would be highly misleading to conclude that those who endorsed S.R. items did so because, accepting that they were men of power, they were thereby expressing a deep conviction that their economic objectives should be re-evaluated in the context of a whole number of other and disparate alternatives.

It may be, of course, that some businessmen do think in this way. Indeed, though they may reach slightly different conclusions, the notion that the businessman has great power, and therefore a definite responsibility to decide how to use it, has been central to the work of Eells,[1] in America, and Goyder, in Britain. However, most Northern City businessmen did not seem to be greatly troubled with any such sense of duty and in this sense the idea conveyed by the above quotation (which might suggest that the manager, being a 'man in the middle', was concerned with performing a delicate balancing act) is rather misleading. In fact, with the exception of the businessmen at Zed Ltd the closest that our interviewees came to accepting

[1] Richard Eells, *The Meaning of Modern Business*, N.Y., 1960, p. 65.

Goyder's general standpoint was to accept his organicist assumptions about company structure.

Most of them, we feel sure, would have shared his evident delight in discovering that the derivation of the word company is 'cum panis'—literally 'a bread-sharing organization'—and also of course his evident chagrin that is not often recognized as such.[1] Similarly, there can be little doubt that they would agree with Goyder that most workers want to remain workers—this being 'their function, their contribution to industry'—and since they were, whether formally acquainted with 'human relations' literature or not, fully aware that 'management is getting things done through people', they might even have had some sympathy for Goyder's depiction of the company as a 'social organism', 'a human association—a company of human beings'.[2] Indeed, in this context, we would suggest that the only thing our interviewees might have held against Goyder was his eloquence. But accepting that many of our interviewees shared Goyder's organicist assumptions it must be emphasized that this was as far as the similarity went because, for Goyder, the observation that industry consists of a multiplicity of contributors necessitates that they be explicitly recognized as such, both in practice and at law.

One of the implications of this, namely that service to diverse groups should be considered as a constituent part of the *objectives* of a company was, by contrast, very far removed from what most Northern City businessmen envisaged when they talked in terms of social responsibility. With the possible exception of some minor examples which they gave of socially responsible behaviour (see Chapter XV) their conceptions of social responsibility did not necessitate the introduction of policies at odds with those general objectives of growth and profitability which it is to be expected that most companies will set themselves. (See Chapter IX.)

As far as we could judge they did not consider socially responsible behaviour to be an alternative to other possible behaviours which they could adopt. Furthermore, if we may put it this way, they assumed that their companies were already in a state of 'moral equilibrium' and that the rewards accruing to

[1] *The Responsible Company*, p. 47.
[2] *The Future of Private Enterprise*, pp. 28-29, 23; cf. L. F. Urwick, *Management of Tomorrow*, London, 1933, pp. 10-11.

P

the various contributors were already fair. Everything, they agreed, could be improved upon in the sense that if everyone pulled together—especially employees and management—then even greater benefits would accrue to each and every contributor and as they pointed out, it was sometimes necessary to make accommodations to different groups because 'if you don't act responsibly to your employees you won't have any shareholders. If you don't have any shareholders well . . . '. But despite the fact that the language of social responsibility may imply that businessmen are continually preoccupied with preserving a just 'balance' between the interests of the various 'partners' we gained the distinct impression that, at least in Northern City, such moments of profound decision never arrived. Similarly, there was no suggestion in any of the interviews—again with the very definite exception of those at Zed Ltd—that these businessmen's 'definition of business responsibility (left them) at sea without a compass'.[1]

Indeed, though we made no systematic attempt to investigate this, our interviewees made it abundantly clear to us that they felt themselves to be continually buffeted by competition from home industry selling the same products, from new technologies and also by overseas competition.[2] In addition to this, they often complained of the way in which their autonomy was constricted by government and 'unreasonable' or 'irresponsible' demands from trade unions.

In short then—and we feel bound to stress this in view of some of the assumptions built into popular discussion of business social responsibility—these businessmen did not think of themselves as powerful figures who were in a position to redress some moral, social, or economic imbalance, of which, in any case, they gave no real sign that they were aware.

In fact, in a special sense, some Northern City businessmen implied that even to consider the partners to industry as disparate entities was at odds with the facts. They indulged in what, in the language of the role theory, can only be termed 'role-scrambling'. The possibility of role-substitutability has of course long been a central assumption of those who have sought

---

[1] *The American Business Creed*, p. 358.
[2] As Schumpeter put it, 'the businessman *feels* himself to be in a competitive situation even if he is alone in the field'. J. A. Schumpeter, *Capitalism, Socialism and Democracy*, London, 1943, p. 84. (My italics.)

to minimize worker-management conflict[1] and it is arguable that, today, the notion that it was 'obviously in the power of industrious, steady, skilful and frugal workmen to become capitalists'[2] has been translated into a bureaucratic setting merely by claiming that they can become managers. But the notion of role substitutability quite specifically implies movement *from* one structurally defined position *to* another and thus, if it is to make sense at all, rests on the assumption that there are differences in the distribution of rewards and authority. In contrast to this, what impressed us in Northern City was the way in which businessmen sometimes represented the position of employee, or customer, or manager, or shareholder as but one of a multiplicity of positions in the directorial role-set which any given role incumbent might occupy.

The implication of this was not that employees *could* become shareholders or managers but that, as they put it, 'as a manager I am an employee', 'some of our employees are our shareholders', 'most shareholders are really ordinary workers in another guise'. And since employees or their wives were in one instance customers too, it was even possible to point out that 'the remedy for higher prices is in the home. We're not "exploiting" anyone —most of the time it's husbands "exploiting" wives'.

It would be foolish to attach any precise significance to these statements, which were often put forward in a humorous sort of way. But they are important in so far as they provide a further gloss to the fundamental assumption that the interests of the partners to industry are indissolubly linked. Like the assumption of interdependence itself, by stressing that the manager is also an employee, the customer 'the real employer', the shareholders just ordinary people,[3] and even that all are 'members of the public', they serve—at least on an ideological level—to effectively

---

[1] See W. Baldamus, *Efficiency and Effort: An Analysis of Industrial Administration*, London, 1961, p. 7.

[2] W. R. Greg, *Mistaken Aims and Attainable Ideals of the Artisan Class* (Trubner), London, 1876, pp. 269–270. (cf. the statements of Lord Shawcross and Mr O. W. Roskill cited in Chapter X.)

[3] The impression that the shareholders are 'just ordinary people' was graphically conveyed in an AEI advertisement (reproduced in B. W. Galvin Wright, 'Projecting the Corporate Image', in *An Advertising Appraisal*, London, 1960, p. 31). This showed a mother, her child, and at her side a giant 'piggy-bank'—it bore the legend '88,000 people own AEI'. Less poetic but similar images were employed by the steel companies against nationalization, see, e.g. 'Who Controls the Steel Industry?', *B.I.S.F. Steel Review*, Oct., 1958.

unite, and in the above case 'scramble', the different interests
which flow from the differential distribution of authority and
rewards within and outside the company. In addition to this,
given that as Mond[1] put it, 'we are all employees', they allow
the businessman to emphasize that the first priority is now 'to
get on with the job'.

At this point, however, it is appropriate to compare further
the assertions and beliefs put forward in the literature of
management with those held by Northern City businessmen
because, though Mond's philosophy of business would appear
to be much more in keeping with the latter's conception of
social responsibility than Goyder's philosophy is, there is reason
to believe that, in their case, it would be misleading to accept
Mond's injunction that 'it is useless to talk about how you
are going to distribute profits unless you have made them'[2] at
its face value. Northern City businessmen would certainly find
such a view quite acceptable but as one of them put it 'in this
job tomorrow never comes—it's push, push, push and then
push harder'. And it is upon this very point, namely of what
happens 'tomorrow', that we find a further clue to why they
were apt to 'confuse' what we termed the L.T.C.I. and S.R.
frames of reference. This 'confusion' is in our own view mainly
explicable in terms of the self and structural representations
held by businessmen themselves of which the two key elements
are first, that they minimize the extent of their own power to
influence events and, secondly, that they perceive the interests
of the parties to industry as interdependent.

No doubt the above comment will be a little mysterious to the
reader and for this reason it is appropriate that we introduce
another example of the meaning of social responsibility, as
represented in the management literature, and then show how,
and use the above suppositions to explain why, this deviates
from the meaning of social responsibility to most Northern City
businessmen. Bowen's[3] rather prescriptive analysis is well suited
for this purpose, for he has written that—

'if a business is to make a profit, and thus to avoid a failure, it must
produce goods that are attractive in quality and price, and it must
produce them effectively and at low cost. These are the primary
responsibilities of being in business at all.'

[1] *Industry and Politics*, p. 62.   [2] *ibid.*, p. 38.
[3] *Social Responsibilities of the Businessman*, p. 48.

Now, up to this point, Bowen is at one with the ideas of Northern City businessmen—but he begins to move outside their frame of reference when he adds, seemingly in a quite straightforward way, 'only then is a business in a position to consider its other responsibilities to society'.

In the scheme of things perceived by most of our interviewees this additional clause was superfluous. In their view, to bring the 'partners' together was to further the social welfare and to do this successfully was to fulfil responsibilities to each of them.

Thus, whereas they believed that there was no longer room in industry for those they referred to as 'the 1926 people', to fulfil social responsibilities to employees, shareholders and so on did not imply a major redefinition of the role of business. On the contrary, when they claimed to do this they were doing little more than expressing the belief that the profit making process is itself a beneficent one. This point is perhaps best illustrated by the comments of a senior production manager at Aye Ltd who chose the S.R. item on 'purpose' in the forced-choice questionnaire. He told us that he had heard Goyder speak and we therefore asked him how his own conception of social responsibility squared with Goyder's. He replied—

'Well, let me put it this way. I've always said that there are three main partners in a company—the shareholders, the customers and the employees—that's what Goyder says, doesn't he? Well, that's good sense. But he's not sitting *here*. This isn't Pall Mall . . . (derogatory comments about Goyder's "time wasting" activities) . . . there's no room for the costs-plus-profit mentality now and what's wanted is not to put employees on the board—the only thing that would come of that is chaos—but a realization that we must all pull together. Industry's about making money—adding to the total sum of wealth if you like—and if we do that, we're doing our job. And when we do that everything else follows. The share-holders do well, the workers get good wages and the customer gets a good deal. Everybody benefits. Now that's real "social responsi-bility" for you. It's not easy but it is possible . . . but to put workers on the board that's just silly talk—it doesn't help *me*, it doesn't help *you* and it certainly doesn't help *them*.'

The above quite clearly expresses two points we have been at pains to stress so far. It begins with a recognition that industry is a partnership and, stripped of non-essentials, concludes with an affirmation that if the company prospers 'everybody benefits'. In short, it shows the way in which certain organicist assumptions about industrial structure are wedded to a predominately materialistic justification for corporate power.

There is, it should be noted, no suggestion that specific policies should be introduced in order to serve the interests of particular groups (i.e. to 'fulfil responsibilities' to them)— and Goyder's notion that the partners should be formally represented as such is 'just silly talk'. Furthermore, and once again this is at odds with what is conveyed to the layman by the language of social responsibility, there is no suggestion in the above quotation that this businessman was considering (or ever had deliberated) which of the many competing interest groups which constitute the company should be given priority. This observation is an important one because it holds true for nearly all the businessmen we interviewed, again except for those at Zed, and irrespective of whether they talked in terms of social responsibility, or chose item B2 on the forced-choice questionnaire, or not. It emerges even more clearly in the following extract from the interview we had with 'Mr Smith', the managing director of a family firm.

Mr Smith referred several times to his company's 'social responsibilities' and we asked him just what this implied in practice.

Q. 'I don't quite follow what you mean by this. I can see that you have these responsibilities but how do you implement them— how, for example, do you decide what to do with the profits? How do you divide them up?

A. 'What a fascinating question. But you see, one doesn't think like that. Taking the long view one does hope that the staff and workpeople will receive better salaries and wages and even better working conditions, that . . . (our products will be further developed) . . . that we will continue to look after our shareholders. One wants to do all these things. But it's what Follet called the "law of the situation" you see (sic), there's always something in the way—new plant, advertising budgets, that sort of thing—so one doesn't get the time to ask oneself this kind of philosophical question . . . (it's "really a matter for politicians" anyway) . . . I suppose the answer is that one is simply too pre-occupied with making a bigger and better "cake" to think who's going to eat each "slice"—and of course if people don't like the taste of their bit they soon let you know, this thing (the phone) sees to that. You see, the fundamental problem isn't to decide how to divide the "cake" up—it's to have the skill that's needed to make the cake at all.'

Now to the extent that most of the above discussion has been guided by our foreknowledge of businessmen making just these kinds of statements it clearly cannot be maintained that the above quotations can confirm the validity of the general stand-point we have adopted. Nonetheless, such statements are not without their significance.

First, they suggest that it may be exceedingly difficult to understand the businessman's frame of reference—and thus to interpret his ideology—without accepting that he is likely to see the purpose of his organization in essentially economic terms. Secondly, they suggest how these same materialistic values, when allied to the businessman's organicist assumptions about the structure of the corporation, make it possible for him to talk in terms of 'social responsibility' without thereby implying that he has, or will, radically re-define the goals of the corporation itself—and without implying that he has, or will, take specific steps to further the (apparently) conflicting interests of diverse groups. Little is to be gained of course—assuming the above points to hold true—by asserting that it is therefore obvious that Northern City businessmen were not *really* socially responsible, or that, in some simple sense, they were not moral either. Indeed, neither of these propositions concern us here.

On the other hand, what does concern us is that the con-ception of social responsibility held by most Northern City businessmen was some distance removed from that advocated or implied in much of the management literature (cf. Berle and Goyder). The key points would seem to be that, as far as Northern City businessmen were concerned, one did not make a profit and then search one's conscience to decide how to apportion the proceeds because (*a*) one did not have (or believe oneself to have) this degree of autonomy and (*b*) because the process of profit acquisition was a continuous one. In short, 'one doesn't think like that'. Furthermore, not only did they not think like that but they did not need to think in these terms to proclaim themselves 'socially responsible'. For them, given that the corporation was a system of interdependent parts then, if it prospered, 'everything else follow(ed)'. And the reverse held true too, which is why we must 'all pull together'—for the company represents the interests of all partners.

It should be noted that the above sort of reasoning does not entirely preclude the businessmen perceiving there to be some conflict of interest between the various members of his role-set and particularly between workers and management. In fact, it is arguable that the stress on co-operation and common purpose rests on an implicit acceptance of this. What on the other hand is precluded is a recognition that those conflicts which do exist are of anything more than a minor or transitional nature.[1]

It should further be noted that the proposition that workers, customers, shareholders and so on have interests in common is, at a particular level, borne out by fact. At given points in time the interests of all these groups, the local community, and many other 'publics', are intimately related to the prosperity of the company. But so, in the same way, would their short-run economic interests be tied to the existence of any economic unit in the sense that were it to cease functioning they would receive no wages, no product and so on. In this sense, then, the above propositions and selective representations do not merit being termed 'ideological' rather than scientific because they are 'not true', but because they are not true inevitably— and because those who put them forward imply that they are.

They divert attention from the possibility that other economic arrangements might serve the above and other interests more or less advantageously and by celebrating the economic excellence of the corporation as a wealth producing agency, they divert attention both from the social needs which any given corporation may or may not serve,[2] and the differential distribution of authority which pertains within it.

It is possible of course that one could seek to explain the statements which businessmen sometimes make about their social responsibilities, their representation of the company as an organic whole, and their stress upon material values, in terms of the observation that, were all these assumptions to be generally and completely accepted, it would be highly con-venient for businessmen themselves. But this is not the point which we have been attempting to make in the latter part of

[1] cf. Child, *British Management Thought and Education*, Ph.D. thesis, Cambridge, 1967, pp. 432, 442.
[2] Businessmen can represent their goals as multiple ones (e.g. as pursuing the welfare of shareholders, customers and employees) whether they produce baby powder or beer: cf. Col Whitbread, p. 219, note 1 and the Johnson and Johnson credo reproduced as Fig. 1, p. 161.

this chapter. What we have been attempting to suggest is that most of these assumptions and values may be seen to arise from the businessman's own work experience, the exigencies imposed upon him by his role within the corporation, and the structurally defined standpoint from which he perceives the corporation itself.

In short, we would suggest that once one thinks in terms of the businessman not as the great arbiter and conscience bearer of our times, but as the great co-ordinator and 'facilitator'; once one thinks in terms of the corporation not as a generator of conflicting interests but as a social organism, the focal point to which diverse interests converge; and once one recognizes that its purpose is not to balance delicately the social welfare but to pursue it by means of economic growth and the multi-plication of wealth, then, at this point, one comes to a much closer understanding of the businessman's own frame of refer-ence. And if it be further accepted that businessmen are most unlikely to consider themselves unethical anyway, or to face moral dilemmas of the sort which, in the case of John Brown, led to the conclusion that 'you oughtn't to be born', then, we would argue, the above discussion may have gone some way to further our understanding of why the businessmen we inter-viewed were prone to confuse the two hypothetically different L.T.C.I. and S.R. frames of reference with which we confronted them.

Such 'confusion' is consistent with the way in which we posit the businessman to perceive the corporation (as a collectivity to which the interests of society converge), the way he perceives his own role (that of co-ordinating these interests) and the way in which he sees the purpose of the corporation itself (to create wealth). In addition to this, such 'confusion' is in keeping with what we posit to be those exigencies which derive from his intra-role conflict situation. These, in the main, take the form of differing economic expectations and do not derive from any fundamental challenge to the directorial role or system legitimacy. And in so far as that government now evaluates the given economic system and its sub-systems in terms of their effectiveness, assessed in terms of profitability and growth,[1] the above confusion—which as we have attempted to show may

[1] For a cogently argued polemic about the extent to which these criteria have been accepted in modern political and economic thought, see E. J. Mishan, *The Costs of Economic Growth*, London, 1967.

not be a 'confusion' at all—leads to the expression of claims which are consistent with these more broadly based expectations too.

Of course the above discussion has neglected many important aspects of modern business ideology. We have not, for example, specifically investigated the role which businessmen attribute to competition, nor have we provided a separate discussion of management-employee relationships. But this has been inevitable in a work of this length in which, in any case, the prime reason for providing a consideration of the ideology of businessmen was to shed some further light upon the plausibility or otherwise of what we have termed sectional and non-sectional managerial theories and the earlier discussion we provided in Part II (especially Chapters XI, XII and XIII). It is a further characteristic of the above discussion that we have largely ignored the possibility that some part of what is often taken to be modern business ideology may be the result of conscious fabrication. Indeed, the particular 'pincer movement' which we have attempted to perform has left little room for such a possibility because having begun with a consideration of the director's intra-role conflict situation, and thus having attempted to draw attention to those 'problems' which business ideology might be expected to 'solve', we have attempted to proceed by suggesting that these 'problems' can be 'solved' in terms of the self and structural representations held by businessmen which, at least in part, appear to derive from their own perception of industrial structure.

However, it must be recognized that even the ideological function of management has been hived off into specialist departments in some large corporations: it could even be that some public relations men are presented with briefs like this—

'It must be our objective to acquaint all sections of the Public with which the company is concerned—employees, stockholders, distributors and agents, customers, bankers, trade union leaders, local community residents and leading citizens, suppliers, Government and general public—with the facts that:

1. To the best of our ability, we discharge our responsibilities to our stockholders by conducting our company profitably.

2. We try to provide for the welfare of our employees by following progressive policies which provide good working conditions and economic security.

3. We endeavour to serve our customers by providing good products at a fair price and ensuring that these products represent

the best in modern technical research, manufacturing skill and study of the customer's needs.

4. We are a forward-looking, public-spirited company, contributing our full share to the social and economic welfare of our country.'[1]

If public relations men are presented with this type of brief one can of course see one glaringly obvious way for them to meet it: nothing could be simpler than to produce a credo which ran—'we believe we have a responsibility to our shareholders, to our employees, to our customers, and to the nation'.

But this sort of 'explanation' is hardly an explanation at all because it begs the question of why public relations men should be presented with such a brief in the first place. Furthermore, it is at odds with the facts because most British companies have not produced such credos, were for some time reluctant to recognize public relations as an essential part of management,[2] and where they have drawn public attention to themselves, as opposed to their products, have been inclined to do so by means of glossy advertisements which celebrate their technical excellence and economic achievement.

On the whole, then, we are sceptical of any attempt to explain the (apparently) radical redefinition of the role of business contained in some statements about 'social responsibility' in terms of a conscious fabrication on the part of a new profession of business ideologists. In fact there must be some doubt about how seriously businessmen take public relations[3] and though we do not question that some companies have better images than others, and that to have a good image may be economically useful,[4]

[1] ICI's publicity controller Galvin Wright provided the above brief (for an imaginary company) in order 'to give some idea of the kind of work involved in carrying out Public Relations, or projecting the corporate image'. See his 'Projecting the Corporate Image', *An Advertising Appraisal*, pp. 28–29.

[2] See the contribution by Lex Hornsby, founder member of the Institute of Public Relations, in *A Guide to the Practice of Public Relations*, prepared by the I.P.R., London, 1958, p. 15.

[3] Item 1 in group D of the forced-choice questionnaire (see Appendix III) vas adapted from B. W. Galvin Wright, 'Projecting the Corporate Image', p. 29: it did not, as we have seen, meet with much approval from Northern City businessmen (see Table 15.2, p. 179).

[4] cf. B. W. Galvin Wright, 'Projecting the Corporate Image', p. 36; Lee H. Bristol, 'Why Develop Your Corporate Image?', in Lee H. Bristol (ed.), *Developing the Corporate Image*, N.Y., 1960, pp. xiii–xiv; A. Lentz and H. Tschirgi, 'The Ethical Content of Annual Reports', *The Journal of Business*, Vol. XXXVI, No. 4, Oct., 1963, pp. 387–393; P. Lesley, 'The "Corporate Image" and the Future Leaders of Business', *Public Opinion Quarterly*, Vol. XXIII, No. 4, 1959, pp. 547–553.

as well as self-satisfying, it seems unlikely, at a time when senior businessmen can often speak to Ministers directly and when, given our interpretation, business is not under 'attack', that public relations men need to do much more than attempt to create a rather diffuse and favourable background image. And this would appear to be just what most of them do.

However, any further discussion of public relations would lead us away from our subject matter. Our intention was not to provide a comprehensive analysis of contemporary business ideology but to discuss those self and structural representations of businessmen which relate to the goals and purposes of industrial companies and to suggest how these may be related to the businessman's values and his perception of industrial structure. This has led us to put forward what, for lack of a better term, we referred to as an argument from identity and we have attempted to complement this with a consideration of the nature of businessman's intra-role conflict situation: the latter having led us to put forward what, again for lack of a better term, we referred to as an argument from interests. Our reasons for proceeding in this way should already be clear to the reader but simply because we have attempted to operate on two analytically separate levels it may be useful to conclude with a short re-statement of the possible implications of these two approaches to our subject.

The Argument from 'Interests'

(i) The introduction of the joint stock company form facilitated the collectivization of private capital and with this a concentration of economic power in the hands of those who govern the large corporations.

(ii) Born of a *laisser-faire* philosophy of the role of business, the large corporation, which is now the central feature of contemporary capitalism, has itself transformed, or at least appeared to vitiate, the principles upon which an earlier capitalist economy was built.

(iii) Consequently—but not of course inevitably—what hostility there is to business today is largely directed not at capitalism *per se* but at the large corporation which appears to have broken some well established rules.

(iv) Possibly, however, it would be more accurate to describe the above as public unease rather than hostility because its focal point is not so much the matter of system legitimacy as the matter of system functioning.

(v) At sub-system level (i.e. at the level of the corporation itself) the same point would seem to hold true because though there is a conflict of interests which, at the most obvious level, takes the form of an economic conflict about how the 'cake' is to be divided up, this is primarily a conflict about directorial role activation, not role or system legitimacy.

(vi) Given that the intra-role conflict situation in which the director is placed is one of role activation conflict, one 'ideological strategy', or attempted form of conflict resolution, is open to him which is not so readily available in cases of role legitimacy conflict. That is, he may lay claim to simultaneously activate the expectations of all parties to his role-set.

(vii) This, in theory, is what those businessmen who talk in terms of their diverse social responsibilities are doing.

(viii) In doing so, they are not only affirming that the 'partners' to industry have interdependent interests and that no radical conflict pertains between them—this being a structural representation which can only make sense to 'sender' and 'recipient' alike if that conflict which exists does not take the form of legitimacy conflict (see vi)—they are also able to depict the corporation itself (see iii) in a particularly beneficent light.

However, taken by itself, the above argument is inadequate. Its greatest value is that it guards us against attempting to explain the content of business ideology in terms of a response to a denial of business legitimacy. But at the most, it can do little more than suggest that some 'fit' can be found between 'social responsibility', 'service', and allied notions, on the one hand, and certain structurally and ideologically generated strains which are associated with the corporation on the other (see (iii) and (iv)).

To regard the above as an 'explanation' would be quite unsatisfactory because, like those arguments which hold that a socially responsible ideology has resulted from the emergence of a non-propertied managerial stratum, it is couched in such general terms that it manages to make no reference to the actual expectations, perceptions and normative orientations of businessmen. This being so, the above type of argument is always exposed to the very real danger of providing explanations for ideologies which may not, in fact, exist.

Thus, since we believe that ideologies cannot be assumed to be conscious fabrications and since they are not inevitably constrained by logic, it is necessary in order to gain a fuller understanding of their significance that we attempt to grasp the frames of reference and selective perceptions of those who give them their existence. This follows because even though ideologies may not always be understandable in terms of some universal logic (meaning) it seems improbable that they have no logic (or are meaningless) for those who adhere to them. Hence of course the necessity for what we have called the argument from 'identity'.

The Argument from 'Identity'

(i) The businessman is likely to define his own role and that of the corporation in essentially economic terms (see Chapter XI).

(ii) However, whether propertied or not, those businessmen involved in active management are largely concerned with co-ordinating the efforts of others and this, in conjunction with (i) above, is likely to have two important implications for those self · and structural representations which constitute part of the business-man's ideology.

(iii) On the one hand, whilst retaining an essentially materialistic justification of corporate power (see (i) above) his managerial experience (deriving from (ii) above) is likely to lead him to conclude that the furtherance of economic prosperity is dependent upon soliciting the co-operation of diverse groups—hence 'human relations', and what we termed the 'L.T.C.I.' variant of business ideology.

(iv) On the other hand, because the businessman does stand at the apex of the organization and because he is concerned with co-ordination, being the manager of a collectivity, he may be likely to perceive the corporation as an organic whole to which the interests of the various 'partners' converge—hence the occasional acceptance of those structural representations ('there are three partners to industry . . .') and those self-representations (particularly that which depicts the businessman as a servant to diverse interests) which are commonly associated with what we termed the 'S.R.' variant of business ideology.

(v) The language of social responsibility, and in particular the affirmation that management has 'responsibilities' to diverse (and competing) groups, might suggest that businessmen deliberately act in such a way as to continuously re-apportion the economic and social costs and benefits accruing to each and every one of them. In fact, however, we know of no evidence to suggest that businessmen typically sit down and decide that shareholders, employees, customers and so on should benefit $\pm x, y,$ or $z\%$, and the number of boards of directors who formally draw up social audits must be very small indeed.

(vi) Modern directors do not in any case generally merit being termed 'professionals' or 'technocrats' (see Chapters VII and VIII) and though they clearly do not generally merit being termed 'capital-ists' either (see Chapter VI) their social experience, pre- and intra-corporate socialization, and not least the survival and growth needs of their companies make it improbable that they will be hostile to the shareholder interest (see Chapters IX and VI, X, XI, XII, XIII *passim*). In this sense, then, one must question whether they can, in practice, be termed neutral or disinterested in the way that the language of social responsibility implies that they are. However, an attempt to investigate what businessmen mean by social responsibility suggests that this assumption may not be necessary anyway.

(vii) On the contrary, it suggests that the language of social responsibility constitutes a rather grandiose and potentially prestige-ful expression of the following beliefs—all of which may arise from the businessman's own experience within the corporation and his own perception of organizational structure and purpose. These are, the belief that economic prosperity, the furtherance of which is a common endeavour, is a good in itself; that the businessman's role is to pursue it; and, given the assumption that the company is essentially a co-operative organization, that by facilitating the achievement of organizational goals the businessman himself is furthering the interests of all the partners who give the company its existence.

(viii) In short, though a formal analysis of 'the socially responsible ideology' must of necessity begin with the assumption that the businessman is separately considering the merits and needs of each of a multiplicity of interest groups such an assumption may lie outside the businessman's own frame of reference. For him, to paraphrase, the corporation is the great provider, the manager, the great co-ordinator, all partners to industry are contributors and—given their interdependence—all are beneficiaries too.

(ix) Given the above interpretation one would not expect businessmen themselves to be able to readily distinguish between what we termed the L.T.C.I. and S.R. frames of reference because the two sets of factors outlined in (iii) and (iv) above are not mutually exclusive ones. Our case study suggests that this is in fact the case: there being but a short 'distance' between these two frames of reference (see Chapter XIV) and a marked tendency for businessmen to explain their preference for one in terms of these notions formally expressed in the other (see Chapter XV).

(x) Thus, whereas it cannot be maintained that the language of social responsibility is meaningless, it does appear to be the case that its meaning *for businessmen* is not radically different from that expressed in terms of that ideological variant we termed L.T.C.I.

To the extent that the above discussion was concerned with the meaning of their own ideas to businessmen it has, when taken in conjunction with Chapters XIV and XV a particular significance for the distributions of ideological preference reported in the tables in Chapter XVI. It suggests that though businessmen with different characteristics may have been more or less likely to fall into the $L.T.C.I._1$ or $S.R._1$ categories it is improbable that these differences can be taken as firm predictors of behaviour, and it underlines our earlier comment that those differences in ideological preference which have the highest validity are those which relate to whether interviewees fell into the L.F.$_1$ category or not. When the data in Chapter XVI is re-evaluated with this in mind evidence is forthcoming to confirm the general expectations of most students of modern business who—whether they be 'sectional' or 'non-sectional' managerialists, or 'Marxists'—are in broad agreement that younger businessmen, and those more in touch with quasi-professional activities, will be less inclined to accept that their companies' objectives can be pursued irrespective of their social and economic consequences for the morrow.

Of course, even this conclusion may require some qualification because the general expectation, at least of managerial theorists, that social origin and graduate status are related to such differences was not borne out by our case study and we take it to be self-evident that all the differences reported in Chapter XVI need to be confirmed by more studies of this type before any definitive generalizations can be made about the ideological correlates of the businessman's pre-corporate and intra-corporate social experience and other non-work affiliations. This, however, brings us to a related point because in the present chapter we have attempted to write about Northern City businessmen in general. It should be noted, therefore, that with the definite exception of the interviewees at Zed, and the possible exception of those in personnel, we think this practice has been a legitimate one.

The interviewees at Zed Ltd expressed anxiety about alienating work from non-work. They depicted themselves as men who were in a moral dilemma. They readily distinguished between those courses of action which they regarded as socially responsible and others which, though they might further the long-term interests of the company, were not. In short, they were beset by just the sort of self-questioning which, given what we take to be the key assumptions of non-sectional theory, one would expect to characterize all businessmen who talked about social responsibility—and for us, the seminal fact is that most businessmen who talked about social responsibility were not.

As we attempted to argue in Part II, and as we have also argued in this chapter, where we attempted to convey to the

reader our own understanding of the businessman's conception
of his own role and that of his company, we think that there
are some theoretical grounds for supposing that this would be
the case. And in so far that the argument we have advanced
holds true not only for Northern City in 1962 but also today,
and more generally, one is led to conclude that our case study
has done more to call into question than to confirm some of the
key tenets of what we have termed 'non-sectional' theories.

At this point, however, and by way of conclusion to Part III,
it is appropriate that we enter two disclaimers.

First, we have no quarrel with Halmos' contention that
'the new habits of tact and consideration substantially reform
the standard of our human relationships'[1]—but we rather doubt
whether it is necessary to posit 'a managerial role change and a
change in leadership ethics' to explain this.[2] Much the same
could be said of 'human relations' policies, irrespective of the
ethics of those who institute them, and as we saw in Chapter XV
the examples which businessmen provided of implementing their
social responsibilities did not imply any radical re-definition of
the goals of industrial companies.

Secondly, and again it is appropriate to refer to Halmos'
work, if only because he is one of the few British sociologists to
enquire into the social responsibilities of business at all, and
because he does to some extent appear to take the talk about
them seriously, we have no quarrel with the proposition that
'if men define situations as real they are real in their
consequences'.[3]

On the contrary, we have taken Thomas' famous dictum
very much to heart because it follows from this that there is
always the danger 'the researcher may unintentionally "define
into reality" that which he seeks without knowledge of his own
involvement in the creation of the product'.[4] For us, this
observation has one severely practical implication. Namely,
that if when men define situations as real they are real in their
consequences, one must attempt to establish just what situations
they are defining as real. Otherwise one's own expectations of

[1] *The Personal Service Society*, p. 28.
[2] cf. Raymond Aron, *The Industrial Society: Three Essays on Ideology and Development*, London, 1967, pp. 117-118.
[3] *The Personal Service Society*, p. 21.
[4] S. T. Bruyn, *The Human Perspective in Sociology: The Methodology of Participant Observation*, N.J., 1966, p. 273.

Q

242 OWNERSHIP, CONTROL AND IDEOLOGY

the consequences of these situations run the danger of being unreal.

It is as a result of this very elementary precaution that we have concerned ourselves with what we referred to as the vexed question of meaning and it is as a consequence of addressing ourselves to this that we have come to be sceptical of Halmos' contention[1] that the 'idealistic definition of the situation materially and substantially changes the situation'. This, we feel bound to point out, holds true only when the definition of the actors concerned is, in fact, an idealistic one. It should be noted, then, that if Northern City businessmen were being idealistic when they talked about their social responsibilities, we find it difficult to interpret the idealism so expressed as anything radically different to a celebration of their companies' own beneficence, this being a beneficence which stemmed directly from their own due regard to the interests of the company itself.

Of course, in a work of this kind which was largely concerned with the clarification and where thought desirable, the re-definition of questions at issue, it is not appropriate to draw up a list of hard-and-fast conclusions. Indeed in many important respects we have felt bound to emphasize that no hard-and-fast conclusions are justified. The question—'are the managers a new class?'—is, for example, one to which no definitive answer can yet be given and our own answer, that in many ways this seems improbable, rests on a similar paucity of data to those answers provided by writers who take the opposite view. Some other questions, for which there is some limited data upon which to provide an answer, for example, those pertaining to the extent to which 'the managers' (i.e. directors and senior managers) are technocrats or professionals, produce answers at some remove from conventional assumptions. Yet other questions, like those concerned with the significance of directorial share-ownership, can even be answered on several analytically separate levels depending upon whether one thinks of such share-ownership as a specific input to the decision-making process, whether one is concerned with its significance for the director's rather general identification or otherwise with shareholders and their interests, as opposed to his identification with employees, customers and so on, or whether one is

[1] *The Personal Service Society*, p. 21.

concerned with the possible implications of this for his class membership.

Our own view upon these and allied matters were put forward in Part II and little is to be gained by repeating them here. What on the other hand does merit mentioning at this point is the possible significance of Part III for recent developments in the economic theory of the firm, because our own observations do seem to suggest that the theories of writers like Marris and Williamson have not been invalidated by their failure to take account of social service objectives. Indeed, though we attempted in Part II to provide the beginnings of a sociological analysis of the probable frames of reference and normative orientations of modern directors this too would seem to complement, rather than contradict, the major conclusions arrived at by Marris.

Furthermore, we think it possible that when allied to the sorts of propositions we advanced in Chapters IX–XIII, 'sectional' micro-economic theories can provide an important meeting point for both sociologists and economists, and that once sociologists and economists do work together on the theory of the firm—which after all should be as much the concern of the former as shop floor behaviour—many of the divisions which separate the 'Marxist' and 'managerialist' schools of thought will be seen as stimuli rather than barriers to the furtherance of our knowledge. At the present time this is not the case because, as we pointed out in Chapter V, those who represent these schools of thought not only arrive at different answers but they are almost bound to do so, for they begin by asking different questions.

We hope that it may have been of value to point this out, first, because little can come of a controversy in which the two participants talk past each other, secondly, because, as we have implied throughout, we think an important basis for progress in this field lies with empirically based sociological analyses of directorial values which will attempt to wed the sectional managerialist theories of writers like Marris to the traditional subject matter of the Marxist school. The starting point for such analyses would lie outside the boardroom and this being so they would begin with an explicit recognition of the socio-cultural differences which pertain between industrialized societies.

These are matters which, at present, lie outside the main stream of managerial theory because just as the lack of empirical investigation into the businessman's frame of reference has been facilitated by a whole number of assertions about his motivation, which themselves often lack any empirical basis, so too has the assumption that the separation of ownership and control has predictable consequences for class structure and company policy been facilitated by the absence of any real attempt to consider the historical and cultural context from which the non-propertied directors of different industrialized societies have emerged.

It is true, of course, that a recent comparative study by Haire and his colleagues[1] has pointed to important similarities in the thinking of British and American (top and middle-level) managers—and even suggested that such thinking characterizes managers in most of the 14 countries they studied. However, it seems possible that Haire's British sample over-represented those managers who are generally termed 'progressive' (a term which, in British management, is often used to refer to acquaintance with, or acceptance of, American techniques and styles of thinking). In addition, that study was mainly concerned with the motivation and in-plant attitudes of management. Consequently, there was little or no investigation of those cross-cultural differences which might relate to the role managers see themselves and their corporations playing, or which they believe they ought to play, within society, the extent to which they feel obligated to the corporation outside the work situation, their perception of class structure, professional self-identification, attitudes toward the rights and functions of government, shareholders, trade unions, and so on.

It is in just such matters as these that one might expect to find evidence of cultural diversity. It is, of course, for this reason that we have avoided the assumption that, in future, a technocratic-meritocratic managerial elite will necessarily emerge whose members have common characteristics in all highly industrialized societies. For example, Humblet[2] has suggested that British technical managers are less likely to

---

[1] M. Haire, E. E. Ghiselli and L. W. Porter, *Managerial Thinking: An International Study*, N.Y. and London, 1966.

[2] J. E. Humblet, *Les Cadres d'Entreprise: France, Belgique, Royaume Uni*, Paris, 1966.

identify themselves as a technocratic elite than those in France. Factors such as this may tell us as much, if not more, about the behaviour and values of modern British management than can be inferred from the fact that there may be proportionately fewer qualified directors in Britain than in other countries,[1] or from the fact that, today, the typical British giant corporation is not actively managed by giant capitalists.

It was not of course our purpose here to provide a full analysis of the type suggested above, for that would require much more information and time than we have at our disposal. However, we do hope to have shown the way in which it could begin, to have questioned some commonly held assumptions about the ideological and, by implication, behavioural correlates of the often proclaimed shift toward meritocracy and technocracy in business, and to have shown not only that many questions have not yet been answered but that some do not seem to have been asked. If we have succeeded in doing this we have done what we set out to do and simply because this was our purpose the most fitting conclusion to this work is to indicate what is required if further progress is to be made. Accordingly, we present below a dozen areas which would repay much fuller investigation.

In each case—and the following list is by no means exhaustive—our present knowledge is severely limited and whereas their investigation would not of itself present us with a new theory, for as we have argued certain assumptions may need re-examining too, such studies would in our view bring us much closer to an understanding of the values and behaviour of the modern British business elite than is possible at the present time. Broadly based historical predictions and pre-scriptive evaluation cannot and should not provide a substitute for this, nor indeed can logically derived sociological theories which, as at present they must, rest on a similar paucity of empirical data.

[1] For other European businessmen see N. Delefortrie-Soubeyroux, *Les Dirigeants de l'Industrie Française*, Paris, 1961; *Les Dirigeants de l'Entreprise de l'Economie Belge*, University of Louvaine, Brussels, 1960; D. Granick, 'Functional Divisions of Company Management: A Reflection of National Styles', *Journal of Industrial Economics*, 1962, pp. 100–117, *The European Executive*, N.Y., 1962; H. Hartmann, *Authority and Organisation in German Management*, Princetown, 1959; D. S. Landes 'French Business and the Businessman: A Socio-Cultural Analysis', in E. M. Earle (ed.), *Modern France: Problems of the Third and Fourth Republics*, Princetown, 1951.

The Need for Empirical Studies—A Dozen Examples

1. Multi-disciplinary and systematic studies of policy formation in business[1] (see especially Chapters VI, IX and XIII).

2. Studies of shareholder expectations and the perception of these by businessmen (VI, IX, XIII).

3. Studies of the sources of directorial and managerial satisfaction and the relation of these to specific company policies (VI, IX, XIII).

4. Comparative studies of the frames of reference and objectives of businessmen in large private, joint stock, and nationalized companies (VI, IX, XIII).

5. Historical studies of changes in business recruitment[2] (X, XII).

6. Longitudinal studies of the careers of businessmen and studies of factors related to the choice of business as a career, including the role expectations of potential managers, and the selection and promotion procedures of large corporations (X, XI, XIII).

7. Studies of the behavioural and attitudinal correlates of professional training and the occupancy of different management positions (VII, VIII, XVI).

8. Studies in depth of the value orientations and attitudes of prominent businessmen (XIV, XV, XVI, XVII).

9. Studies of the non-work activities, affiliations, and social life of businessmen (VI, IX, XII, XIII).

10. Replications of the Northern City study in different areas, at different authority levels, and using more sophisticated techniques (XIV, XV, XVI, XVII).

11. Studies of the public's attitudes to, and evaluation of, private business and businessmen[3] (XVII).

12. Further studies of the attitudes of trade union leaders to management/shareholder-employee conflict (IX, XVII).

---

[1] cf. the detailed study of R. M. Cyert, H. A. Simon and D. B. Trow, 'Observation of a Business Decision', *The Journal of Business*, Vol. 29, 1956, pp. 237-248.

[2] cf. Mabel Newcomer, *The Big Business Executive*, N.Y., 1955.

[3] cf. B. R. Fisher and S. B. Withey, *Big Business As the People See It*, Ann Arrbo, 1951.

THE NORTHERN CITY DATA

The Selection of Companies and Individuals

THE information gained in this survey relates to the views and social characteristics of 65 directors and senior managers in 15 different companies. In order to determine which were the largest companies in Northern City we approached the Ministry of Labour who provided us with a list of 27 'main factory occupiers'—as measured by number of employees.

We decided to make no approach to 8 of the 27 companies. Four were excluded on the grounds that they were subdivisions of other companies which we intended to contact, two because they fell below the anticipated minimum size (500 employees), and one because it was in the flour milling industry which was already well represented in the original 27. One further company was found to be a large publicly owned enterprise. This was excluded because we were interested solely in private (i.e. joint stock) companies. Following this initial sorting procedure there were 19 companies left. When approached, 16 of these agreed to co-operate. Of those which refused, one simply did not reply to repeated enquiries, one refused on the grounds that it was undergoing radical reorganization and one on the grounds that it could not spare the time. In one further case, though the company agreed to co-operate, the managing director had not informed his colleagues what to expect and the interviewer's (unanticipated) arrival led in this case to such hostility being directed at him (and the managing director) that it was not felt worth while to proceed. With this one exception, however, it was found possible to interview all the 65 businessmen selected from within the remaining 15 firms.

The interviewees themselves were selected following an informal discussion with the personnel director or, more often, the managing director, in which we asked about the structure, origins and products of the firm and attempted to obtain details of the role specifications of its senior executives. Thus, once we knew who occupied the senior positions we were then able to select individual interviewees in such a way that we could achieve some overall balance between the various management specialisms. However, because they were generally inaccessible we made it our policy not to interview non-executive directors.

Although we did not take a 'sample' in the strict statistical sense we feel reasonably sure that the businessmen and businesses included represent a fair cross-section of those in Northern City. Ten of the interviewees were chief executives (defined as chairman and managing director, etc.); 26 occupied line positions (deputy managing director, works and general manager, and 'chief executives' of the organizational unit visited if they reported to a higher (main) board); 29 occupied non-line positions (including directors and senior managers in personnel, sales, finance, and technical and R. and D. directors). The number of interviewees selected from each company was governed by the size of its top management staff; it ranged from only one in the smallest firm, which had only 500 employees, to 13 in the case of the largest company, which had 7,000.

Out of the 15 firms in the study 10 would be termed 'management-controlled' on most commonly accepted criteria (e.g. those adopted by Florence in 1961) and 5 would either be termed 'owner-controlled', or were known to be actively managed by large shareholders or family representatives. The majority of companies had between 1,000–4,000 employees on the sites visited.

The companies in which interviewing was carried out were operating in the following industries: Chemicals (18 interviewees), Heavy Engineering (13), Light Engineering (8), Pharmaceutical (8), Flour Milling and Animal Foodstuffs (7), Distribution and Allied (6), Packaging (5).

The Method of Investigation

In the majority of cases our first contact with the interviewee was in the presence of the managing director, chairman or, occasionally, the personnel director. What generally happened was that after we had selected the interviewees (during our conversation with the managing director), he would take us along to see his colleagues. Upon meeting them we would emphasize that their anonymity would be safeguarded and when, as they all did, they agreed to co-operate we would present them with a copy of the forced-choice questionnaire.

We emphasized that altogether we would take up no more than one hour of their time and having made a special point of requesting that they did not discuss the survey or their opinions with their colleagues, we made an appointment with them to be interviewed and took our leave. Sometimes it was exceedingly difficult for the interviewees to keep these appointments so that although all the firms were contacted as early as April 1961 it was not until October 1962 that the interviews were finally completed. However, as we stated above, we did find it possible to interview all the businessmen chosen in 15 companies.

When we arrived for the interview the forced-choice questionnaire had already been completed. Thus, we were able not only to ask the interviewee the questions on the interview schedule but also to ask him to explain why he had made particular choices on the forced-choice questionnaire.

As expected, the interviews generally took about one hour. In one instance we were forced to rush through in 30 minutes but in many other instances the time was (voluntarily) extended so that we were treated to highly coloured, but extremely useful, expositions about the state of British industry in general and Northern City in particular.

The only difficulty encountered in the interviews concerned questions which we asked about the Economic League and Aims of Industry. We believe that asking questions about them was partly instrumental in causing the hostility we encountered in the firm we decided to cease interviewing in. Other directors whom we had asked about them generally gave the impression that they were unaware of their precise function or doubtful of their value. But given one awkward experience we felt it wiser to remove them from the questionnaire. In other respects the questionnaire gave rise to no major problems. This may in part be associated with the policy we adopted of not asking questions about salary and share ownership. In retrospect, however, we received such good co-operation that we doubt whether the inclusion of such questions would have affected the response rate, and we now regret that we were so cautious.

The Reliability of the Interview Data

Given the nature of the sample we attempted to treat our 65 businessmen in some depth. By doing so, and particularly by following the forced-choice questionnaire with an interview, we hoped to gain information not only about what businessmen said they believed but also about what, in their own words, such beliefs meant to them. In the last resort, of course, we have no guarantee that businessmen were 'telling the truth', or that they did not discuss their choices on the questionnaire with their colleagues. However, the nature of our contact with them did allow us ample opportunity to cross-check statements: indeed, we were often fascinated by the way in which businessmen were able to hold two, for us, contradictory views without themselves perceiving any conflict between them. Furthermore, the frequency with which the interviewer was subjected to a rather cunning kind of probing—e.g. 'I suppose Mr Jones chose this'—may perhaps be taken as an indication that they did not generally know just which choices their colleagues had made.

Since the Northern City survey was primarily conceived as an attempt to study the businessman's ideology it is incumbent upon us to say something about the sort of 'public' with which businessmen associated the interviewer. The interviewer tried to represent himself as an interested outsider who had chosen to find out something about directors—as a change from studying workers. However, because he was a social scientist he seemed to be regarded as some sort of a mongrel efficiency engineer-cum-moral crusader. In the minds of those interviewed a sociologist would appear to be depicted either as a man preoccupied with increasing productivity and/or being more than usually nice to nasty people. If then any conclusions can be drawn about interviewer bias, it is probably that the interviewees tended to represent themselves as being more 'socially responsible' than would otherwise have been the case. *Prima facie*, the same sort of conclusion might be drawn from the two main deliberate elements of bias in the sample, namely, the over-representation of younger businessmen and of those in personnel. (See Chapter XVI.)

THE INTERVIEW SCHEDULE

Position

Age

Religious Belief

Father's Occupation
  (At age you started work)

  Details:

Own Age at Leaving School

Type of School Attended
  Elem.   Name:
  Sec. Mod./Tech./Comp.
  Grammar/Non H.M.C.Pvte.
  Public/Private H.M.C.

University
  Ox.   Subject:
  Camb.
  Other

Brief History of Career

                    Formal Quals.
                    How first management
                    position obtained

Management Training
  Training/Courses *Prior* to Becoming Manager

  Management Courses *Since* Becoming Manager

Participation in Activities of Management Bodies
  (e.g. B.I.M., I.I.A., I.P.M.)

  Attends Meetings
          Conferences
          Speaks/Writes

Opinion of 'Management Bodies'

Reading in 'General Field of Management'
Books   Periodicals

Heard of Elton Mayo?
  (Hawthorne?)

Any experience of American Management
                          Yes/No
                          Opinion

Do You Regard Yourself As a Professional?
                          Yes/No/DK
                          If 'yes'—Why?

What Do You Think About Management Consultants?

What in Your Opinion Makes a Good Manager?
  (For a position like yours)

Do You Take Part in Local Community Affairs?
                          Yes/No
                          If 'yes' specify

                          (In own right or for firm)

Any Contact with the Economic League or Aims of Industry?
                          Yes/No
                          Opinion of

What Do You See as the Function of Works Councils?

What Would You Say Was the Greatest Need of Industry Today?

Would You Say Your Responses Would be Reasonably Typical for This Firm?
                          Yes/No
                          If 'no'—specify area of
                          disagreement

Do You Think This Firm Is Reasonably Typical of the . . . Industry?
                          Yes/No
                          If 'no'—differences

THE FORCED-CHOICE
QUESTIONNAIRE

THE following represent statements by prominent businessmen and theorists. They are arranged in four groups, each group consisting of three statements.

Tick the statement nearest to your own opinion in each group.

Group A

1. It is common knowledge that the secure contented employee, who is aware that management is concerned for his welfare, will work better; and to this end some form of redundancy payment is desirable.

2. Provision for employees against redundancy is no part of management's responsibility. No firm wants unemployment; it is simply a risk which all those in industry have to bear.

3. Management has a moral responsibility to guard against redundancy and provide for the workers' security should it occur.

Group B

1. A firm exists for one purpose only: to satisfy a need at a profit. Managers should not, and cannot, be concerned with social and moral consequence; if they were, the country's economic position would be undermined and with it the welfare of us all.

2. A business conducted solely for the profit of shareholders is unethical. A firm is a social institution; it exists to further the social welfare. The management is an arbiter with responsibilities to serve the social and economic needs of employees, customers, shareholders and the local and national communities.

3. Profit is the one absolute in business and it is to the nation's benefit that this be so. But in the interests of long-term survival every firm must gain the sympathetic understanding and co-operation of all people directly or indirectly within its sphere of interest.

Group C

1. Every worker has the right to full information of his own and the company's position and, excepting trade secrets, every company has a moral duty to provide such information.

2. Not only does the provision of information serve no useful purpose, since employees do not want it, but its circulation may have deleterious results for the firm.

3. In an age of increasing mass production and bigness the provision of information to employees is a means whereby the individual can be made to feel an important part of the team and his potential to co-operate with management increased.

Group D

1. The public must accept businessmen as thinking people actively contributing to the national weal. Public speeches are a powerful form of public relations and directors should accept invitations to write and speak on public platforms, associating themselves, in honorary or executive positions, with as many important groups as possible.

2. Every business has a social responsibility to the community. It is the duty of senior executives to fulfil this by contributing their skills and knowledge to public life.

3. A manager has work enough to do without becoming a leading figure in the community. If he wishes to do so that is his affair, but as a manager his place is with the firm.

Note: the L.F. set of items are A2; B1; C2; D3. The L.T.C.I. set of items are A1; B3; C3; D1. The S.R. set of items are A3; B2; C1; D2.

BIBLIOGRAPHY

Note: The dates given below refer to the edition of
the works cited in the text

BOOKS ORIGINALLY PUBLISHED BEFORE 1900

GREG, WILLIAM RATHBONE, *Mistaken Aims and Attainable Ideals of the Artisan Class* (Trubner & Co.), 1876.

MARX, KARL, *Capital*, 3 Vols. (Charles Kerr & Co.), Chicago, 1909.

URE, ANDREW, *The Philosophy of Manufactures, or, An Exposition of the Scientific, Moral, and Commercial Economy of the Factory System of Great Britain* (H. G. Bohn), London, 1861.

MORE RECENT WORKS

AARONOVITCH, S., *The Ruling Class*, London, 1961.

ACTON SOCIETY TRUST, *Management Succession: The Recruitment, Selection, Training and Promotion of Managers*, London, 1956.

ANDERSON, P. (ed.), *Towards Socialism*, London, 1965.

ANDREWS, P. W. S. AND BRUMMER, E., *The Life of Lord Nuffield: A Study in Enterprise and Benevolence*, Oxford, 1955.

ARNOLD, T. W., *The Folklore of Capitalism*, New Haven, 1937.

ARON, R., *The Industrial Society: Three Essays on Ideology and Development*, London, 1967.

——, *Eighteen Lectures on Industrial Society* (trans. M. K. Bottomore), London, 1967.

BALDAMUS, W., *Efficiency and Effort: An Analysis of Industrial Administration*, London, 1961.

BARAN, P. A. AND SWEEZY, P. M., *Monopoly Capital: An Essay on the American Economic and Social Order*, N.Y., 1966.

BAUMOL, W., *Business Behavior, Value and Growth*, N.Y., 1959.

BENDIX, R., *Work and Authority in Industry: Ideologies of Management in the Course of Industrialisation*, N.Y. and London, 1956.

BERLE, A. A., *Economic Power and the Free Society*, N.Y., 1958.

——, *Power without Property*, London, 1960.

——, *The Twentieth Century Capitalist Revolution*, London, 1955.

—— AND MEANS, G. C., *The Modern Corporation and Private Property*, N.Y., 1932.

BERLINER, J. S., *Factory and Manager in the U.S.S.R.*, Harvard, Cambridge, 1957.

BOWEN, H. R., *Social Responsibilities of the Businessman*, N.Y., 1953.

BRADY, R. A., *Business as a System of Power*, N.Y., 1943.

——, *Crisis in Britain: Plans and Achievements of the Labour Government*, London, 1950.

BRISTOL, LEE H. (ed.), *Developing the Corporate Image*, N.Y., 1960.
BURNHAM, JAMES, *The Managerial Revolution*, London, 1962.
BURNS, T. AND STALKER, G. M., *The Management of Innovation*, London, 1961.
CHEIT, E. F. (ed.), *The Business Establishment*, N.Y. and London, 1964.
CHILD, J., *British Management Thought and Education: Their Interpretation of Industrial Relationships*, Ph.D. thesis, Cambridge, 1967 (Part I of which is contained in *British Management Thought—A Critical Analysis*, London, 1969).
CLARK, D. G., *The Industrial Manager: His Background and Career Pattern*, London, 1966.
CLEMENTS, R. V., *Managers, A Study of Their Careers in Industry*, 1958.
COLE, A. H., *Business Enterprise in its Social Setting*, Harvard, 1959.
COLE, G. D. H., *Studies in Class Structure*, London, 1955.
COLLINS, O. F., MOORE, D. G. AND UNWALLA, D. B., *The Enterprising Man*, Michigan, 1965.
COPEMAN, G. H., *Leaders of British Industry*, London, 1955.
COTGROVE, S. F., *Technical Education and Social Change*, London, 1958.
CROSLAND, C. A. R., *The Conservative Enemy*, London, 1962.
——, *The Future of Socialism*, London, 1956.
CYERT, R. M. AND MARCH, J. G., *A Behavioral Theory of the Firm*, N.J., 1963.
DAHRENDORF, RALF, *Class and Class Conflict in Industrial Society*, London, 1957.
DALTON, M., *Men who Manage: Fusion of Feeling and Theory in Administration*, N.Y. and London, 1959.
DAVENPORT, N., *The Split Society*, London, 1964.
DIAMOND, S., *The Reputation of the American Businessman*, Cambridge, Mass., 1955.
DOBB, M., *Capitalism Yesterday and Today*, London, 1958.
DRUCKER, PETER, *The New Society*, London, 1951.
EMDEN, P. H., *Quakers in Commerce*, London, 1959.
ERICKSON, C., *British Industrialists: Steel and Hosiery, 1850–1950*, Cambridge, 1959.
FISHER, B. R. AND WITHEY, S. B., *Big Business As The People See It*, Ann Arbor, 1951.
FORTUNE, the editors of, AND DAVENPORT, RUSSEL W., *U.S.A.: The Permanent Revolution*, 1951.
FLORENCE, P. SARGANT, *Economics and Sociology*, London, 1964.
——, *The Logic of British and American Industry*, London, 1953.
——, *Ownership, Control and Success of Large Companies*, London, 1961.
GALBRAITH, J. K., *American Capitalism: The Concept of Countervailing Power*, London, 1957.
——, *The New Industrial State*, London, 1967.
GEIGER, THEODOR, *Die Klassengesellschaft im Schmelztiegel*, Cologne and Hagen, 1949.
GERSTL, J. E. AND HUTTON, S. P., *Engineers: The Anatomy of a Profession*, London, 1966.
GOFFMAN, E., *Encounters*, Indianapolis, 1961.

R

GORDON, R. A., *Business Leadership in the Large Corporation*, Berkeley and Los Angeles, 1961.
GOYDER, GEORGE, *The Future of Private Enterprise*, Oxford, 1951.
——, *The Responsible Company*, Oxford, 1961.
GRANICK, D., *The European Executive*, N.Y., 1962.
GUTTSMAN, W. L., *The British Political Elite*, London, 1963.
GUZZARDI, W., *The Young Executives*, N.Y., 1964.
HAIRE, M., GHISELLI, E. E. AND PORTER, L. W., *Managerial Thinking: An International Study*, N.Y., 1966.
HALMOS, P. (ed.), *The Development of Industrial Societies*, Sociological Review Monograph, No. 8, Keele, 1964.
HARBISON, F. H. AND MYERS, C. A., *Management in the Industrial World*, N.Y., 1959.
HARTMANN, H., *Authority and Organisation in German Management*, Princetown, 1959.
HUMBLET, J. E., *Les Cadres d'Entreprise: France, Belgique, Royaume Uni*, Paris, 1966.
HURFF, G. B., *Social Aspects of Enterprise in the Large Corporation*, Pennsylvania, 1950.
HUTTON, G., *We Too Can Prosper: The Promise of Productivity*, London, 1953.
INSTITUTE OF PUBLIC RELATIONS, *A Guide to the Practice of Public Relations*, London, 1958.
IVENS, M. AND DUNSTAN, D. (eds.), *The Case for Capitalism*, London, 1967.
JURAN, J. M. AND LOUDEN, J. K., *The Corporate Director*, A.M.A., N.Y., 1966.
KATONA, G., *Psychological Analysis of Economic Behavior*, N.Y., 1951.
KEYNES, J. M., *Essays in Persuasion*, London, 1931.
KOLKO, G., *Wealth and Power in America*, London, 1962.
LANDSBERGER, H. A., *Hawthorne Revisited*, Cornell, 1958.
LEE, JOHN, *Management: A Study of Industrial Organisation*, London, 1921.
LEIBENSTEIN, H., *Economic Theory and Organisational Analysis*, N.Y., 1960.
LEVY, A. B., *Private Corporations and their Control*, London, 1950.
LEWIS, R. AND STEWART, R., *The Boss: The Life and Times of the British Business Man*, London, 1963.
LIPSET, S. M. AND BENDIX, R., *Social Mobility in Industrial Society*, Berkeley, 1959.
MACKENZIE, NORMAN (ed.), *Conviction*, London, 1958.
MANNHEIM, KARL, *Ideology and Utopia: An Introduction to the Sociology of Knowledge*, London, 1960.
MARCH, J. G. AND SIMON, H. A., *Organisations*, N.Y., 1958.
MARRIS, ROBIN, *The Economic Theory of 'Managerial' Capitalism*, London, 1964.
MASON, E. S. (ed.), *The Corporation in Modern Society*, Harvard, 1960.
MCCLELLAND, D. C., *The Achieving Society*, N.J., 1961.

McGIVERING, I., *Personnel Management in Large Manufacturing Firms in Liverpool*, M.A. thesis, Liverpool, 1960.
——, MATTHEWS, D. AND SCOTT, W. H., *Management in Britain: A General Characterisation*, Liverpool, 1960.
MILLS, C. WRIGHT, *Power Elite*, London, 1959.
——, *White Collar*, N.Y., 1953.
MISHAN, E. J., *The Costs of Economic Growth*, London, 1967.
MOND, Sir ALFRED (later LORD MELCHETT), *Industry and Politics*, London, 1927.
MORGAN, E. V., *The Structure of Property Ownership in Great Britain*, London, 1960.
MOUZELIS, N. P., *Organisation and Bureaucracy: An Analysis of Modern Theories*, London, 1967.
NEWCOMER, M., *The Big Business Executive*, N.Y., 1955.
NICHOLS, W. A. T., *Ownership, Control and Ideology*, M.A. thesis, 1968.
ORWELL, GEORGE, *The Collected Essays*, London, 1961.
PARKINSON, H., *Ownership of Industry*, London, 1951.
PARSONS, TALCOTT, *The Social System*, London, 1952.
P.E.P., *Attitudes in British Management*, London, 1966.
RAISTRICK, A., *Two Centuries of Industrial Welfare: The London (Quaker) Lead Co., 1692–1905*, London, 1938.
RENNER, KARL, *Wandlungen der modernen Gesellschaft: zwei Abhandlungen über die Probleme der Nachkriegszeit*, Vienna, 1953.
RIZZI, BRUNO, *La Bureaucratisation du Monde*, Paris, 1939.
ROBERTS, D. R., *Executive Compensation*, Glencoe, 1959.
ROBINSON, JOAN, *Economic Philosophy*, London, 1962.
ROBSON BROWN, Sir WILLIAM, *Management and Society*, London, 1961.
ROGERS, K., *Managers, Personality and Performance*, London, 1963.
ROLL, ERIC, *A History of Economic Thought*, London, 1961.
ROSENBERG, M., *Occupation and Values*, Glencoe, 1957.
SAMPSON, ANTHONY, *The Anatomy of Britain*, London, 1962.
SAYLES, L., *Managerial Behavior*, N.Y., 1964.
SCHLATTER, RICHARD, *Private Property: The History of An Idea*, London, 1951.
SCHUMPETER, J. A., *Capitalism, Socialism and Democracy*, London, 1943.
SELZNICK, P., *T.V.A. and the Grass Roots*, Berkeley, 1949.
SERING, P., *Jenseits des Kapitalismus*, Nurnberg, 1947.
SHELDON, O., *The Philosophy of Management*, London, 1923.
SIMMEL, GEORG, *Conflict and the Web of Group Affiliations* (trans. K. H. Wolfe and R. Bendix), Glencoe, 1955.
SOFER, C., *The Organisation from Within*, London, 1959.
STEWART, R., *Managers and their Jobs*, London, 1967.
STRACHEY, J., *Contemporary Capitalism*, London, 1956.
STROTHER, G. B. (ed.), *Social Science Approaches to Business Behavior*, London, 1962.
SUTTON, F. X., HARRIS, S. E., KAYSEN, C. AND TOBIN, J., *The American Business Creed*, Cambridge, Mass., 1956.

SWEEZY, P. M., *The Present as History*, N.Y., 1953.

URWICK, L. F., *Management of Tomorrow*, London, 1933.

—— AND BRECH, E. F. L., *The Making of Scientific Management*, 3 Vols., London, 1949.

VEBLEN, THORSTEIN, *The Engineers and the Price System*, N.Y., 1921.

——, *Absentee Ownership and Business Enterprise in Recent Times*, N.Y., 1923.

WALTON, C. AND EELLS, R. (eds.), *The Business System: Readings in Ideas and Concepts*, 3 Vols., N.Y. and London, 1967.

WARNER, W. LLOYD AND MARTIN, NORMAN, H. (eds.), *Industrial Man: Businessmen and Business Organisations*, N.Y., 1959.

—— AND ABEGGLEN, J. C., *Occupational Mobility in American Business and Industry*, Minneapolis, 1955.

WEBB, S., *The Works Manager Today*, London, 1917.

WEBER, MAX, *The Protestant Ethic and the Spirit of Capitalism* (trans. Talcott Parsons), N.Y. and London, 1930.

WHITEHEAD, T. N., *Leadership in a Free Society*, Harvard, 1947.

WHYTE, W. H., *The Organisation Man*, London, 1957.

——, *Is Anybody Listening?*, N.Y., 1952.

WILLIAMSON, O. E., *The Economics of Discretionary Behavior: Managerial Objectives in a Theory of the Firm*, N.J., 1964.

PAMPHLETS AND SHORTER RESEARCH REPORTS

AN ADVERTISING APPRAISAL, The Times Publishing Co., London, 1960.

ALLEN, G. C., *Economic Fact and Fantasy: A Rejoinder to Galbraith's Reith Lectures*, I.E.A. Occasional Paper 14, 1967.

ARGYLE, M. AND SMITH, T., *Training Managers*, Acton Society Trust, London, 1962,

BARNA, T., *Investment and Growth Policies in British Industrial Firms*, N.I.E.S.R., Occasional Paper xx, Cambridge, 1962.

BIRNBAUM, N., 'The Sociological Study of Ideology (1940–60): A Trend Report and Bibliography', *Current Sociology*, Vol. 9, No. 2, 1960.

BOWEN, H. R., *The Business Enterprise As a Subject for Research*, Social Science Research Council, N.Y., 1955.

BRITISH INSTITUTE OF MANAGEMENT, *British Business Schools*, Report by the Rt. Hon. Lord Franks, London, 1962.

CAMBRIDGE, DEPT. OF APPLIED ECONOMICS, *The Owners of Quoted Ordinary Shares: A Survey for 1963, A Programme for Growth, No. 7*, London, 1966.

COLLIN, A., REES, A. M. AND UTTING, J., *The Arts Graduate in Industry*, Acton Society Trust, London, 1962.

DAHRENDORF, RALF, *Conflict After Class: New Perspectives on the Theory of Social and Political Conflict*, London, 1967.

ECONOMIST INTELLIGENCE UNIT, *A Study of Industry's Contribution to Science, the Arts, Education and the National Welfare*, London, 1957.

FEDERATION OF BRITISH INDUSTRIES, *Nationalisation*, Nov., 1956.

——, *Public School and Grammar School Boys in Industry*, Dec., 1954.

GLENNERSTER, H. AND PRYKE, R., *The Public Schools*, Young Fabian Pamphlet No. 7, Nov., 1964.

FINER, S. E., *Private Industry and Political Power*, London, 1958.

HALMOS, P., *The Personal Service Society*, Inaugural Lecture, delivered at University College, Cardiff, May 17, 1966.

HARRIS, A. I. AND CLAUSEN, R., *Labour Mobility in Great Britain*, Government Social Survey for the Ministry of Labour, H.M.S.O., 1966.

LAZARFELD, P., HAIRE, M. AND DAHL, R. A., *Social Science Research on Business*, N.Y., 1959.

LITTLE, I. M. D. AND RAYNER, A. C., *Higgledy Piggledy Growth Again*, Oxford, 1966.

LONDON STOCK EXCHANGE, *How Does Britain Save?: A Summary of the Results of a Survey Conducted for the London Stock Exchange by the British Market Research Bureau Limited*, London, 1966.

N.B.P.I., *Top Salaries in the Private Sector and Nationalised Industries*, Report No. 107, Cmnd. 3970, H.M.S.O., London, 1969.

N.E.D.C., *Management Recruitment and Development*, H.M.S.O., London, 1965.

NEW YORK STOCK EXCHANGE, *Shareownership U.S.A.: 1965 Census of Shareowners*, N.Y., 1965.

P.E.P., *Graduate Employment*, London, 1958.

SINGH, A. AND WHITTINGTON, G. WITH BURLEY, H. T., *Growth, Profitability and Valuation: A Study of United Kingdom Quoted Companies*, Cambridge, Dept. of Applied Economics, Occasional Paper 7, 1968.

THOMAS, G., *Labour Mobility in Great Britain, 1945–49. An Enquiry Carried Out for the Ministry of Labour and National Service*, Report No. 134, n.d.

THOMPSON, S., *Management Creeds and Philosophies*, A.M.A. Research Study, No. 32, 1958.

TITMUSS, R. M., *The Irresponsible Society*, Fabian Tract No. 323, London, 1960.

URWICK, L. F., *Is Management a Profession?* Urwick Orr and Partners, 1954.

ARTICLES

ALCHIAN, A. A., 'The Basis of Some Recent Advances in the Theory of Management in the Firm', *Journal of Industrial Economics*, Vol. 14, Nov., 1965.

'The Anatomy of the Board', *The Director*, Jan, 1965.

BALDWIN, W. L., 'The Motives of Managers, Environmental Restraints and the Theory of Managerial Enterprise', *The Quarterly Journal of Economics*, Vol. LXXVIII, May, 1964.

BARAN, P. A. AND SWEEZY, P. M., 'Monopoly Capital', *Monthly Review*, Vol. XIV, Numbers 3 and 4, July-August, 1962.

BARRATT BROWN, M., 'The Controllers', *Universities and Left Review*, No. 5, 1959.

BARRITT, D. P., 'The Stated Qualifications of Directors in Larger Public Companies', *Journal of Industrial Economics*, Vol. V, July, 1957.

BEED, C. S., 'The Separation of Ownership and Control', *The Journal of Economic Studies*, Vol. 1, No. 2, Summer, 1966, pp. 29–46.

BENDIX, R., 'A Study of Managerial Ideologies', *Economic Development and Cultural Change*, Vol. v, No. 2, Jan., 1957.

BERLEW, D. E. AND HALL, D. T., 'The Socialisation of Managers: Effects of Expectations on Performance', *Administrative Science Quarterly*, Sept., 1966, pp. 207–223.

BLEASE, J. G., 'Institutional Investors and the Stock Exchange', *District Bank Review*, Sept., 1964, pp. 38–64.

BURNS, T., 'What Managers Do', *New Society*, Dec. 16, 1964.

CHILD, J., 'Quaker Employers and Industrial Relations', *Sociological Review*, Vol. 12, No. 3, Nov., 1964, pp. 293–315.

COCHRAN, T. C., 'A Plan for the Study of Business Thinking', *Political Science Quarterly*, Vol. 62, 1947, pp. 82–90.

CYERT, R. M., SIMON, H. A. AND TROW, D. B., 'Observation of a Business Decision', *The Journal of Business*, Vol. 29, 1956, pp. 237–248.

DAHL, R. A., 'A Critique of the Ruling Elite Model', *American Political Science Review*, Vol. 52, 1956, pp. 463–469.

'The Director Observed', *The Director*, April, 1966.

'The Director Observed Away from the Desk', *The Director*, May, 1966.

EARLEY, J. S., 'Business Budgeting and the Theory of the Firm', *Journal of Industrial Economics*, Nov., 1960, Vol. IX, No. 1, pp. 23–42.

——, 'Marginal Policies of "Excellently Managed" Companies', *American Economic Review*, Vol. XLVI, March, 1956, pp. 44–70.

——, 'Recent Developments in Cost Accounting and the "Marginal Analysis".' *Journal of Political Economy*, Vol. LXIII.

GOLDTHORPE, J. H., 'Attitudes and Behaviour of Car Assembly Workers: A Deviant Case and a Theoretical Critique', *British Journal of Sociology*, Vol. XVII, No. 3, Sept., 1966.

—— AND LOCKWOOD, D., 'Affluence and the British Class Structure', *Sociological Review*, July, 1963, pp. 133–163.

HALMOS, P., 'The Personal Service Society', *British Journal of Sociology*, Vol. XVIII, No. 1, March, 1967, pp. 13–26.

HEALD, M., 'Management's Responsibility to Society: The Growth of an Idea', *Business History Review*, Vol. XXXI, 1957, pp. 376–384.

HENDERSON, R. F., 'Comments on Company Finance', *Lloyds Bank Review*, Jan, 1959.

HENRY, W. E., 'The Business Executive: A Study of the Psychodynamics of a Social Role', *American Journal of Sociology*, Vol. LVI, Jan., 1949, pp. 286–291.

HORNE, J. H. AND LUPTON, T., 'The Work Activities of "Middle" Managers', *Journal of Management Studies*, Vol. 2, Feb., 1965.

'The Insiders', *Universities and Left Review*, No. 3, 1958.

KAYSEN, C., 'The Social Significance of the Modern Corporation', *American Economic Review*, May, 1957.

KLEIN, L. R. *et al.*, 'Savings and Finances of the Upper Income Classes', *Bulletin of the Oxford Institute of Statistics*, Nov., 1956.

KRATZ, L. A., 'The Motivation of the Business Manager', *Behavioral Science*, Vol. V, 1960, pp. 313–316.

LADINSKY, J., 'Occupational Determinants of Geographic Mobility Among Professional Workers', *American Sociological Review*, Vol. 32, No. 2, April, 1967, pp. 253–264.

LENTZ, A. AND TSCHIRGI, H., 'The Ethical Content of Annual Reports', *The Journal of Business*, Vol. XXXVI, No. 4, Oct., 1963, pp. 387–393.

LESLEY, P., 'The "Corporate Image" and the Future Leaders of Business', *Public Opinion Quarterly*, Vol. XXIII, No. 4, 1959, pp. 547–553.

'The Life and Times of the Director', *The Director*, Oct., 1959.

LINTNER, J., 'Distribution of Income of Corporations among Dividends, Retained Earnings and Taxes', *American Economic Review*, May, 1956, pp. 97–113.

LITTLE, A. AND WESTERGAARD, J., 'The Trend of Class Differentials in Educational Opportunity in England and Wales', *British Journal of Sociology*, Vol. XI, No. 4, Dec., 1964.

LUPTON, T. AND WILSON, S., 'The Social Background and Connections of "Top Decision Makers",' *Manchester School of Economics and Social Studies*, Jan., 1959.

MACHLUP, F., 'Theories of the Firm; Marginalist, Behavioral, Managerial', *American Economic Review*, Vol. LVII, No. 1, March, 1967, pp. 1–33.

MASON, E. S., 'The Apologetics of Managerialism', *The Journal of Business*, Vol. XXXI, No. 1, Jan., 1958.

MYRDAL, GUNNAR, 'The Relation Between Social Theory and Social Policy', *British Journal of Sociology*, Vol. 4, No. 3, pp. 210–242.

NIVEN, M. M., 'The Beginnings of the Institute', *Personnel Management*, March, 1957.

PAPANDREOU, A. G., 'Some Basic Problems in the Theory of the Firm', in B. F. Haley (ed.), *A Survey of Contemporary Economics*, Vol. II, Illinois, 1952, pp. 183–219.

PARSONS, TALCOTT, 'The Motivation of Economic Activities', *Canadian Journal of Economics and Political Science*, Vol. VI, May, 1940, pp. 187–200.

——, 'The Professions and the Social Structure', *Social Forces*, Vol. 17, No. 4, May, 1939, pp. 457–467.

PATERSON, T. T., 'The New Profession of Management', *The Listener*, December 6, 1961.

POOL, I. S., 'The Head of Company: Conceptions of Role and Identity', *Behavioral Science*, April, 1964, pp. 147–155.

PORTER, L. W., 'Where is the Organisation Man?', *Harvard Business Review*, Nov., 1963.

PUGH, D. S., 'Role Activation Conflict: A Study of Industrial Inspection', *American Sociological Review*, Vol. 31, No. 6, Dec., 1966, pp. 835–842.

ROGERS, D. AND BERG, I. E., 'Occupation and Ideology: The Case of the Small Businessman', *Human Organisation*, Vol. 20, No. 3, Fall, 1961, pp. 103–111.

SAMUEL, R., 'The Boss As Hero', *Universities and Left Review*, No. 7, 1959.

SCHEIN, E. H., 'Attitude Change During Management Education', *Administrative Science Quarterly*, March, 1967, pp. 601–628.

SCITOVSKY, T., 'A Note on Profit Maximisation and its Implications', *Review of Economic Studies*, Winter, 1943, pp. 57–60.

SILVER, M., 'Managerial Discretion and Profit Maximising Behavior: Some Further Comments', *Journal of Industrial Economics*, Vol. 15, April, 1967, pp. 157–163.

SIMON, H. A., 'Theories of Decision Making in Economic and Behavioral Science', *American Economic Review*, Vol. 49, June, 1959, pp. 253–283.

STOVER, C. F., 'Changing Patterns in the Philosophy of Management', *Public Administration Review*, Vol. 18, No. 1, 1958, pp. 21–27.

TURNER, R. H., 'Role-taking, Role Standpoint, and Reference Group Behavior', *American Journal of Sociology*, Vol. 61, No. 4, Jan., 1956, pp. 316–328.

VILLAREJO, D., 'Stock Ownership and the Control of Corporations', *New University Thought*, Chicago, Autumn, 1961 and Winter, 1962.

WALD, R. M. AND DOTY, R. A., 'The Top Executive—A firsthand Profile', *Harvard Business Review*, July, 1954.

'Who Controls the Steel Industry?', *B.I.S.F. Steel Review*, Oct., 1958.

WRONG, D. H., 'The Oversocialised Conception of Man in Modern Sociology', *American Sociological Review*, Vol. 26, 1961, pp. 183–193.

ZETTERBERG, H. L., 'Complaint Actions', *Acta Sociologica*, Vol. II, No. 4, 1957.

AUTHOR INDEX

Aaronovitch, S., 41n, 68n, 74n
Abrams, M., 80, 115n
Alchian, A. A. 96n
Allen, G. C., 108n
Andrews, P. W. S., 100n
Argyle, M., 89n
Arnold, T., 176n
Aron, R., 28, 153m, 241n

Baldamus, W., 227n
Baldwin, W. L., 103, 123n
Banks, J. A., 129n
Baran, P. A., 41n, 55n, 108n, 123n
Barber, B., 84n
Barnard, C., 99n, 121
Barratt Brown, M., 41n, 69n
Barritt, D. P., 80n
Baumol, W., 54n, 97, 120
Beed, C. S., 147n
Bendix, R., 34, 49-50, 134, 148n, 208, 209, 211, 217n
Berg, I. E., 209n, 212
Berle, A. A., Chapter I, 12, 15, 31, 35n, 36-9, 43, 211n, 231
Berlew, D. E., 196n
Berliner, J. S., 123n
Birnbaum, N., 212
Blackburn, R., 41n, 64, 65n, 74n
Blease, J. G., 25n
Bowen, H. R., 153, 160n, 228-9
Brady, R. A., 36n, 37
Bristol, L. H., 235n
Brummer, E., 100n
Bruyn, S. T., 241n
Burnham, J., Chapter II, 12, 14n, 26, 30, 41, 43, 63
Burns, T., 154n

Cheit, E. F., 214n
Child, J., 139n, 160, 204n, 206, 210n, 218, 232n
Clarke, D. G., 80, 82, 90, 91, 113n, 114, 115n, 116, 117, 119, 129, 132

Clausen, R., 113n
Clements, R. V., 113, 114n, 116, 117, 130, 132
Cole, A. H., 99n
Cole, G. D. H., 33
Collin, A., 126n
Collins, O. F., 100n
Comte, A., 12, 28
Copeman, G. H., 80, 115, 116, 117, 119n, 159n, 214n
Crosland, C. A. R., 36n, 41, 50, 52, 63, 66, 72, 76n, 104, 143n
Cyert, R. M., 95n, 246n

Dahl, R. A., 153
Dahrendorf, R., Chapter III, 12, 33, 35, 38, 63-4, 110, 112, 113, 118, 126, 133, 134, 137, 144, 152
Dalton, M., 182
Davenport, N., 40n, 65n
Davenport, R. W., 26, 48, 50
Delefortrie-Soubeyroux, N., 245n
Dobb, M., 68n
Dublin, R., 154n

Earley, J. S., 123
Eells, R., 24n, 56n, 224

Farrow, N., 117
Fisher, B. R., 246n
Florence, P. S., 20, 21, 53, 68, 69n, 71-7, 92, 106, 107n, 109n
Fox, A., 159

Galbraith, J. K., 14, 24n, 47, 95n
Geiger, T., 41
Gerstl, J. E., 130
Ghiselli, E. E., 99n, 151, 244
Glennerster, H., 117n
Goffman, E., 206n
Goldthorpe, J. H., 125n, 135, 145n

265

Gordon, R. A., 21n, 96n, 99n, 152n, 154n
Gower, L. C. B., 23n
Goyder, G., 160, 218n, 224, 225, 228, 229, 230, 231
Granick, D., 245n
Greg, W. R., 227n
Guttsman, W. L., 116
Guzzardi, W., 89n, 202

Haire, M., 99n, 151, 244
Hall, D. T., 196n
Halmos, P., 155, 159, 241, 242
Harris, A. I., 113n
Hartmann, H., 245n
Heald, M., 214n
Heller, R., 117
Henderson, R. F., 107n
Henry, W. E., 100, 101
Humblet, J. E., 244
Hutton, G., 84
Hutton, S. P., 130

Katona, G., 53, 99n
Kaysen, C., 22n, 53n
Keynes, J. M., 53
Klein, L. R., 74n
Kolko, G., 41n, 134, 143
Kratz, L. A., 54, 98n

Ladinsky, J., 119n
Landes, D. S., 245n
Landsberger, H. A., 88n
Lee, J., 218n
Leibenstein, H., 99n
Lentz, A., 235n
Lesley, P., 235n
Lewis, R., 122, 159n, 215n
Levitt, T., 185-6
Lintner, J., 25n, 94, 106, 109n
Lipset, S. M., 148n
Little, A., 114n
Little, I. M. D., 107
Lockwood, D., 135
Lupton, T., 140n, 154n

Machlup, F., 95n
Mannheim, K., 211
March, J. G., 95n, 96n, 246n
Marris, R., Chapter IX passim, 54, 56, 76n, 77, 92, 120, 125n, 139, 143, 144, 151, 152, 243
Marx, K., 12, 41, 44, 64

Mason, E. S., 23n, 24n, 31n, 53n
McClelland, D. C., 100
McGivering, I., 139n, 150n, 159
Means, G. C., 15, 22, 35n, 36
Mills, C. W., 12, 25n, 33, 40-1, 43, 67, 122, 143
Mishan, E. J., 235n
Mond, Sir Alfred, 160, 218n, 228
Mouzelis, N. P., 34n
Myrdal, G., 213n

Newcomer, M., 148n, 246n
Nichols, W. A. T., 193n
Niven, M. M., 197n

Orwell, G., 34

Papandreou, A. G., 145n
Parsons, T., 84n, 217
Penrose, L. S., 68n
Poggi, G., 69n
Pool, I. S., 119n
Porter, L. W., 99n, 121n, 151, 244
Pugh, D. S., 220-1, 222

Raistrick, A., 139n
Renner, K., 41, 44
Rizzi, B., 34n
Robinson, J., 219n
Rogers, D., 209n, 212
Rogers, K., 100, 101
Rosenberg, M., 130n

Sampson, A., 37
Samuel, R., 37n
Sayles, L., 154n
Schein, E. H., 204n
Schlatter, R., 216n
Schumpeter, J. A., 226n
Scitovsky, T., 108n
Selznick, P., 124n
Sering, P., 41, 112
Sheldon, O., 160, 218n
Silver, M., 107n
Simon, H. A., 95n, 96n, 246n
Singh, A., 106n, 107, 109n
Stewart, R., 122, 154n, 159n, 215n
Strachey, J., 66
Strother, G. B., 154n
Sutton, F. X., 163-4, 208, 209, 210-12, 219n, 226n

Sweezy, P. M., 34n, 41n, 55n, 108n, 123n, 143

Thomas, G., 113n
Thomas, W. I., 241
Thompson, S., 160n
Thompson, V. A., 99n, 124
Titmuss, R. M., 25n
Touraine, A., 220n
Trow, D. B., 246n
Tschirgi, H., 235n
Turner, R. H., 110n

Ure, A., 139n, 218
Urwick, L. F., 89n, 114n, 225n

Veblen, T., 12
Villarejo, D., 41n, 69n, 103

Wald, R. M., 100n
Walton, C., 24n, 56n
Warner, W. L., 148n
Watson, W., 181n
Weber, M., 33, 218n
Westergaard, J., 114n
Whitehead, T. N., 213n
Whittington, G., 106n, 107, 109n
Whyte, W. H., 85n, 121n
Williamson, O. E., Chapter IX passim, 54, 120, 146, 151n, 243
Withey, S. B., 246n
Wright, B. W. G., 227n, 230-1, 235n
Wrong, D. H., 151n

Young, M., 35

Zetterberg, H. L., 103n

SUBJECT INDEX

Accountants, 81, 89
Action approach, 145
Advertising, 216, 230, 235
Age of businessmen,
  and ideological preference, 193-6, 240
  and management education, 90
  and Northern City sample, 250
  and secondary education, 114, 117
Aims of Industry, 216n, 249
American management, 22, 27, 32, 45n, 62, 84, 85, 148, 186, 187, 209
Anglo-American Productivity Teams, 84-5
Aye Ltd., 173, 183, 184, 193n

B.A.T., 75, 76
Bee Bros., 173, 183, 193n
B.I.M., 127
B.S.A., 104
Bureaucratization, 31, 32, 50, 98, 119, 121
Business ideology, 15, 56, 162, 164, 186-9, 206-7, 208ff
  and business theorists, 210, 225, 228, 229-230, 231
  and choice, 164-5, 168ff
  and conflict, 212, 220
  and consistency, 164, 167, 170-2, 188, 209
  and cross-cultural similarities, 209, 244
  full definition of, 208
  and ideology of businessmen, 26, 209, 211
  and industrialization, 49-50, 209
  and interdependence, postulate of, 223ff
  and interest theories, 165, 207, 212ff, 236-7
  and logic, 187, 219n, 238
  and meaning, 15, 162, 168, 182, 211, 238
  and organicism, postulate of, 224ff
  and power, 208, 232
  as problem solving device, 207, 211ff

  and public relations, 234-6
  and role strain theory, 209, 212, 219n
  and self-conception of actors, 207
  as symbol-meaning system, 212, 219n
  and 'truth', 232, 250
  see also, Hypothetical ideologies, Social responsibility
Business schools, 85
Businessmen, defined, 12n

Capitalists, motivation of, 29, 45, 52-3, 55, 94, 97-9, 125, 134, 139
Capitalism, 12, 22, 25-6, 29, 32, 35, 38, 42, 45, 50, 63-5, 66, 153, 215
  attack on and defence of, 211, 214ff
  and conflict, 45-6, 66-7, 212
Charitable donations, 155, 184n
City influence, 175-6
City journalists, 65
Club membership, 141
Company credos, 160-1
Company size,
  and directors' shareholding, 72, 75
  and organization men, 121
  and performance, 106, 109
  and qualifications of businessmen, 81-2
Compartmentalization, 176
Competition, 98, 140, 149, 150, 216, 226
Conservative Party, 66, 148
Consumer sovereignty, 213, 216
'Control', criteria used to assess, 19-20, 63, 69n
  and limitations of criteria, 21
  see also, Separation of ownership and control, Statistical method and 'control'
Corporate conscience, 24ff, 77
Corporate state, 31-2
Corporation, see Joint stock company
Countervailing power, see Pluralism
Courtaulds, 76
Cultural lag, theory of, 126
Culture shock, and management recruitment, 130

Decentralization, 124
Decision making, 61, 95-6, 145, 155
Dee & Co., 173
Dividends and capital appreciation,
    76-7, 94, 104, 109, 147
Dunlop, 75-6, 77

Economic League, 249
Economic theory, Chapter IX, 53, 54,
    145-7, 149, 150-1, 163, 243
Education,
    of directors' children, 131n
    secondary, 114, 116-8, 127, 193
    university, see Graduates
    see also Public schools, Management
        education
Embourgeoisement, 36n, 135
Engineers and technical directors, 89,
    130, 132, 197, 244
Ethics in business, 50-51, 139, 167, 172,
    181-7, 202-3, 206, 241
Esso, 160
European management, 31-2, 244-5

Fabian intellectuals, 215, see also
    Labour Party
Family firms, 42, 125, 150n, 230, 248
Ferranti, 50, 135
Finance directors, 197
Forced-choice questionnaire, 166ff, 189,
    209, 254-5
Full employment, 149, 187, 213

Gee Ltd., 173, 193n
General Motors, 187
Government and business, 213, 215,
    233, 236
Graduates in industry, 80ff, 112-3, 115,
    116, 127, 129, 130, 191-2, 199-200,
    240
    in America, 85
    expectations of, 129
    Oxbridge, 83, 115, 116, 118, 127,
        129, 130
Grammar schools, 114
Growth,
    and idea of social responsibility, 225
    and internal financing, 107
    and profits, 97, 109
    and shareholder interest, 104, 109,
        149
    and theories of the firm, 54, 95ff, 149
'Guinea-pig directors', 143

Human relations, 49, 62, 88n, 89n,
    210n, 213, 220, 223-4, 241
Hypothetical ideologies, types of, 164,
    166ff, 182
    revised types, 189-90

I.C.I., 50, 75, 76, 235
Idealism in business, 175, 204, 242
Ideology, see Business ideology
Ideological preference, 191-207, 239-40
    and age, 193-7
    of directors, 191
    of graduates, 191-2, 199, 240
    and length of management ex-
        perience, 193-7, 201
    of line managers, 191, 200, 201, 204
    of non-line managers, 191, 197-8, 201
    and professional participation, 199
    of senior managers, 191
    and social origin, 192, 240
Imperial Tobacco, 76
Imperialism, 66
Interlocking directorships, 41, 141, 143
Internal financing, 63, 65, 94, 106ff,
    147
Intra-unit orientation, 69, 103
Inverted ritualism, and managers'
    goals, 123

Johnson & Johnson, 160, 161
Joint stock company,
    and anomie theories, 125, 224, 226
    and capitalist mode of production,
        38, 40, 42, 44, 50
    as a collectivity, 224ff
    Government evaluation of, 233
    introduction of, 213
    legal position of, 22-3, 136-7, 141
    and planning, 49, 95
    property of, 20, 42
    and rationality, 108, 122ff, 131, 150
    and rules of capitalism, 216
    as social organism, 225ff
    as soulful, 22
    voluntary socialization of, 23, 29

Kay & Co., 183

Labour Party, 36-7, 66ff, 147, 215
Legitimacy crisis in business, thesis of,
    214ff
Leverhulme, Lord, 75

Management bodies,
    attitudes to, 86-90, 198, 205
    and ideological preference, 198ff
    participation in, 85-6, 198ff, 240
Management clichés, 205
Management consultants, 89, 123
Management education, 84, 85, 129,
    204-5
    and universities, 85
Management journals. 160
Managerial class, idea of, Chapter
    XII, 31ff, 91, 119, 133, 144, 242
Managerial motivation, 54, 99ff, 123,
    146ff, 163, 218n
Managerial performance, assessment of,
    122ff
Managerial revolution, 38n
Managerial spiralists, 181
Managerialism, 12n
    sectional and non-sectional types, 43
Managerialists and Marxist schools,
    logics of analysis, 68-70
    overlap between, 12, 13, 111, 243
    strengths and weaknesses, 143-4
Marxism,
    adapted, 35
    inverted, 29
Marxist school, see Managerialist school
Marxist tradition, 41, 43-4, 63-4, 68, 144
Meritocracy, 28, 36n, 114
Mobility,
    cross-functional, 132
    geographical, 119
    inter-firm, 109, 119
    inter-generational, 113, 114, 116,
        118, 131, 148
    intra-generational, 88n, 113, 130-2
    see also Social origin
Monopolies Commission, 216

N.A.M., 160n
Nationalization, 66, 67, 138, 215
Nepotism, 115
Neutral technocracy, idea of, 24ff, 31,
    37, 55, 142
New Left, defined, 67n, see also Politics,
    left wing
Northern City study, methodology of,
    13-14, 163-9, 247-55
Nuffield, Lord, 75, 100n

Organization man, 121
Organizational identity, 155, 196

Ownership and control, see Separation
    of, Statistical method and 'control'
Oxbridge, 83, 115, 116, 118, 127, 129,
    130

Paternalism, 139
Personnel managers, 89, 132, 197-8,
    200, 201, 204, 240, 250
Personnel policies, 49-50, 63, 150n, 183
Pilkington's, 50, 135
'Plough-back', see Internal financing
Pluralism, 46-8, 66, 67, 187, 209n
Politics,
    left-wing, 41, 66ff, 74n, 215
    right-wing, 65, 216n
    voting of directors, 148
    see also Conservative Party, Labour
        Party
Private companies, 50
Private property, 138-9, 142
    and idea of social duty, 28-9
    see also Shareholders, Wealth
Productivity, the promise of, 222
Professional managers, Chapter VIII,
    51, 127, 130, 141, 151, 191, 198ff
Profit,
    acquisition of, 109, 120, 231
    as beneficent, 229
    maximization of, 53, 55, 95, 97, 98,
        105, 108, 120, 123-4, 143, 149,
        150, 153, 161, 215
    as process, 231
    utilization of, 150, 230
Propertied and non-propertied direc-
    tors, difficulty of distinguishing,
    136ff, 152
Public consensus, idea of, 24ff, 77
Public schools, 65, 116-8, 127, 129, 131,
    193
Public sector,
    and managerial revolution thesis, 31ff
    qualifications of directors in, 81, 90
    salaries in, 137
Public relations, 25, 178n, 187, 234-6
Purpose of industrial companies, 166,
    168-9, 179, 182, 223, 225, 231

Quakerism, 139, 218
Qualifications of businessmen, 127, 128,
    130, 132, 133
    lack of, Chapter VII, 129
Qualities of businessmen, 90, 122, 125ff,
    185, 223
Quality press, 37

Ranks, 50
Reading habits of businessmen, 89, 198
Redundancy, 166, 168-9, 177, 179, 180, 182, 183
Re-investment, see Internal financing
Resale price maintenance, 216
Restriction of output, 62, 123n
Retarded development, thesis of, 91, 126
Role, 103n, 122, 138, 148, 152, 221
businessman's perception of, 129, 132, 159, 222ff
re-definition of, 119, 231
scrambling, 226-8
strain, 184-5, 206-7, 209, 212, 219n
substitutability, 226-7
Role set, of businessman, 221
and conflict, 220ff
Russian managers, 62, 123n

Salaries of businessmen, 135, 137, 142
Sales managers, 197
Satisficing, 53, 95
Selection and promotion, 26, 53, 122ff, 186
and culture shock, 130
and ideological preference, 193
Self-help, idea of, 217
Separation of ownership and control,
and entrepreneurial authority, 48-50
problems of concept, 20-1, 35, 63, 102-3, 144-5
and secondary evidence, 63
see also Statistical method and 'control'
Share options, 76, 123n, 143
Shareholders,
directors as, Chapter VI, 65, 91-2, 118, 137-8, 140, 145, 148, 152, 153-4, 242
expectations of, 62, 104, 109, 150, 153, 221
institutional, 24-5, 41, 104, 105n, 109, 143, 154
legal position of, 22-3, 110, 136-7
management's alleged independence of, 19, 21, 22, 31, 52, 94, 107, 147
as 'ordinary people', 227
passivity of, 103-4, 110, 147
personal, 19, 42, 52, 78-9, 91, 105, 109, 118
Shareholder-oriented conscience, 77, 79, 138ff, 148, 150, 182

Social origin, Chapter X, 110, 114-5, 130-1, 143, 147, 148, 191, 192, 199, 200, 240
see also Mobility, inter- and intra-generational
Social power, 63, 149
compared to mechanical, 21, 147
Social responsibility,
and Christianity, 186n, 209n
and the community, 179-80, 183, 184
as display of role distance, 205-6
and economic theory, 94ff, 100, 154-5, 161-2, 186, 243
as form of words, 190ff
and human relations, 213, 241
interpretation of in management literature, 228ff
long history of, 217ff
self and structural representations of, 208-9
see also Business ideology, Ideological preference
Social sciences, 11-12, 13, 62, 88, 90, 151, 152, 160, 167, 250
Socialist economics, 31-2, 153
Sociology of knowledge, 15, 163-5, 208-12, 214ff
Statesmanship in business, 206
Statistical method and 'control', 19-20, 21, 68-9, 92, 102-3, 141, 144-5, 147
see also Separation of ownership and control

Take-overs, 96, 143-4, 148, 216
'Theory', attitude toward of businessmen, 87ff
Trade unions,
management and, 48, 140, 213, 226
officials, 181, 221
Tube Investments, 213-4

Unilever, 50, 73, 76
Universities, see Graduates, Oxbridge
U-Products, 173, 174, 181-2, 193n

Valuation ratio, 96ff

Wealth, concentration of private, 41, 66, 78-9, 148
Weinstock, Arnold, 135

Woolworths, 50
Workers,
  businessmen's attitudes to, 48, 139,
    140, 182, 205, 217, 223, 225, 226
  and company information, 166,
    168-9, 179

as 'exploiters', 227
  managers as, 227-28
Workers' control, 215, 230

Zed Ltd., 173-9, 181, 189, 224, 230,
  240